Changes in the Therapist

Changes in the Therapist

Edited by

Stephen Kahn
Erika Fromm

LAWRENCE ERLBAUM ASSOCIATES, PUBLISHERS
2001   Mahwah, New Jersey   London

Lawrence Erlbaum Associates, Inc., Publishers
10 Industrial Avenue
Mahwah, NJ 07430

Cover design by Kathryn Houghtaling Lacey

Library of Congress Cataloging-in-Publication Data

Changes in the therapist / edited by Stephen Kahn and Erika
   Fromm.
         p.   cm.
   Includes bibliographical references and index.
   ISBN 0-8058-2382-4 (cloth : alk. paper)
1. Psychotherapist and patient—Case studies.
   2. Countertransference (Psychology)—Case studies.
   3. Psychotherapists—Psychology—Case studies.
   4. Change (Psychology)—Case studies.
   5. Intersubjectivity—Case studies. I. Kahn, Stephen,
   1950-   . II. Fromm, Erika.
RC480.8.C43 2001
616.89′14—dc21   01-033165
                                                       CIP

Books published by Lawrence Erlbaum Associates are printed
on acid-free paper, and their bindings are chosen for strength
and durability.

Printed in the United States of America
10 9 8 7 6 5 4 3 2 1

In Loving Memory of Joan Fromm Greenstone

Contents

Foreword

It has been said that the greatest obstacle to self-analysis is the countertransference. Although that may be true, something happens in the interpersonal domain that rarely occurs when one is alone. It is the opportunity of another person to remake one's own possibilities in light of relating to another person. What goes on in psychotherapy is far more than cognitive reappraisal. It is the experience of being with another person who cares about you, who can react to you as a person when you show them your insecurities, discuss your fears, traumatic experiences, or your relationship difficulties. In the psychotherapy of Post-Traumatic Stress Disorder (PTSD), for example, patients need to work through their own conflict over guilt and worthlessness versus vulnerability: Did I deserve what happened to me (and thereby I had and have control over being hurt), or was I rendered helpless by bad fortune or someone else's malicious intent? In order for a therapist to help such a patient, the therapist must be able to tolerate vulnerability by identification, to acknowledge that if it could happen to the patient, it could happen to the therapist. Such patients, in turn, want to see if the therapist can be empathic, can feel for them, indeed *with* them, in reliving and grieving losses that accompanied the traumatic experience. They can come to accept themselves, vulnerabilities, misjudgments, and all, if they feel acceptance and caring from the therapist. But therapists have to be able to tolerate the fear, terror, sadness, and pain that come with such experiences and express caring to their patients despite knowing what they know about them. In other words, therapists have to be willing to change if they expect their patients to do so. The work demands no less of them if they expect patients to come to terms with themselves and their lives.

This book is rich with existential issues: death, loss, serious injury, traumatic stress. My work with patients suffering from life-threatening illness such as cancer has changed me. I am often asked if it is demoralizing to work with patients who die with such distressing regularity. I have done such work for more than 20 years, and I could not bring myself to continue if I did not find it challenging and inspiring. I have been to more memorial services than I would like. But I find the confrontation with death that these patients undergo with me invigorating, a reminder of what matters in life (and what does not). They have taught me to value what is most precious, savor time with family and friends, not to prepare for life but live it, and to dump unnecessary burdens. Confronting mortality means facing the fact that a time will come when my time too has gone, but I feel stronger when doing it. I can recall one transforming group meeting with my metastatic breast cancer patients that occurred immediately after I had attended the memorial service for a dear friend who had died of a glioblastoma. I was quite overwhelmed by my own grief and received tremendous warmth and support from the group, who turned the tables for an hour and focused on my loss rather than theirs. Being open to receiving help was what I needed then, and it also conveyed my respect for them. It has helped me to put in perspective the minor tribulations of life.

More than that, changing with patients is a reminder that respect is conveyed in both giving and receiving help. If we want our patients to be open to change, we must let them change us as well, a dynamic that one sees daily in group psychotherapy. Group members initiate and consolidate major changes in themselves as they help others to do the same.

As Irvin Yalom reminded us in his excellent books on psychotherapy, such as *Love's Executioner* (1989), and the recent *Momma and the Meaning of Life* (1999), it is a good therapist who can learn from the relationship with a patient, making it a bidirectional give and take. The existential issues in psychotherapy are powerful ones. The challenge is to examine the obstacles to having an authentic relationship and remove them by being honest and open, using one's here-and-now reactions as fuel for the fire of therapy. This means modeling as well as promoting change, showing patients that you respect them enough to change with them. There is an old saying that it is a smart hypnotist that knows who is hypnotizing whom. Smart therapists know how to grow with their patients. This book is thoughtfully put together and provides a broad range of well-described experiences from seasoned psychotherapists. Enjoy it and let it change you.

—David Spiegel
Stanford University School of Medicine

REFERENCES

Yalom, I. (1989). *Love's executioner & other tales of psychotherapy.* New York: Basic Books.
Yalom, I. (1999). *Momma and the meaning of life.* New York: Basic Books.

Introduction

Stephen Kahn
Erika Fromm

The idea for this book began some years ago during a discussion we had about the changes over the years in the practice of psychotherapy and, as a result, the changes in ourselves. We realized that as the view of the therapist's role changed, so did the nature of our involvement in the therapy. The therapist used to be seen as immutable and omniscient, speaking from a position of authority and giving advice to or helping the patient cope or deal with his or her conflicts. That is, the therapist was considered to be the person who need not or does not change, whereas the patient was the one who was expected to change. Therapy thus had been regarded as a one-way street; it was the patient who got "cured" or at least who became able to suffer less, while the therapist remained the same.

But modern therapy has changed its emphasis to focus on the interpersonal field and on *mutuality of influence*. The therapist and the patient are now seen as participating in an ongoing feedback loop, with each influencing the other. This set of interactions, sometimes called *intersubjectivity*, has brought therapists and their reactions more to the foreground. Could the patient be the cause or source of an essential change in the psyche of the therapist? Perhaps the street could go both ways.

We talked to a few of our associates who felt that they, too, had undergone changes as part of the therapeutic process with certain patients. We decided to send a letter out to over 100 of our colleagues, asking them to contribute to an edited volume that would focus on this mutuality of influence—possible changes in themselves as well as changes in their patients. We did not specify the kind of change—it could be either personal or professional, as long as it was the result of doing therapy with a particular patient. The response was very positive: "It's about time someone wrote such a book" said one. Another said, "I was working on something else until I read your letter. Now this is my number one priority."

We received some powerful case studies, extraordinary in the way that both patient and therapist dealt with existential issues, extraordinary in the way the patient may have faced devastating trauma or tragedy, and extraordinary in the way that the therapist responded to them. These are the studies that comprise this volume.

Deep, lasting, existential changes do not, of course, occur in the therapist with every patient. For instance, changes in views about life and death may be experienced only a few times in a therapist's life. But the cases that give rise to them are illuminating and their memory suggests the same kind of potential with each new patient. Some of the authors used the job of writing to further consolidate the changes they had undergone. The process begun with the patient clearly does not end with the termination of the therapy. Consolidation can sometimes occur years later or may be more strongly brought into focus with successive patients. Each new patient who enters therapy has a potential for change. The therapist not only harnesses that potential but begins to realize his or her own potential in the process. Ultimately, the process comes to fruition, sometimes all at once, with a single patient and sometimes only after reflecting on the process at a later date or after seeing a number of similar patients.

Before discussing the cases themselves, we seek to illuminate the intersubjective process by exploring the experience of hypnosis and the concepts of empathy and of transference–countertransference.

HYPNOSIS

In asking therapists about their experiences, we elected to focus on therapists who use hypnosis in their practice because in contemporary permissive hypnosis a particularly strong interaction usually occurs between patient and therapist. *Hypnotherapy,* or *hypnoanalysis,* is a powerful, intimate relationship between two people, the therapist and the patient. It can enhance the level of empathy and intimacy because it is experiential, and because it uses imagery, it taps into a deeper dimension of emotion, creating a more powerful bond in the process. In addition, aspects of earlier relationships are more available in hypnosis, which further intensifies the relationship (see Banyai, 1998; Diamond, 1987).

To give the reader a feel of what modern permissive hypnosis is, let us give you an example. In trance, as in dreams, people tend to think more in images than in language. Imagine a hanging lamp, which when near the ceiling sheds its light over the entire room, making everything visible. When entering hypnosis, it is as if the light is pulled down to just above the therapist and patient so that it shines more intensely on them both and the rest of the room is rather dark. The focus is entirely on the two of them and what transpires between them. The room and its contents have all but disappeared, and what is left is only the process between the two people, patient and therapist.

It is this intensive interaction and the changes that develop as a result that are the subject of this book. Although not all the cases in this volume involved hypnosis, all did involve this powerful connection that, while it ebbs and flows during the course of therapy, it engages both therapist and patient intimately.

EMPATHY

Empathy is one of the driving forces that dynamically enhances the intersubjectivity of the therapy. As therapists become more intimately involved, it is their empathy that creates a process that is alive, one that can proceed beyond the more familiar ground, or even transcend some of the traditional roles prescribed by the field of psychology. As they progress through this process, therapists frequently also change. Thus, a therapist's empathy is core to the changes that go on in therapy not only for the patient but for the therapist as well.

Therapists must be able to understand their patient on the patient's own terms and from his or her own perspective. Therapists must feel themselves into the very soul of the patient and deeply understand the hurt and other painful emotions found there. In putting themselves in the shoes of the patient and taking on the deep inner feelings of various patients, we, the therapists broaden our perspectives, and expand our own personalities. As Erika Wick (chap. 4, this volume), discussing therapist change in her chapter, put it: "Therapist change is the natural outgrowth of a therapeutic involvement, a chance to grow and broaden horizons. I have felt growth when sharing in human experiences not close to my own field of awareness, as they activated my access to deeper layers of the collectively human realm in which I am participating." Empathy is the starting point, but alone it is not enough; one must also be courageous enough and open enough to confront one's own limits and perhaps travel to uncharted territory beyond the normal and the familiar.

What is it that invites the change? It is through our empathy for the patient that we may come in contact with a part of ourselves that needs to change as we observe the change process in our patients. We are brought face to face with an aspect of the human condition that causes us to change as persons. Wick (chap. 4) states, "all our experiences affect and influence us. Often the effects and ensuing changes are so subtle that we may not notice them as they occur. We only become aware of them when the cumulative effect of the received input expresses itself in new thoughts, feelings, attitudes or behaviors." In the powerful interaction of patient and therapist, the therapist is most definitely affected.

It is the interpersonal nature of the relationship that is so profoundly influential. The word *interpersonal* refers to something that transpires between two people, not a process that goes in one direction only. A therapist who is open to the experience comes to this interaction ready to change, although perhaps not specifically with the intent of changing. It is this openness to the relationship and to the process that sets the stage for what is to follow. As the patient delves deeper in his or her psyche, the empathic therapist tries to understand the patient's perspective and becomes drawn into the patient's point of view. At some point along the way, the boundaries may become a bit blurred so that the therapist may temporarily adopt some of the distortions of the patient. Over time, more and more of the irrational behavior, concerns, preoccupations of the patient become fully understood. It is at this juncture that the situation calls on the therapist to be extraordinarily responsive; it moves him or her to react in a new way that speaks to the specific needs of the patient. Here, the intimacy that is engendered is profound as are the changes that are effected (with the therapist involved as much as, or almost as much as the patient). The therapy then becomes something fresh and alive as it emerges from the organic relationship between patient and therapist. In carrying this further, the therapy may travel beyond the traditional or well-worn pathways to retain this precious vitality. As therapists venture beyond the familiar, they must carefully scrutinize their boundaries and the boundaries of the therapy. It is at this point that they may decide to alter these boundaries, and in so doing, create a lasting change in both patients and themselves.

There must be compelling reasons to go beyond the traditional bounds of therapy. These reasons must emerge from understanding the patient deeply and the real empathy the therapist has for the patient's suffering. Only in unusual cases, when there are powerful reasons stemming from the suffering of the patient, which the therapist understands and feels with the patient, may the therapist go beyond the general rules of the therapy.

Let us give a few examples. Every form of therapy has traditional rules (i.e., boundaries beyond which the therapist generally does not go). For instance, psychoanalysis has a rule that the patient should never be touched by the therapist because the patient might conceive of such a touch as being seductive. However, when the patient weeps because of the death of a spouse, it may be worth the risk to empathically put your hand on the patient's arm.

Other, more general rules are rules that hold for all kinds of therapy, such as the patient should not be allowed to smash the furniture of the therapist's office when he or she is angry, or the patient comes to the therapist's office and not that the therapist comes to the patient's home. These traditional rules of therapy are important and necessary. However, there may be times when the therapist breaks such a rule, out of understanding and empathy for the patient, or lets the patient break the general rule. For instance, when a close member of the patient's family has died, and the patient is mourning deeply, the therapist may decide to go and visit the patient at home. Or the therapist may decide to reveal certain aspects of his or her own life, or bring a part of his or her life into contact with the patient.

TRANSFERENCE AND COUNTERTRANSFERENCE

Our conceptualization of change expands on the ideas of transference and countertransference. In the former, the patient transfers old childhood feelings and unresolved difficulties that he or she has had in relationship to his or her parents, siblings, and other important childhood figures onto the therapist. The patient who has had a highly authoritarian and strict father will at sometime in the therapy, or probably for most of the time in the therapy, conceive of the therapist as authoritarian and strict, regardless of whether the therapist is authoritarian or not. Thus, in the traditional idea of transference, the patient attributes characteristics of important figures of his or her childhood to the therapist, and in his or her relationship with the therapist he or she works out these conflicts. More recently, transference has come to encompass all the feelings that the patient has toward the therapist—including those that may emerge from the here-and-now relationship.

Traditionally, countertransference referred to the therapist's unconscious childhood fantasies and conflicts that are brought to light by the patient, which undercut the therapist's neutrality and therefore compromised the therapeutic process. In recent years, countertransference has also come to be defined more comprehensively to include any feelings the therapist has about his patient. The more recent rendition of the concepts of transference and countertransference will clearly be the focus of this book. However, if the more traditional definition were used, then these unconscious conflicts coming to the foreground would only represent a part of our focus. We would, in addition, include the here-and-now relationship on both conscious and unconscious levels in our formulation.

To some degree, we also have to consider the here-and-now reality of the patient's perception of the therapist as the person he or she really is. If the therapist is a mild, protective, and giving human being, then the patient will, with some small (still reality-oriented) part of himself or herself, real-ize that. If the therapist is a highly artistic person and has beautiful pictures hanging around the office, the patient can easily conclude that the therapist is sensitive and artistic. If the therapist is a warm and mothering kind of in-dividual, then some, perhaps smaller, part of the patient's psyche will feel this nurturance and at least from time to time react realistically in relation-ship to the therapist. He or she may like or not like the actual maternal feel-ing, or the paternal, or risk-taking, or very cautious personality encountered in the here-and-now relationship. But there will be a response to the actual person. Just as the patient responds to the kind of person and the reactions the therapist has to him in the present, so, too, does the thera-pist respond to the reactions of the patient and to the patient's reactions to the situation as well.

Changes in the Therapist

The examination of this process of change in the therapist as the result of doing therapy, and in particular, hypnotherapy, has, to our knowledge, never been undertaken. This volume represents a beginning effort to assess both the kind of changes therapists go through and the way they go through them. The changes were not uniform; some therapists reported profound transformations, others only mild ones.

By change, we mean an alteration in the way a person interacts with the surrounding world. This alteration can affect only a circumscribed area of one's life, say a change in therapeutic technique or way of looking at a ther-apeutic problem. At the other end of the spectrum, an alteration can effect one's entire worldview—a change in Weltanschauung in which assump-tions about the world and about oneself as part of this world undergo radi-cal transformation. We conceive of all of these changes as falling along a developmental continuum similar to Skovholt and Rønnestad's (1992) three stages of therapist change. They see the process as starting with as-similation of technique and imitation of the experts, evolving into separa-tion from traditional roles and finally into self-reflection and integrity, a stage where the therapist's reflections transform ways of thinking and act-ing in both professional and personal life. This final stage of Skovholt and Rønnestad's was what we wanted to focus on in this book.

In the case studies we received from the senior therapists who are our au-thors, we could discern three kinds of changes that occur as they move through this final stage of self-reflection. The first type of change we call *New Approaches*. This refers to changes in specific areas, with relatively brief self-reflection and without ongoing ramifications in one's personal life. This does not mean that the change is not personally meaningful; on the contrary, it is very powerful. However, the effects are circumscribed—it is primarily found in the treatment arena, although there are reverberations felt in other parts of the therapist's life.

The second type of change we have termed *Individuation*, which refers to a more complex, deeper, and pervasive change. A modification of therapeutic endeavors represents the beginning. Beyond this, it involves a clear disjunction from the past that also affects ones personal life and is experienced at both an intellectual and emotional level. A personal exchange with the patient sets the stage for this kind of change, but the interaction is more the occasion of the change than the cause of it. That is, the seeds of change reside more within the therapist than in a series of interactions with the patient.

The third type of change we call *Transformation*. This refers to an even more complicated process, one that not only can reconstruct the past but can transform past understanding into knowledge as used in the present and sets the stage for future interactions. Like Individuation, Transformation reaches beyond professional development. The professional relationship, rather than being one of distance, is transformed and transforming. The relationship is transformed by becoming more real, more authentic than many of the others in one's life (this can apply to both therapist and patient). This relationship in turn transforms a difficult circumstance (e.g., death or other serious situation in the patient's life) to one that can be negotiated or put in perspective. A profound and powerful existential issue is encountered in which one's basic assumptions or stance toward life is changed. The involvement with the patient not only sets the stage for change but is crucial to it. It is through this mutual exchange that *both* individuals move toward the unknown and the uncertain that life (and death) may hold, and *both* can eventually learn to transcend or accept these seemingly overpowering forces.

When examining these case studies, we discovered that the treatment evolved through clearly discernable phases. These phases seemed most evident when a Transformation occurred, although some could be seen in the other two types of change.

Phase 1

The patient undergoes some powerful experience, such as the death of someone close or confrontation with the imminence of his own death. Or, an ordeal, a gut-wrenching experience, produces a formidable change in the way a patient lives his or her life. Their difficulties become so vivid and so involving, particularly when using hypnosis, that the therapist becomes highly focused on the patient and what he or she is going through.

Phase 2

The therapist enters the world of the patient, experiencing it, feeling it in all its complexity and pathos. The bond of empathy becomes so strong that the therapist experiences many of the emotions of the patient. At times, it can become difficult to keep boundaries clear and to keep things entirely in perspective. There may be some minor difficulties in adaptation or even distortions.

Phase 3

In the third phase some of the emotions of connection and empathy are transmitted in various ways to the patient. All the different shades of emotion that have been shared by patient and therapist and that have become part of their mutual exchange feed this. Of course, this kind of empathy is vital to doing dynamic psychotherapy. However, the way it is played out here is different. Because of the empathic attunement, dealing with the crisis calls for the therapist to be strongly responsive. He or she even may go beyond the usual bounds of therapy to respond to the situation. Many of the therapists in this volume took some unusual and sometimes dramatic steps on behalf of their patients.

Phase 4

In the fourth phase both patient and therapist process the meaning of moving beyond the usual boundaries, the results of taking that extra step. A change is effected in both patient and therapist. Although this may occur on a conscious level, for many it remains a part of an unconscious, but strongly felt change in the relationship. It is the way an infant feels a shift in the mood of its mother by the way the mother reacts to the child and the child to the mother. Stern et al. (1998) called this a shift in *implicit relational knowing*. If this shift occurs in the relationship, it inevitably leads to the patient changing.

Phase 5

In the fifth phase the patient goes on to cope with his or her life situation, using the shifts and changes assimilated in the therapy; the therapist continues to process this change, adapting it to his treatment and to his life.

These five phases may not have been explicitly stated for each of the authors but were present for many when we tried to elicit more of the details of treatment. Some therapists spent less time focusing on the changes in themselves. In fact, quite a few spent only a page or less on their own experiences. These therapists seemed reluctant to focus on themselves because their attention usually has been devoted entirely to their patients. As we asked them to rewrite their chapters and become aware of what happened in their own psyches, the phases described earlier became more apparent.

We have divided the chapters into five sections based on the focus or content of the therapy. Certain foci, like dealing with the death of a patient, can cause profound changes which result in a Transformation. Other chapters dealt more with changes that emerged during treatment and consequently fell into the Individuation category. Still others represented a change in technique (i.e., a New Approach).

PART I: CHANGES IN ATTITUDE ABOUT DEATH

The four chapters in this section comprise reports of therapists whose patients died during the course of therapy. In dealing with such a powerful experience, the therapist must confront his or her own mortality in order to help the patient through the process. Changes in the therapist's perspective follow and flow from this. These changes fall in the category of *Transformation* described previously.

Chapter 1

Marlene Eisen worked for 8 months with Larry, a 46-year-old man dying of liver cancer, to help him cope with the stages of dying and to enhance his relationships with his family. She learned to be more openly expressive of her own feelings about Larry as he went through the process, including her own grief, anger, and disappointment about the fact that he had to die, as well as her hope for him and elation whenever he seemed to get better. Listening to him, she became inspired by the depth and breadth of the human spirit.

Chapter 2

Stephen Kahn also worked with a dying cancer patient, a 64-year-old woman, and helped her to die with dignity notwithstanding the fact that in the process the patient and the therapist became aware of incest experiences from her childhood. During that time, Kahn became and acted not only as a therapist but also like a supportive friend of the patient. He learned that there are occasions when the therapist, although still remaining the therapist, must go beyond the ordinary limits of therapy when facing the process of dying. As a result, he learned to fear death less than he had and to be courageous in the face of approaching death with patients who are dying.

Chapter 3

Rita Rogan worked with a cancer patient as well, but this was a young man. She worked closely with him and his immediate family and family of origin, helping them all come to terms with his death by changing their relationship during the time he had left. Her relationship to him changed dramatically as well. She learned how to cope with mortality while becoming more open to the surprises and twists and turns of life.

Chapter 4

Erika Wick worked to revive a comatose patient using variations on hypnotic techniques. When the revived patient later suffered life reversals, he became furious with her for "bringing him back." She realized that this form of therapy went well beyond the usual, and she struggled with how much one can make a life-and-death decision for a patient and how much should be left up to the patient.

PART II: CHANGES IN THE ABILITY TO MOURN PARENTS

The two chapters in this section explore the confrontation with the death, loss, and reintegration of ones parents as the therapists work with their patients. These fall in the category of *Transformation* but not as decisively as the first four chapters.

Chapter 5

David Soskis used hypnotherapy with Malcolm, a middle-aged bank executive, to help him stop smoking. The treatment, although initially successful, was followed by a relapse and led to a significant change in the treatment approach. Soskis recognized a parallel process in himself in terms of rebellion and independence and the need for a positive authority. This stimulated him to work through the grief over his own parents' deaths approximately 1 year earlier and to integrate their positive authority with him. It then made it easier for him to be fatherly or motherly when this patient and the patients that came after him, needed it.

Chapter 6

Linn LaClave treated a 12-year-old boy for posttraumatic stress. He saw his father shoot his mother, his aunt, and then turn the gun on himself. With hypnosis, she helped him to work through and integrate this trauma. LaClave came to experience the strong affect around the boy's grieving as stimulating her own process of grieving. She was amazed at the strength and perseverance of this boy as he confronted his loss. This helped her to better confront and integrate the loss of her own parents.

PART III: CHANGES IN PERSPECTIVE OF THE SELF

The five chapters in this section involve changes which lie on the continuum between Transformation and Individuation. Each are discussed independently.

Chapter 7

Brenda Bursch and Lonnie Zeltzer, in a highly complicated case, accepted their own uncertainty and supported each other after they realized how their own insecurities about their treatment of a child mirrored the dynamics of the child's parents. They came to see that their own independence issues had affected the process, and both feel now that professional interdependence is helpful and often crucial in doing good treatment. It went beyond the treatment in that they both confronted their personal issues around independence. This is partly a change in technique (New Approaches), but it also had ramifications in their personal lives (Individuation) and thus may lie in between the two.

Chapter 8

Phyllis Alden became able to accept her own physical handicap (congenital near-blindness) after empathically listening to a paraplegic patient maintain hope in the face of her paraplegia. The patient was able to obtain relief from her chaotic past and the burdens of shame she was carrying. By helping the woman to feel deeply understood and to experience a profound sense of relief, Alden was able to put her struggles with her own blindness in perspective. This is a case of Individuation rather than Transformation because it was not the outcome of ongoing therapy but the outgrowth of one session.

Chapter 9

Joan Murray-Jöbsis, a very giving, mothering female therapist, to whom maternally giving to others is a natural need, learned from her patient that not everyone wants to be mothered. Eventually, she learned to tolerate the rejection of her maternal feelings and that mothering at times may mean holding back on expressing mothering feelings. She also accepted the infantile rage her patient felt toward her and learned to trust the process of therapy to work all these complex emotions through. These changes fall under the category of Transformation.

Chapter 10

Judith Rhue worked with a patient who felt responsible for the death of her younger sister, a toddler who was severely burned and later died. The patient's feelings of guilt were undeserved and excessive. Rhue learned to tolerate the pain and guilt of her patient, instead of talking the patient out of these feelings. She allowed herself the compassion to suffer through these emotions with her patient empathically while standing by her and helping her work them through. Tears could be shed by the therapist as well as the patient, and this important realization about suffering together changed both patient and therapist together. This also falls under the category of Transformation.

Chapter 11

Mary Jo Peebles-Kleiger grew up in a religious environment in which the world was interpreted as all sweetness and light. She came to recognize that there are also powerful negative feelings in the patient, in herself, and in the world. She also learned that her patient's idealization fit with her own need to be a rescuer. These feelings had to be worked through in order to set limits with the patient. Her worldview could now incorporate the possibility of gratuitous ill will and that her goodwill could not cure her patient. This definitely represented a change in Weltanschauung for her and therefore can be classified as a Transformation.

PART IV: CHANGES IN TECHNIQUE

The two chapters in this section discuss alterations in therapeutic approaches and by definition, are categorized as New Approaches. Although elements of change in aspects of themselves beyond their technique are apparent, the primary thrust of the change centered on the therapists' treatment perspectives and methods.

Chapter 12

Stanley Krippner treated a patient with hypnosis who could experience no joy in his life or in relationships. As the patient progressed, Krippner learned to trust hypnosis and himself more fully, and came to feel that he could pass this on to others in the field by teaching them to use hypnosis responsibly.

Chapter 13

Albert Ellis reformulated his approach to his rational-emotive behavior therapy (REBT) by weaving a permissive hypnosis into the process. He changed his view of hypnosis as antithetical and instead found that hypnosis helped overcome resistance. The evocative, emotional quality that is engendered by using hypnosis supports and rounds out REBT. When he reached the limits of his approach, he became doubtful and self-critical but used his own techniques on himself. His change involved broadening his approach as well as overcoming doubts about himself.

PART V: CHANGES IN TOLERANCE FOR UNCERTAINTY

The three chapters in the following section recount major changes in therapists as they face the limits of their professions, each undergoing Transformation.

Chapter 14

John Van Eenwyk questioned his basic tenants for doing therapy as he treated a torture survivor. Van Eenwyk worked through how involved he should get with the external situation of his patients (even to the point of being involved in rescue efforts). He struggled with going beyond the bounds of traditional therapeutic interpretation and treatment and in resolving this struggle changed both himself and his approach in therapy.

Chapter 15

Karen Olness, a successful pediatrician, treated Denise, a child suffering from cyclic vomiting. As she worked to help her and her family through the medical system, Olness became very involved and intertwined with Denise and worried about her own objectivity. She later realized that this was important to their relationship. Olness also learned a tolerance for uncertainty and for the limitations of the medical profession.

Chapter 16

Richard Kluft worked with a childhood sexual abuse patient. Much to his chagrin, he learned that the abuse was still ongoing and that work had to be done to stop it. Kluft struggled with the intellectual, political, and emotional issues surrounding therapy, struggling through not only anxiety about current situations but also about the effectiveness of recovering memories, and the anguish of dealing with the suffering of his patient.

Kluft became convinced that the clinician must allow himself to be informed by the science of the field but must sometimes rise above it to fight for the recovery of his patients.

It is our hope that through these cases, we all become more aware of the potential for change in all those whose life path we cross. Each new person we see represents a new possibility—another chance for him or her to share trials and travails and another chance to relieve himself or herself of these burdens while negotiating a new path. As we observe the process of therapy and participate in it, the same potential is there for us—to change, to grow, and to become more than we are now.

ACKNOWLEDGMENTS

It is with pleasure and gratitude that we acknowledge the authors who contributed to this volume. Each searched deeply within themselves to put words to a most difficult and sometimes elusive process. What was most inspiring was their willingness to carve this from their personal lives and present it for public inspection. Thanks to you all.

In addition, we would like to thank especially David Wark for his time, effort, and support of the manuscript and particularly for his insights. David Spiegel also contributed his time and support; his efforts are shown in his outstanding foreword. Patricia DeJean read and commented thoughtfully (along with some members of her family) and was wonderfully helpful throughout. Mitzie Eisen not only contributed a chapter but worked with us on the introduction.

We are also appreciative of the support of our assistants, Kendall Sharp, Gunella Fecadu, Elena Weinstein, and Leah Williams, who would often give that extra effort that helps so much.

Finally, we would like to thank all those who gave so generously along the way: their flashes of insight, their thoughtful inquiry, or just their plain helpfulness in the long and protracted process of publication. May their reward be in the changes this volume can help to bring.

REFERENCES

Banyai, E. (1998). The interactive nature of hypnosis: Research evidence for a social-psychological model. *Contemporary Hypnosis, 15*(1), 52–63.

Diamond, M. J. (1987). The interactional basis of hypnotic experience: On the relational dimensions of hypnosis. *International Journal of Clinical and Experimental Hypnosis, 35,* 95–115.

Skovholt, T. M., & Rønnestad, M. H. (1992) *The evolving professional self: Stages and themes in therapist and counselor development.* West Sussex, UK: Wiley.

Stern, D., Sander, L., Nahum, J., Harrison, A., Lyson-Ruth, K., Morgan, A., Bruschweiler-Stern, N., & Tronick, E. (1998). Non-interpretive mechanisms in psychoanalytic therapy: The 'something more' than interpretation. *International Journal of Psychoanalysis, 79,* 903–921.

I

CHANGES IN ATTITUDE
ABOUT DEATH

1

From an Artist's Palette

Marlene R. Eisen

INTRODUCING LARRY

It has been 2 years since Larry died; time enough to have processed the experience, to weave together the threads of a therapeutic relationship that endured only 8 months, yet that has had a deep and abiding impact. In that brief time, the nature of our joint endeavor created a strong and unforgettable bond between us. What Larry and I confronted together was his battle with liver cancer. "We'll try radiation," the doctors said. "We may be able to slow the process down."

Larry insisted that he was too young to die. At 46 he was at the peak of his talents and at the top of his professional field. "I have so much to do," he moaned. "What happens to a man's dream when his hope of a future is snatched away?" He came to me because he found it awkward to speak of his situation with anyone else. "People turn away or they give me all kinds of advice," he said. "They tell me I should get another opinion or go on a macrobiotic diet, or meditate. Some folks tell me about people they know who have had cancer and survived. In fact the only thing nobody seems able to do is to let me talk about the cancer. What is it they can't tolerate, my pain or their discomfort?"

This was not Larry's first bout with a life-threatening illness. Ten years earlier he had a brain tumor, which was successfully removed. He was married at the time, but his young wife, unable to face the responsibility of taking care of a sick husband, fled the marriage. This was a devastating experience for him. He said he could understand her feelings and held no bitterness toward her. Since that time however, Larry was careful not to show any sense of vulnerability to others.

His life began on the flat plains of middle America. His farm family did not know what to make of this strange son who wanted to be an artist and go off to New York or Chicago, places that seemed foreign and dangerous to them. As a boy, whenever he sat sketching or reading a book, his father would take him to task for not being more usefully occupied. Only his grandmother understood his dream and supported him emotionally and financially. She praised his artistic efforts and encouraged him to reach beyond the narrow confines of his small world. "I believe she was living out her own dream through me," he said, smiling at some warm memory the thought evoked.

He recalled that the first time he really cried was at his grandmother's funeral. His father belittled him for his "unmanly" emotional outburst. No man ever talked about feelings in Larry's world. It was considered a sign of weakness to express fear or sadness. Anger was the only acceptable feeling state for a "real" man and it always had to be carefully controlled. Larry's mother felt free to express "weak emotions" like her interminable sadness, and then it became Larry's task to make her feel better.

He described his family as kind but distant. "We are like separate planets circulating in the same universe but rarely connecting." He could not recall much conversation of any kind among the members of his family. When he tried to bring up images of family events whether in trance or in our conversations, they were always rather static; people sitting around, engrossed in their own activities. When there were verbal exchanges, they were usually in the form of commands or complaints. Larry wondered aloud whether this legacy of silence could be the source of the difficulty he had expressing himself. I pointed out to him that he seemed quite articulate when we spoke. "I feel safe here," he replied. "I come here expecting to tell you how I feel and you ask the right questions and actually listen to my answers."

As our work together progressed, Larry often expressed surprise at how readily he was finding words to describe his feelings during our sessions. "You can use these words with others when you are ready," I assured him.

Larry was in analysis for several years before the cancer was diagnosed. His psychiatrist responded to this news with the suggestion that perhaps they should terminate therapy. He expressed the concern that Larry would be so involved with medical issues that he would not benefit from further therapy at this time. Larry felt strongly that the doctor could not deal with the situation, and just as his wife deserted him 10 years earlier, this man was "jumping ship" rather than face the possibility that he would be expected to confront, with Larry, the specter of death.

It was with great trepidation that he initially contacted me. A friend had suggested hypnosis as a way of treating the cancer, and got my name from another therapist. When Larry called he asked if I had ever treated a cancer patient, and only when I assured him that I had treated many, did he make an appointment. On his first visit he laid out his history. "People accuse me of being cold and unemotional," he said, "but I am just protecting myself. They invite me to be totally open with them, but in fact they only want to hear the pleasant things. The minute I start telling anyone about my doubts or fears, a curtain comes down, eyes glaze over or they turn away." As a consequence of his experiences, Larry did not allow himself to feel close to the many people who called themselves his friends. He even held the woman who loved him at an emotional distance. "She wants to share everything with me, she says, but I know that if she knew how dark my soul is right now, she would run like the others."

COURSE OF TREATMENT

Watching this man struggle, I wondered if I could tolerate his pain. It was palpable in the room around us. It reawakened in me a memory of all the losses I had experienced in my own life. I wanted to save this talented, creative person from his fate ... and knew I could not. I felt that he deserved a companion on the difficult road before him. As I look back on the experience, I feel privileged to have played that role.

One of the first reactions to a diagnosis of cancer is outrage (Newton, 1983). "How could this body betray me so?" The reaction that follows almost immediately is a sense of helplessness and hopelessness. Our relationship with our bodies is based on the assumption that if one takcs reasonably good care of it, the body will function well and long without additional thought or effort. The onset of a chronic or terminal illness destroys that assumption and sends us spinning into the chaos of unpredictability. Larry, who exercised regularly and ate carefully, felt bewildered by the turn of events.

When I tried to explore his feelings with him during one of our early sessions, I hit a brick wall. "I don't know what I feel," he replied. "What is a person supposed to feel at a time like this?" "Well, there are several possibilities, I suggested; "You might feel angry or sad or scared." "I can't let myself feel those things," he replied. "They would get in the way of my work and interfere with my life."

I tried a new tactic, to help him express these blocked feelings. "What are you experiencing right now?" I asked. Close your eyes and think about it for a moment before you respond. He replied in a quiet voice, "I feel very tired … I just want to sleep. I feel like I am in a strange place without a road map. Something is not right, but I can't do anything about it." "Tell me about the something you can't do anything about," I asked softly. "What does it look like? What does it smell like? What color is it?" "It is dark, black, shapeless," he responded. "It smells rotten. I feel drawn into it. It is like quicksand. I can't escape. I am too tired." He opened his eyes, looking somewhat bewildered.

Drawing from my knowledge of Larry's work as an artist, gleaned from our first session, I wondered whether he could articulate his feelings as paintings in his mind. He had described so vividly the scenes of his childhood on the vast plains of the Dakotas, that I could see them before my eyes. He drew me into those early images of endless horizons, flaming sunsets, a lone house outlined against the barren vastness. His life would have been as barren as those images except for his grandmother who provided her shy, quiet grandson with her vision of a world beyond the boundaries of their homestead through stories and songs. She encouraged him to sketch the world around him, providing him with an alternative way of communicating. On the canvas of his mind, he could use the palette of his imagination to paint the images necessary to confront the end of his life.

With this in mind I asked; "If you could paint your present feeling, what would the picture look like? Close your eyes and see if you can imagine it." He closed his eyes and sat quietly for a few minutes. Then, with his eyes still closed as if he were scanning something, he spoke: "It is a dark hole in the middle of a vast wilderness. Nothing but barren plains with an occasional scraggly, leafless tree. The sun is a great red ball in one corner. It is like some of the places around where I grew up, especially in the winter time." "That is a wonderful vision," I told him. "What would you title that picture?" "I would call it 'Loneliness.' It is how I have felt much of my life. I just never gave it a name." "Perhaps one of the things we can work on is a vocabulary for feelings," I suggested. "Do you think you might find that helpful?" "I don't know. Maybe if I have words for these feelings they will hurt more." "That is possible. An alternative possibility is that it will allow you to communicate more openly with people who love you and you won't feel so lonely." "It's worth a try," he shrugged.

In our early sessions, we spent time getting to know one another, establishing his goals for therapy, and seeking some common language we could share. During our third session I introduced him to hypnosis, explaining the process, and guiding him through a simple relaxation exercise. He was delighted with the feeling of calm he attained. "I haven't felt this relaxed in ages!" he proclaimed. "I didn't think I could do it."

Over the weeks that followed, Larry learned that through hypnosis he could alter his bodily sensations, replacing tension with calm, pain with relaxation. He used Simonton style (Simonton, Matthews-Simonton, &

Sparks, 1980), representations of the destructive cancer cells being over-whelmed by healthy antibodies as his body fought the disease. He discovered through these techniques that he could regain a higher level of energy, sleep better, improve his appetite and, in general, function pretty much as he had before the illness. His initial success with trance work brought a flood of elation, a feeling in him that he could "beat this thing yet."

Larry went through the five stages of mourning as described by Kubler-Ross (1969). Stage 1: After the initial shock of the diagnosis comes *denial*. The person believes there has been a mistake, this could not be happening to him or her. Stage 2: *bargaining* with the doctor, with God; "if I eat healthy food, if I am good, if I pray, I will beat this thing." Stage 3: *anger*; "why me? I have had enough trouble in my life." Stage 4: *depression*; when everything seems hopeless and the person feels like a helpless victim. Stage 5: *integration* is that moment of acceptance, of acknowledging the reality in one's everyday life that leads to whatever accommodations are necessary.

As I shared his experience with him, Larry went through all these stages of mourning; not in a linear fashion, but back and forth, from one phase to another, triggered by both internal and external cues. When he came for his first visit, depression hung about his shoulders like a heavy cloak. He slumped like an old man, his head hanging forward, his voice without timbre. He had heard about hypnosis but was not sure it would work for him. When he discovered how successfully he was able to use trance, there followed a period of optimism. In a state of euphoric denial, he began to talk about healing and about his future. He took on a formidable new project without fear that he would not be around to complete it. He began to hold his head high, even to swagger a bit in his new found state of well being. His doctors were delighted with the change in him, and although somewhat cautious, were willing to join him in the pleasure he felt.

Larry began bargaining with the world. "If I work with my images religiously, eat healthy foods and exercise, I should get well, right? If I only think positive thoughts this nightmare will go away, isn't that so?"

I found myself sharing Larry's denial with him. "We'll work on it," I said. "Miracles do happen." I prayed hard that he would be allowed to continue his work, his life, for just a few more years. I was bargaining too. Then he had a relapse. The doctors decided radiation was necessary. Larry became angry. "One of my colleagues had lung cancer. He was on his deathbed. They did a lung transplant and now he's just fine. We were already mourning him. Now he's going to live and I'm going to die. It's not fair!" I was angry too. Not that his friend was going to live but that this man was in such emotional pain. "He has suffered enough!" I cried to the Universe. "Can't he have a reprieve?" I found myself reading avidly about people who had survived miraculously from devastating cancers. My own emotions swung from anger to anticipatory grief, to prayerful hope. I became a mirror that reflected his emotions and validated them for him. He told me that many of his friends and family were uncomfortable when he exposed his feelings, so most of the time he either avoided contact or put on a show of good spirits. It was a relief for him to share his feelings and know that I could take it.

Larry was always acutely aware of the impact of his disease and treatment on every aspect of his life: personal and professional. When the radiation left him drained of energy, he had to hire a colleague to help him with his big project. "I have to keep pushing," he said, "or no one will ever hire me again. Once they find out how sick I am my career is finished."

His hypnotic imagery reflected the depression that followed on the heels of his anger. Although he often struggled to find words to describe his emotional state, he had no difficulty picturing his internal landscape. Having come from a place where the prairie stretched for miles around and the horizon was forever, Larry visualized a house alone in the prairie. "Looks like my grandmother's house," he said. He described a house that looked run down, unlived in. Its rooms were empty. While he was in trance I suggested that he furnish the rooms and add people to them. Being an artist, this was a task to which he could readily respond. He created a kitchen where grandmother cooked and he sat eating cookies fresh from the oven. He felt warm and loved there. In the living room his mother sat and sewed, his father read the paper, his sister did a jigsaw puzzle, and he lay on his belly on the floor reading the funnies. He felt lonely and disconnected from the rest of the family. In both these scenes he was a young boy. His third image was of a dining room where contemporary friends sat around a large table with the adult Larry sharing a feast. He felt the warmth of friendship in the room, yet some sense of separation at the same time; almost as if he were watching a scene in a play. This reconstruction took several sessions, as we did one room at a time and then talked about what the visions he created meant in his life. He compared the empty house with his own sense of emptiness and alienation from family and friends since his illness, and his wish to reconnect. But he also expressed the fear that people would feel sorry for him, treat him differently, and that he would feel responsible for making them comfortable.

He was particularly concerned about the reactions of his parents to his situation. He would like to draw support from them but because of their ages and his history with them he thought the shock would be too great for them. I suggested that parents are stronger than their children give them credit for, just as children are more resilient and resourceful than their parents think they are. Perhaps he could enlist the help of his sister and see if together they could find a way of including his parents in his experience. "I don't have the energy to take care of them," he said. "I know what my mother will say. 'Oh my God, what have I done to deserve this!' It will become her pain, and I will have to comfort her." "That is a risk," I agreed, "but maybe, just this once, it will be different, and if it isn't, perhaps you are strong enough now to handle it."

It took him some time, but Larry did finally talk to his sister, who encouraged him by her own solid support and offered to help him find a way to approach their parents. The results were better than he hoped. Whether the sister had warned them, or they had become wiser in their later years, they seemed to be able to be fairly supportive, without demanding too much in return. Through this process he was able to re-establish ties, especially with his sister, and to a lesser degree with his parents, which would stand him in good stead through the months ahead.

Together, as we examined his concerns about the responses of family, friends, and colleagues, I was forced to look in myself and explore my countertransference issues. I had become extremely fond of Larry. My own mourning process as I dealt with the issue of his impending death, paralleled his. With every improvement, no matter how small, I clutched at hope. With every setback, I was sad and angry. I asked myself how helpful it was to Larry to know what I was experiencing? Should I be honest with him, or pretend that I was maintaining "therapeutic neutrality?" I decided to use these feelings as grist for the therapeutic mill. I also felt that in describing my emotional states, I could model a way of talking about feelings that might be helpful to him. So I shared what I was experiencing. I assured him that it was not his task to "take care of me," but I wanted him to know the strong feelings his situation evoked in me. I also remarked that though he spoke frequently of his icy detachment I had found him to be warm, approachable, and articulate.

He responded in a very positive way. He expressed relief at my honesty, saying that so many of the reactions he was getting felt artificial. He perceived the interactions he was having with people as being stiff and unnatural. He preferred to be with strangers who did not know him and therefore responded to who he was at the moment rather than to "Larry, the cancer patient." Consequently, he had been avoiding most of the efforts friends and family had been making to connect with him and was becoming more isolated. He often chose to go to neighborhood bars and have a few beers with strangers. Although his relationship with his parents had improved somewhat, he still avoided direct contact. He kept putting off a visit to them and telling them he was too busy to have them come to see him. I suggested that he could try to be honest with those close to him just as I was honest with him about my feelings although I had some concerns about the consequences. He could tell each person what he needed from him or her, and let each person decide whether he or she could respond appropriately.

It was a very hard thing I was asking Larry to do, for he had a history of doing for others, while keeping his own needs hidden. He believed that expressing need was a sign of weakness. In the past his sense of self-worth was based on giving, not receiving. Now, at his most vulnerable, I was asking him to go out and ask for something he needed. Could he do this in his hour of need? Yes, he could and he did.

In a sense, Larry was calling back the parts of himself that he had been giving away most of his life. And the response was heartening. He discovered how many people cared about him, how rejected and cheated they felt, how much they wanted to form a loving circle around him, and, most importantly, how much he needed them. "The amazing thing is," he said, in some bewilderment, "I feel stronger with all this support around me, not weaker."

Rather than taking work away from him, people came asking that he get involved in their projects, to the extent he was able. Now that he was openly expressing his state of being, he could ask for assistance or time out, and it could be given without discomfort on anyone's part. In earlier sessions he told me that he was not sure how valued he was professionally. "If I could live longer, I would have more time to prove myself, to make a real name for myself," he said. When the requests for his work began coming in, he expressed surprise and pleasure. "I guess people do respect my work," he said. "Perhaps I have already proven myself. It is pretty sad to have to get cancer to find out how much you are valued." Sometimes the thing we look for all around us is right there all the time.

I shared with Larry my perception that although he had difficulty finding a vocabulary for emotional expression, in his art he was extremely expressive of a wide range of intense feeling states. There was something so spare and simple, yet so evocative in his artistic expression. With just a few lines, a dash of color, a simple structure, he conveyed the whole range of human experience. Like the empty house on the vast prairie, there was so much embodied in so little.

I asked him where his ideas come from. "I just sit quietly," he said. "Suddenly a picture begins to form in my mind. No words, just a picture. I don't really know where it comes from." "Did that happen to you when you were a boy?" "Yes," he said. "That is why I would go off by myself and sketch. It was my way of talking to myself."

After establishing a solid therapeutic relationship during which difficult topics are brought into the open I frequently ask the question, "What gift has this experience brought you?" Larry's response echoed many others I have queried in this way. "I have learned the importance of telling the people in my life what I feel about them and what I need from them. I have found a way to feel close to people that I never thought was possible for me. I have learned to read the love in the eyes of my friends. How sad that I learned these things so late," he mourned. "But how wonderful that you learned them before it was too late," I replied.

As he described the changes he felt taking place in him, he likened the experience to an iceberg thawing. Having been accused of being icy and unapproachable in his relationships, he was very pleased with his analogy. Perhaps he was free to expose himself because he felt he had nothing more to lose. The results felt good enough that he was not concerned about explaining it.

It can often be effective to have the patient go to a quiet place deep within himself or herself, where his *spirit guide* dwells. The spirit guide represents the wise inner voice available to all of us if we can quiet those voices on the surface of our minds who natter and chatter about "shoulds" and "ought tos" and "don'ts" (Spiegelman & Vasavada, 1989). I am forever in awe of the wisdom of that inner voice, the truth of the images evoked in that inner space. Larry used his inner voice to very good effect. He recognized, after a while, that his art had long been informed and guided by that inner voice. When asked if his spirit guide had a form, he described him as an Indian brave, strong and solemn, sitting on a great horse. He expressed surprise as he recalled this image as one that had come to him in dreams in the recent past. Toward the end of our work together, when Larry had become dreadfully weakened by the various treatments he had undergone, we spoke of death and what it meant to him. His greatest fear was going alone into the unknown. It was of great significance that his last image, which he actually sketched out, was of his spirit guide, sitting on his horse, a shield on his right arm, standing behind a slim, naked youth, looking across an expansive, empty plain. "I am the boy," he said, "about to embark on a great journey. My guide is right there with me, protecting me with his shielding strength. I know now that I will not be alone on that journey."

THE IMPACT OF THERAPY ON THE THERAPIST

My involvement in this therapeutic process has informed my work in so many ways. The courage with which Larry and other cancer patients face the painful road leading to recovery or death has a soul-changing effect. Despite what I learned in my traditional psychodynamic training years ago, I now believe that neutrality is not always helpful. When a person is in deep pain, for another to sit protected by a wall of professionalism can disrupt the therapeutic alliance. It may be more comfortable for the therapist to maintain distance, but then the patient is trapped with one more person whom he or she has to protect by silencing his or her pain. Larry was in therapy with a psychoanalyst for several years. When the cancer was diagnosed, the analyst abruptly terminated the analysis. Larry and I discussed that issue and decided together that the analyst probably did the right thing. He was admitting, in his own way, that he could not deal with Larry's pain. It helps the therapist to be comfortable with the grief of others if he has looked deeply and come to terms with his own experiences of grief and loss.

I struggled with the question of whether I had the right to ask Larry to act in ways that, for him, might be emotionally difficult, when he was so vulnerable. Suggesting that Larry go against a lifetime habit and ask for what he needed from his family and close friends may seem like it was asking too much. But time was of the essence. Larry needed his support system immediately, and the risk seemed worth it. The very gratifying consequences of that risk-taking behavior reinforced my sense of the inherent goodness in people. If a loved one in pain reaches out in an honest and open way, people respond actively, relieved to know what they can do that will be most useful.

Watching this man who was so verbally inarticulate about his feelings find a way to express those feelings through his art opened a new way of thinking about the personal expression of deep emotions. In his work, he represented a whole range of emotional states without ever connecting them to himself. Through trance-induced imagery he was able to make the connection between his art and his emotions.

We are so accustomed to thinking of words as the only way to express our deeper selves. Allowing ourselves the freedom to express feelings through other channels can release areas of creativity ordinarily left untapped. Perhaps we can all become artists in the way we create our lives if we do not limit our means of self-expression.

Through my deep commitment to the therapeutic alliance Larry and I formed, I found the courage to express my own feelings openly. If I were to ask him to be honest in his emotional expressions, I had to model that behavior myself. Larry watched me as I reacted to his experience with a whole range of feelings that included anger, grief, disappointment, frustration, and moments of hope and elation. There was always the clearly defined understanding that I could express these feelings without any expectation that he do anything about it. We talked about the fact that feelings simply exist. They belong to some deep part of ourselves and are evoked by trigger cues that we might not even recognize. We are not responsible for our feelings, but we are responsible for our behaviors. I pointed out that he could also express his feelings and I would not consider it my job to make them go away. In fact, the healing comes from being able to express one's feelings openly and honestly, while a companion just sits in supportive silence. I thought about all the sympathetic statements people make when others come to them in pain. We say "don't worry, everything will be all right" or "what can I do to make you feel better?" What we may communicate to the sufferer is, "please don't suffer out loud, it makes me uncomfortable." I hope I never resort to such platitudes again.

Sharing difficult moments with another person without any expectations for the other to do something is a profoundly soul-changing experience. "Not doing" is one of the hardest things for any of us. We are programmed to "do," we are valued for what we do and how we do it. There are times in therapy, however, when not doing is clearly what is called for. The healing value of not doing was reinforced for me in my work with Larry.

Having had this experience with other patients also reinforced for me the power of hope. Each time Larry could find a way to work on one more project, he was filled with prodigious energy. When hope failed, he was like that empty house he had imagined. Eventually, the hope took form in imagery: In the image of the empty house that he filled with the important people in his life; in the image of the spirit guide riding beside him across the Great Plains on his final journey, this man who had felt so isolated and alone, had populated his world and gained strength through connection. He had found within himself, a strong companion for the frightened child who would take that last trek across the prairie. Even in his complete vulnerability, as represented by the nakedness of the boy, he found strength.

With a surge of energy after a long period of weakness, Larry decided to go back to his hometown. He wanted to see for himself the houses, the prairie, the people, that he had visualized in trance and in dreams. So he gathered his strength and went. It was a healing time. His family really responded. They cried for him, not for themselves, they reminisced, they shared real feelings. He felt they would never again be the closed-off people they had been. Through his confrontation with the most vulnerable parts of himself, Larry had finally broken through the walls that separated him from the significant people in his life. That was the gift he had given them.

Two weeks before he died, Larry decided to have a party on his birthday. With the help of some very close friends, he invited all the people who meant something to him. He collected things of his that he thought each person might like and gave them as gifts. He had a wonderful time. People laughed and cried, ate and drank, sang and hugged. It was the ultimate birthday party.

I saw Larry for the last time in the hospital a week before he died. He was thin, pale, and very weak. Nevertheless, his eyes sparkled when he saw me. His roommate, an elderly man, said to him, "Hey Larry, its hell to grow old." "I don't think that's something I'm going to have to worry about," retorted Larry with a wink at me. I think I will always remember that moment and that wink.

The power of the human spirit inspires me over and over again as I walk with people through their life experiences. The privilege of sharing these painful and courageous journeys has touched my soul in a profound way. I have come to believe deeply in the value and beauty of life and its natural conclusion, death, each an integral part of the human experience. I found within myself the capacity to sit with the intense feelings evoked by the suffering of another person. This empathic response brings with it, along with the pain, a deep sense of peace. Accepting whatever the patient needs to bring to the therapeutic relationship has also taught me to accept the expressions of the deepest feelings in myself, expressions I once thought unacceptable. The grieving over losses I have experienced in my own life, reawakened by my work with patients like Larry, somehow seem to take on a different meaning. I now find these feelings deepening my understanding and enlarging my capacity to respond effectively without boundaries. I have learned that the more I acknowledge my own fragile humanity, the more I have to offer those who come to me in pain and the more meaningful my work becomes to me.

REFERENCES

Hilgard, J. R. (1970). *Personality and hypnosis.* Chicago: University of Chicago Press.

Kubler-Ross, E. (1969). *On death and dying.* New York: Macmillan.

Newton, B. (1983). The use of hypnosis in the treatment of cancer patients. *American Journal of Clinical Hypnosis, 25,* 104–133.

Simonton, C. O., Matthews-Simonton, S., & Sparks, F. T. (1980). Psychological intervention in the treatment of cancer. *Psychosomatics, 21,* 226–233.

Spiegelman, J. M., & Vasavada, A. U. (1989). *Hinduism and Jungian psychology.* Phoenix, AZ: Falcon.

2

A Matter of Life and Death: The Case of Jan

Stephen Kahn

> It is one of the most beautiful compensations of this life that no man can seriously help another without helping himself.
>
> —*Ralph Waldo Emerson*

Jan was a patient I will never forget. She came to me to help her come to terms with her death, and in the 9 months I treated her, we dealt with that and much more. In that short period, I, too, changed in ways that I still am discovering. Not only did I help her to die with dignity, or, as she put it, "with her head held high," but I, too, felt I had encountered my own mortality and what it meant to be alive in the present. I also learned more about the power of therapy and of hypnosis, and how we as finite beings can come to terms with our finitude.

JAN'S JOURNEY

Jan's voice trembled as she spoke. She managed to stammer out: "I've been given 6 months to live—I'm frightened.... I want to see you as soon as I can." I imagined her face overcome by this desperate sense of panic and terror, and I was glad that I could meet with her the next day.

Jan, a tall, stately, and attractive woman, looking much younger than her stated age of 64, walked in my office in a tense and hurried fashion, but with an engaging smile. Her angular face with its aquiline features and highly

15

contoured cheeks framed two piercing eyes. She seemed healthy and was lively and quite energetic, despite the fact that she had undergone a modified radical mastectomy, radiation, and chemotherapy over the past 2 years. It did not take long for this unperturbed appearance and manner to give way to the desperation that lay just below the surface. She was given a "death sentence" as she called it. In the next 6 months, her red and white blood counts, now dangerously low, would continue to drop until she could no longer sustain life. This was the tragic outcome of a radical and risky new cancer treatment, one, she said with an ironic twist, that "cured me of cancer but also happened to kill me." She wanted me to help her to come to terms with her dying and felt that hypnosis and therapy both would be helpful. She also wanted to better manage her anxiety and to deal with some of the physical pain she would be experiencing. She had used meditation in the past to relax and to gain control over claustrophobia and panic attacks and felt that it helped immeasurably. In general, she wanted to overcome her helpless feeling and gain some sense of control again. We decided to meet 3 hours every 2 weeks, 2 hours on Thursday afternoon and 1 on Friday morning to accommodate her long trip with her husband from her home in Wisconsin over 3 hours away. We met more often at first and later supplemented the sessions with phone calls.

THE JOURNEY BEGINS: ESTABLISHING THE ALLIANCE

During the first few sessions she focused on her rage: at her oncologist, at herself for not investigating this new chemotherapy more fully before going ahead with it, and at her body for developing the cancer in the first place. She had not felt such intense rage before in her life except when her adult daughter, Becky, had been killed in a car accident about 8 years previous. Her rage and the sense of "why me" were overwhelming to her then and seemed no less intense at present. Feelings of anger and guilt over her inability to prevent either her daughter's or her own death were themes that dominated our early sessions. It was a distinct relief for her to vent and express such intense emotions: "Anger feels good!" she remarked after a particularly bitter tirade.

It was then we began discussing, although treading very lightly, her feelings about dying. When it seemed to be the right moment, I asked her directly about *crossing over,* using that term to lessen the finality of it all. She retorted, with a half-smile, that if I ever called it that again, she would leave and never come back. She was going to die, and "there would be no sugar coating it." I was immediately drawn to Jan, not only because she was in such dire straits but because of her depth of feeling, her clarity and directness. I also admired her ability to forge ahead.

She did, however, have trouble envisioning what her dying would be like, or what death actually was. She was not sure whether she believed in God or in an afterlife, but she felt she had a sense of "something beyond" when listening to music and walking around her farm, smelling the smells and feeling the sun, and watching the lake. But death was something she knew she had to face alone and this, along with the terrifying idea of simply ceasing to be, was very frightening to her. She imagined what it would be like to die; going through it would mean totally relinquishing control and would be "scary like losing your breath … stifling and suffocating."

I noticed her unusual imaginative capabilities and creativity (she was writing a piece of fiction) and hoped to harness her talents to help her explore and overcome her fears through hypnosis. The first goal was to establish hypnosis (and me) as a friend and guide—not something that would deprive her of control—and to build on her positive experiences with meditation. In the first hypnosis session, the focus was on deep breathing to help her to relax and feel in control as well as be aware of her body as alive. This clearly helped her to breathe a little easier. The image of herself walking on the farm by her favorite tree and then down a path to the lake gave her a sense of peace and soothing. It also gave her the sense of the divine she had talked about previously. She could feel the strength of nature shimmering on the waves, wafting about in those full and luxurious smells, enveloping her body in the radiant sunlight and welling up inside her, allowing a deep calm and serenity to flow over and into her body. We used this body sense as an anchor for the calm breathing and the imagery, something she could use to ground herself in the future. She called a few days later to say how helpful the hypnosis had been, and I rejoined by remarking on what a wonderful hypnosis talent she had.

In the next session, we began making tapes for her to use at home. As she played the first tape at home she reported an orange glow was surrounding her body and that the tree in her imagery was growing taller and more supple and resilient (a metaphor describing her body and her sense of herself). We incorporated these new images in the next tape in the following session. She was quite adept at forging such images and using them to the fullest. Her ability to enter and utilize trance for relaxation, for comforting and soothing, and for feeling good about her body again increased rapidly.

She continued using the tapes at home—and we made new ones each session—creating a more finely tuned yet flexible repertoire for handling negative emotions and for feeling more at one with her body. The kinds of light she used evolved as well; the orange glow assumed a pinkish hue and eventually became an iridescent white glow that she could see shimmering on the waves and surrounding her body. Over time, she came to use the light as the induction and to envision it healing her body and increasing her white blood count. Her energy increased, and she felt she was somehow mitigating her death sentence.

CONQUERING DEATH BY RESOLVING LIFE'S REGRETS

With this sense of renewal and grounding, Jan turned to resolving issues in her life. There was much that Jan wanted to do before she died. Despite how she and the family came together in times of crisis, she felt her relationship with her children needed enhancement. Although there were no major rifts between her and her son, she wanted to feel closer to him. Jan and her other daughter, Ruth, enjoyed a close relationship, but Jan felt that somehow she had not given her the wherewithal to get married; she felt she somehow had abridged her autonomy. She also worried that her relationship with Becky, her older daughter who had died after being hit by a car while bike riding, had stifled this daughter's life, as well. Becky had been injured in a similar situation a number of months before, and Jan feared that Becky was suicidal because of their enmeshed relationship. This stifled/stifling feeling was emerging as a theme in her relationships, one that she wanted to set right. As she had felt so stifled by her parents, she wanted to be sure she did not have this effect on her children. She began to discuss these feelings with them and wished she could have talked to Becky. This desire was fulfilled in a hypnosis session a short time later.

After an induction, Jan imagined herself on the beach at her farm on the lake. I gave her the open-ended suggestion that she would come upon something that would help her deal with the problems she wanted to work out. She could make out a figure in the distance, barefoot and walking toward her. Soon, she came face to face with a young woman with a hood drawn over her face. A sense of fear and dread came over Jan as the woman pulled the hood back. "It's Becky," Jan whispered and gasped at the same time. A bone-chilling shiver ran through me, but it was clearly only half as powerful as what Jan was experiencing:

> She is taking me by the hand—I don't know where we are going. We are just walking. I'm afraid but she's calming me. Now, we are sitting down on the sand to talk. It's so good to see her, to be with her. She makes me better, better than I am. [She will say something that will help you.] Jan began to cry softly. She says "don't be scared" and smiles—she looks aside at me with one eye, then the other and says "I love you, Mom. Don't worry—I'm all right. You should have been okay with me ... the way I left you" I'm trying to believe her. "It's all right, Mom ... all right." She's putting out her hand for me to hold ... I'm taking it in mine ... it's so good to be with her.

By this time, the tears were streaming down Jan's cheeks. Her closed eyes served as pockets to hold the small pools of tears that had welled up.

The intensity and depth of feeling was palpable; she held out her hand for me to hold. I knew that this violated a taboo against touching patients. I also knew that at this particular moment, I would create a powerful connection, a link between me, Jan, and Becky, one creating possibilities all for the good but not without complications. Would I be moving too close too soon? Would I be uncomfortable with the intensity and have to pull back? With some trepidation, I stretched out my hand. She grabbed hold and seemed to be clinging on for dear life.

When we met the next day, Jan described the immense sense of relief she felt, and instead of walking down the steps to the beach during her induction, she floated down. Becky was not there this time, but did make occasional appearances in later sessions. At this point Jan simply enjoyed the walk along the beach with a new sense of peace, consolidating the gains from yesterday's session.

The focus on family continued in the next session, when Jan remembered an early encounter with death. She made a suicidal gesture when she was 7; she drank Lysol in an angry response to her mother's failed empathy. As Jan continued on, it became clear that there were many conflicts. Her mother, who still was living then, was in poor health. She was a highly narcissistic woman in her 80s, who Jan felt was so fragile that she had to be protected from knowledge of her medical condition. Her father, who was no longer alive, was a powerful man, an advisor to President Roosevelt, and a man whose charisma was well known. Jan harbored some antipathy toward both her parents because they divorced when Jan was 10. Her father was a womanizer and wanted more freedom; her mother was severely wounded by his affairs and by the divorce. We discussed how Jan's early gesture was a manifestation of her parents' conflicts and how painful it was to have been caught in the middle.

When Jan saw something was not right, she, in her own determined way, wanted to resolve the difficulties straight away. Resolving the anger at both parents and conflicts with her mother was a tall order to be accomplished in the next few months; we resolved to do what we could. In this mode, we began working through her thoughts about her mother.

Jan railed, at times quite bitterly, at her mother's failures to notice her and her feelings. She was raised by a series of governesses and felt her mother could not invest time or energy in her. Her older sister was needy and seemed to absorb all the mother's attention. As Jan grew up, she also felt uncomfortable about her sexuality, concerns that were later ameliorated as she had more relationships and finally got married. In trance, the images helped Jan work through some of this wrath at her mother and father. At the end of each trance, we used an imaginary plastic spray to cover her all over, giving her a sense of safety and a permeable and flexible coating that could protect her.

Our meetings were almost weekly the first month in therapy. Once, in between sessions, Jan called because she had been overcome by feelings of guilt about being angry with her dead father. She felt depressed and asexual, but felt relieved by our last visit in which she discussed her angry feelings at both her parents. She also began writing a long letter to her mother that she was undecided about sending.

In our next session, Jan found herself on the beach again, but this time with her mother (after her mother divorced her father):

> I can see Mom is hurt. I want to tell her ... I want to confront her, but I'm just not able to. She never lets me get close. I can see her gray hair; it's kind of a shock. She was always wearing wigs. ["It's OK to see her like this."] Now she is kissing her new boyfriend; I didn't want her to leave Daddy. I am afraid. I am afraid of Daddy.... ["Something will come up that will tell you more about what you are afraid of."] I'm not sure what I'm afraid of ... oh, I've thrown up all over this nice white dress. I want Mom to pick me up. I didn't want to get dirty but I couldn't help it.

She realized from this that her mother had never paid as much attention to her as she needed and that the divorce heightened this. Again, she found herself in the middle of the conflicts between her parents. There was also an association between her fear of her father and vomiting, and wanting comfort for soiling this pure white dress. This symbolism became clearer later as her sense of her highly charged relationship with her father emerged more fully.

Although Jan was able to find some relief working through her anger, her body was reacting to her disease and to some of the stress she was under. She discussed some of the physical pain she was now feeling and also discussed her fear of eventually contracting fatal pneumonia. She contracted it before and was worried that this might be something that might eventually kill her.

During this time, Jan was writing furiously. She desperately wanted to complete her book. The more her anger flowed in the therapy, the more the writing seemed to flow for her at home. I discussed how much was going on with her in her life, particularly working so hard on writing the book and trying to work through all these emotions with people both dead and alive. While I encouraged her to decrease the pressures on herself to achieve so much, she kept reminding me that she was "working on a deadline."

She also began to feel some vulnerability around her fear of her father. This vulnerability emerged as the feelings about her mother became more resolved. In the next hypnosis session, Jan found herself going down the stairs. But this time they changed to the stairs in her father's house (after he had separated from her mother). The stairs felt very big, and she had to proceed cautiously:

I am down the stairs now to a dirt floor. There's a room here; I'm not supposed to be here. There's a door to a second room. It is cold and small and I can't get out. There are a lot of ugly little animals here. Rats.... I can't get out; there's no ... air. I am afraid. ["You'll find that you can breathe a little more easily and that something is changing."] I'm in the garden now; there's a large heart there. It's white and full. And now it's turning into a pure white, beautiful bird with its mouth open. There's the heart there on a chain in its beak; it's a prism and rainbows are coming from it. I'm feeling the bird ... stroking it. It's so big, it's bigger than I know what to do with. I can almost fly holding onto it. There's also a sad feeling (she begins to cry). I don't want this to end, it's so beautiful. The bird is climbing higher and higher, and I am getting more afraid. ["The clouds can catch you."] I'm taking the white heart on a chain and putting it on. It feels good. I'm not afraid anymore.

When Jan approached these frightening, suffocating images, terror would threaten to overwhelm her. But she was able, sometimes with my help and sometimes with her own images, to create an atmosphere of safety and beauty imbued with a soft and gentle tenderness. The beach with its backdrop of security and a sense of contact with the divine had become the meeting place for those whom Jan had to confront. She began talking about her fear now of meeting her father on the beach, talking more about her anger at him, how much of a ladies' man and a flirt he was. He once told Jan about his cheating on his second wife, along with the details of his sexual life. It was apparent that there were some sexual issues between Jan and her father. As she spoke more of her father, she also talked about that little room, the fear of no air, the fear of this rotten little cellar, and connected it up with the fear of dying from pneumonia. She began to have a number of fears about dying. At this point, she asked if I could be there when she died. Again, I was uncertain as to how to answer that, not wanting to raise hopes, not wanting to violate the boundaries. In the end, I told her that if at all possible I would be there.

In the next session, Jan consolidated some of the gains she made in the previous one. The heart chain could be used as a talisman to soothe and calm her when she was assailed by the fear of dying and of not being able to breathe. During hypnosis, she went down to the beach on her farm, but suddenly had found herself again in the little room, suffocating and feeling helpless:

There is no air here. No light either. I'm feeling all alone and helpless ["The talisman in your hand can light up the room."] Yes, that helps.... I can leave the room if I want, or I can come back if I have to. I need to be able to be in there without the talisman. I am less afraid now, but there is something else here; there is some kind of monster or something that I cannot see.

We soon found out what or who this monster was. It was the end of our second month of therapy and we spent the time talking about the strong attachment she had to her father when she was a young teenager. When she was 14, her father asked to paint her, and later clarified that he wanted to paint her in the nude. The idea was abhorrent to her but also pleased her. It made her feel so much more an adult, a woman, to be treated this way. He began by painting her with her top off. Later on, he would, as he painted, come over to make an "adjustment" by moving her breasts with his hands. Along with these memories came a strong sense of rage, first at her father and then at herself, for somehow enjoying it and "leading him on."

A week later, she reported that her platelets had decreased and her physical pain had increased. We began using hypnosis for both pain management and to decrease her sense of fatigue. We were uncovering a great deal, and the resulting stress may have precipitated some physiological reactions. But Jan did not wish to slow this down; she was on a mission to complete not just her book but the book of her life before she died. She wanted to know more about her feelings about her father and more about what had happened. However, pushing into these things may have been causing her health to deteriorate. I felt we had to slow things down. This made Jan furious. At this time she also became afraid and distrustful of me. We discussed these feelings at length and how they became more powerful as we got closer to these feelings about her father.

Other scenes emerged in hypnosis. The first was her father on the beach coming toward her. She suddenly became a little girl and climbed up on some rocks to get away from him. Many games of chasing and hiding followed, some of which were fun for her, but some of which were quite frightening. Another scene was one of her father tickling her, which was fun and pleasurable at first, but later left her again gasping for breath. These two scenes expressed or typified the feelings of enjoyment that her father gave her but also the fears and sense of suffocation that his closeness engendered. This tickling scene brought out a good deal of Jan's animosity and venom toward her father.

By the end of the third month, more of these feelings were emerging and being worked through. Imagery like the following was very healing:

> I'm at the beach. I'm getting onto a small raft, it's floating down … I can steer it with a long pole. I'm going down the beach a ways.… Oh, God, it's my father; he's swimming toward me. He's getting up on the raft. He is dripping wet. I can see his genitals in his trunks. He looks so strong, and he's moving toward me. I take the pole and begin hitting him with it. I'm hitting him with it over and over again. There's a big dent in his head. It's all so awful.

The pole guides her journey, and it also protects her. Jan wept and sobbed in horror at the intensity of her anger at her father. Throughout this scene, she held my hand fast. I wanted to help her to reconcile herself to and integrate this anger. I told her to look at the bottom of the pole. "You can see another hand on that pole." "Yes, I can see it now" she responded. "It's my hand," I said. "I'm there … to help you." The relief was evident on her face and in the fact that she had loosened her grip. My being involved in her rage at her father, even helping her to keep him at bay, however violently, made it acceptable. In the next few sessions, we discussed her rage and outrage at her father and his advances toward her.

In a later session, Jan had what she termed a *flashback* during hypnosis:

> I am walking through these tall grasses, on the grounds where I lived with my parents…. I hear my father calling me. He is lying in the grass. I am just a little girl, but I can see him. There he is, with his penis out, hard and erect. And he's laughing, and he's saying, "This is the biggest mushroom on the whole farm." He asks me to come closer, still laughing. I now have the sensation of tasting it, licking it. It tastes awful.

The tears flowed throughout this session as well. The scene was so graphic and clear. I was with her as all this transpired; the scene seemed so real, I could almost see it myself. It sounded so much like her father's sadistic humor. Yet, a sense of doubt pervaded my thoughts. Had this really happened? It seemed all too classic and dramatic; yet her reaction left her devastated. Was she somehow acting? As we discussed this, she too would express doubts as to whether this happened, and I realized that some of my doubts were coming from her wish to deny all this, as she had done for the last 50 years.

On the one hand, I knew we could never be absolutely certain. On the other, I did not want to hide behind this principle. I felt so conflicted that it took a number of sessions with my supervisor before I could begin to resolve it and allow myself to believe that something clearly had happened.

I did tell her that despite the intensity of these images, we could not say exactly what had transpired. Although she remembered her father's fondling her as a teen, this was not proof positive of the veracity of this new scene. But I also believed that part of these doubts represented denial on both our parts. Certainly the sense of her father's inappropriate sexuality was a theme woven throughout her childhood, and her feelings about this was something we could work on. I told her also that I was incensed about what her father had done to her despite the fact that we could not be sure about exactly what it was.

We ended this and many sessions following by using hypnosis to help calm her, to center her, and to help her feel more integrated. Her ability to be relieved although only temporarily was also a relief to me. In the next 3 weeks, we processed her intense and burning rage at her father both through imagery in hypnosis and through discussion. Jan also expressed some of these feelings by typing out her novella, typing "till my hands hurt." She had been writing the story feverishly the past few weeks and had come to the final chapters. Some of the book imagery dealt with her anger and the justification for it. One of the main characters, a male, was burned up in a fire. The connection to her father became more and more apparent.

Her sense of abuse at the hands of her father left her feeling "terrible, bad, dirty and soiled." Some of the images dealt with hitting her father; other images were more symbolic. One of these found her and her father underwater, where he was riding a huge goldfish. She was able to squash the goldfish flat. This led to her taking him and "putting that fucker in a goldfish bowl. He is the one not able to breathe. In fact, he's afraid, he's claustrophobic." It was then that she realized that it was her father creating the feelings of claustrophobia and not being able to breathe that surrounded death. "Perhaps," she conjectured, "this is all about my father." Indeed, the anxiety attacks that she experienced earlier on in her life, her fears about sexuality (and some of the minor difficulties with her husband), and finally her thoughts about death as losing one's breath, now all seemed to stem from their eroticized relationship. She went further with this and interpreted that not being able to breathe was perhaps due to her father forcing himself on her, either with oral sex or some form of lying on top of her.

Although she obtained much relief from coming in to see me, there was still more to process, something hurtful and grotesque. Again, although her platelet count for a time had stabilized, it began dropping once more; the intensity of the sessions may have been adding to her deterioration. I became worried about this and would reign in her drive to experience these things so fully and intensely and spend more time soothing and covering over. Many times, she grew impatient.

Jan's sister was coming in for a visit and Jan wanted to talk with her about these memories. We discussed the pros and cons of her telling her sister of her experience with her father. The advantage was that she might learn more; the disadvantage was that her sister might not believe her at all and might defend their father. Jan felt that it was worth the risk, and she was right; her sister did respond quite well. She believed Jan and trusted her experience, although she herself had no such memories and could provide no corroboration. The visit was quite fruitful.

In hypnosis, Jan returned to the beach. Her father did not appear. Instead, there was a peaceful sense, a silvery light reflecting the moon on the lake, with wonderful shades of midnight blue surrounding her. She could hear a white owl hooting nearby, and the sounds of children playing, as well as some very peaceful music, all symbols of resolution and safety.

The next 3 weeks, we went through one scene after another depicting a burning rage at her father. I helped her to express these feelings as well as reconcile herself to the intensity of the rages she felt. Her acceptance of her anger was furthered when she began to feel some of this toward me, particularly when I was away for a few days. Jan began to worry about her dependence on me, and she felt angry that I was not there for her. A number of angry letters to me followed. She realized after discussing these in the session that as the time drew nearer to the end of 6 months, she began to feel totally dependent on me. The anger at me helped to distance her and to help her to feel more autonomous, and my encouragement to express these to me helped her accept them both with regard to her father and to me.

A couple of weeks later, I was taking a long weekend in Wisconsin. At the end of the session before I left, Jan expressed a wish to somehow remain in contact. An inclination to gratify this need welled up in me, and I spontaneously offered to visit her and her husband at the farm on the way back from my vacation. This is something I would not usually do. Particularly because of the poor boundaries with her father, I felt keenly the need to keep the limits of therapy clear. In a direct response to her wish, however, I felt the need to visit her, to see these places that her hypnotic imagery embodied, to actually witness and go with her to the beach of which I had only a vague image. These unusual circumstances and the sense that "she has only a little time left" helped me to decide to make the visit. We both benefited.

At the end of the fourth month, she began the beach scene with a new person on the beach with her—me. She appreciated my presence; she was feeling secure and unafraid. Suddenly her father appeared in swim trunks.

> He is there now, but he's looking old and sad. I want to talk with him, but he can't seem to hear me. He's saying, "Didn't we have good times together, me and you? I wanted us to, but I do know how awful you felt." [She cries.] It's hard to hate him when he's like this, but I can't, I just can't, forgive him. I gave it all I had, and it was still not enough.

We talked about how it was not necessary that she forgive him for this, but it was helpful to see him less powerful and to feel his good wishes toward her, despite the fact that he had harmed her.

A few sessions later, Jan connected the mushroom scene to the taste of taking Lysol when she was a little older. This was the part of her that wanted to punish herself for doing as her father bade her. As she worked through these feelings about her father, she began to talk more with her son, who had moved to Albuquerque a number of years previously, perhaps to put some distance between himself and his family. Jan felt particularly good about these conversations; the gulf between them was finally being bridged.

A short time later, a platelet crisis landed Jan in a nearby hospital. Although death was not imminent, I did drive up to Wisconsin to help allay some of her fears, and to show her that I was intent on keeping my promise. When I arrived, she cordially, and with a bit of poking fun, offered me a Coke, my favorite beverage. Then she began telling me about some of the work that she did while semiconscious. There were some very powerful images of an Indian larger than life, perhaps twice life-size, wrapped in a blanket and standing on her favorite beach. He was immersed in a white light, and it was very soothing. He stood by a fire from which rings of white smoke floated upward to the sky. The white owl she talked about previously flew through these rings and, with its head held high, flew to the top of the sky, where the heavens were opening. There was a deep sense of peace and equanimity that enveloped her as I watched her face glow with this light.

She also asked me if I would miss her; I told her directly that I would. I told her also that ending therapy was always difficult for me. You may never hear again about someone whose life became important to you. This way of ending therapy seemed even more difficult.

The end of the 6 month period that she was allotted by the doctors had come and gone. Although she was frail, she was not faltering. Her energies were low, but she had finished her novel as she wished.

The next few weeks represented a consolidation of a new set of images that were used not only when facing her deteriorating health but also in dealing with some of the angry feelings that still lingered about her father during this time. Also, Jan had a number of conversations with her daughter encouraging her to get married.

At the end of 8 months, Jan and her husband went on a trip to Alaska that lasted 3 weeks. This was a wonderful, freeing trip for the both of them. She had always wanted to see Alaska, and brought back a number of powerful experiences with its frosty white lights that were both austere and clear. These lights surrounded and seemed to come from the moon above the mountainous terrain of Alaska. For the most part, her health was quite good during this trip. When she returned, she added much of this rugged terrain and this soothing white light that seemed to follow her wherever she went, into her hypnotic imagery. Her control over the emotions about her father was expressed in the following hypnotic image: Her father would be chasing her. She would find the strength to stop and turn to face him. She would then stare at his boots. When she did this, the boots would begin walking him in another direction, farther and farther away. As he became smaller and smaller, her fears would diminish, until her father became just a speck on the horizon when her fears would vanish.

THE JOURNEY'S END

At the end of 9 months, Jan's platelet count became seriously depleted. She continued her "good talks" with both her children. Her relationship with her husband continued to flourish. She was able to visit her son over Thanksgiving, but while there had to be hospitalized. After about 1½ weeks in the hospital, and a number of calls to me, Jan asked me to fly down. When I arrived, she was on a respirator, and could only communicate through written words. Even then, the first thing she did was offer me a Coke. I was deeply touched by this, as well as amazed that even at death's door one could maintain a sense of humor.

Though communication was not easy, she was able to convey her fear and continued anger at her father. But the scenes of the Indian in a blanket, the Alaskan landscape, and the white light prevailed. I had a number of hypnosis sessions with her where I did the talking, where the emphasis was on continuing to let go by merging into this white light.

It was not clear how long she would live, although it was obvious that she was not going to live much longer. The doctors said that it might be a few days or a week or 2 at the most. I felt torn because I had to return to Chicago, but I did want to be there for her death. I decided to make a tape for her that she could listen to, which used the evolution of images we had created together, particularly the white light, the Indian, and the white owl flying into the heavens through the white rings of smoke. This was the same white light that surrounded her in her relationships with her family and friends, forming a kind of special bond between them. The focus was on letting go, releasing her from her fears and rage. It was to release her from her past and to help her let go in the present. It was also to help her let go of her life when the time would be right.

Two days after I left, surrounded by her family, Jan had the respirator removed. The family turned on the tape for her final hypnotic session. There, bathed in that divine silvery light, connected to her family and friends and to whatever lies beyond, Jan did her final letting go. Immersed in the sense of nature at her beloved lake and farm, she merged into the white light. She confronted death head-on, facing it directly and with clarity. As she had resolved many of her conflicts around living, death was not so fraught with fear and dread. She could face it as she had wanted to, with her head held high.

I was saddened to hear of her death, although I was not as sad as I imagined I would be. I wondered about this but later realized that I was glad to have been able to help so much throughout the process, but particularly by giving her a tape for her final moments. In a way I was there for her death. I helped her to free herself from being stifled by her father's sexuality and by her mother's narcissism and from feeling she was also stifling her family. I also realized that although her death was a loss, she came to terms with her dying ahead of time. Perhaps I did too.

CHANGES IN THE THERAPIST

Through this short time with Jan, I found myself changing in a number of ways: Our journey changed my beliefs about hypnosis, about my sense of the boundaries of therapy, and my perspective on death.

Hypnosis

I viewed hypnosis, to some extent, as a set of techniques or ways to approach treatment rather than as a process. I was aware of the heightened quality of communication and contact inherent in the hypnotic relationship but had never experienced this so fully. Because I could experience her deeper feelings more directly I was able to become more fully involved in Jan's life more quickly. Hypnosis with her involved a unique kind of presence in which my whole being could focus on the heights of her serenity and the depths of her despair. I could be with her in a way that went beyond mere talking in the waking state, a way that went fully to the heart of the matter.

Jan wrote an article on her dealing with a friend who was dying of cancer. She could not decide what kind of gift was right to bring a friend who was in the hospital; in the end, she discovered that the most important present was her presence (her pun). The therapist's being present in the patient's waking state is a powerful support and nurturance; being present with her in hypnosis was even more powerful. Although sometimes doubting the intensity of her emotion (which was perhaps defensive on my part), I came to experience the intensity of her life in both its joys and sorrows through these hypnotic images. Because of the heightened intensity, I often felt I was hanging on to my seat as if on a roller-coaster ride. I did not know what was waiting for me around each turn, nor did she. She, too, was having a bumpy ride; she went up and down, around all kinds of harrowing turns, while moving inexorably toward confronting her own death. The hypnosis work helped us both not only to feel the ups and downs more fully but to keep us strapped in as well. We could always return to the peace and calm of the farm, which I realized was as helpful to me as it was for her. Because of the experiential nature of hypnosis, I was dealing with the fullness and power of Jan's life in all its splendor and in all of its horror. There was no specific formula to follow, no clear pathway, trajectory or protocol. Without clear answers, and with the hypnosis making the experience more palpable, we were thrown on ourselves to trust our direction, to follow our step-by-step process along the way. Hypnosis is a powerful tool. It can be very helpful, but sometimes its intensity is difficult to manage and can even be grueling for both patient and therapist alike. Again we proceeded together, and we both learned to tolerate this intensity. At times I felt exhausted, but I felt we were always forging ahead. I now better understand the value of being there "in the trenches" with a patient. I no longer hesitate or step so gingerly. The process and value of hypnosis as a therapeutic tool that allows one to become so intimately involved became a basic belief.

Hypnosis also brought with it the very sticky question of whether the memories she "recovered" were real. My doubts about how to proceed

and about the dramatic nature of her imagery were at times quite daunting. Was I to believe that these scenes actually occurred? Jan wanted to believe in them but also felt many doubts. She wanted to resolve this by
asking me if I believed this all had happened. This pressure was enormous; could I refuse her this kind of solace? Would it even be helpful to af-
firm my belief that these scenes had actually taken place? Sometimes I felt
she was working herself up into some kind of frenzy about things she
could not control, about mistreatment by her parents and regrets about
her life. At others times, it seemed so real I thought I could touch it; I felt
for her and all the misery she had endured. I wondered if it was helpful for
her to relive it, even if this had happened exactly as she was experiencing
it. I did not want her to have to go through all these painful memories.
Wasn't it enough that she had to deal with her death? Through supervision and struggling with such feelings in myself, I learned to live with the
uncertainty. We eventually came to accepting our mutual doubts while
also accepting our individual but shared rage at her parents. Hypnosis
could not prove the memories were real, but it could give us access to emotions that needed to be healed.

Limits and Boundaries of Treatment

Another change occurred as I faced the limits and boundaries of treatment.
There are prescribed boundaries that each therapist encounters during the
course of his or her work and tends to observe. But there are times to move
beyond the role, to new territory. Part of me wanted to observe these limits
because I was afraid, afraid of violating the rules, but most of all, afraid of
becoming too close to Jan. Would there be too much dependency or attachment? Would I grow angry or impatient? Would I, too, become fearful in the
face of her death? Would I be able to bear the loss of this person to whom I
had become so attached? At times it seemed death was in the room and I
could feel the inevitable for both of us. Because of this, I did violate the
usual and customary boundaries when I held her hand, when I visited her
at her farm, and even when I promised to be there for her death. Particularly
with this last wish, I felt these were unusual and extraordinary circumstances that required the suspension of the normal limits of treatment. It
was appropriate, in retrospect, but at the time, each of these decisions was
fraught with uncertainty and conflict.

I worried for a number of months about the level of Jan's dependency
and how this dependency would be resolved. Piercing the usual boundaries of therapy did create more dependency. But did I even need to resolve
it? Was it not acceptable to have her become so dependent? If I could tolerate it, it would be alright. At the same time, I felt I needed to make this a
good death, which made the dependency feel overwhelming. Was I playing

into rescue fantasies? And who was I trying to rescue? I realize now that my own fear of death played a significant role.

I also worried about whether the therapy was even harming her: Was it adversely affecting her health to endure such trauma? Was it really necessary to enter the thicket of her relationship with her father? At times I felt that the stress on her already heavily stressed immune system was not salubrious. However, it was impossible to tell how much the sessions were influencing her health. We both had to reconcile ourselves to sometimes moderating our pace, despite the deadline we were under, despite her wanting to work through these emotions at any cost. Looking back, I cannot see how I could have chosen otherwise. Jan did what she needed to do, and, with my help, was able to die peacefully, accepting death, although there were still angry feelings about her father that were left unresolved. In a very short time, she worked through many of her feelings about her mother, her father, and her own death. And she enriched and enhanced the relationships with those around her, including her son, daughter, and husband.

Perspectives on Death

Perhaps the most profound and enduring changes that occurred within me were in my perspective and feelings about death. Although Jan had many fears about dying, she had the courage to face them. She brought a great deal of resourcefulness, energy, and just sheer will to the therapy, perhaps even more than she used during her life. I was impressed by her drive and her abilities; perhaps facing death can generate a new kind of courage.

It was my fears that had me referring early on to the process of dying euphemistically as "crossing over." Her willingness to forge ahead and to dive headlong into her fears not only facilitated the therapy, it helped make me more comfortable with my own and other's death. I realized that facing and surmounting the fears surrounding one's own demise could be accomplished.

In addition, seeing her go through the process of dying having resolved much of her apprehensions gave me the courage to help others in the same way. But I can best help others when I too have traversed that path. No, I am not comfortable with the idea of my own mortality or that of those I hold dear, but I can conceive of meeting death with a kind of clarity and openness that I had not felt was possible. The thought of merging to the white light that surrounds us all and partaking in a freeing process of becoming a part of what binds us all together is very consoling and even uplifting. I can now conceive of death as something that has its own kind of beauty and awe; it is not simply losing consciousness for all time. I understand more what Plato meant about looking forward to death because ones soul has been freed and the curiosity about what will happen is over.

Death is inescapable; I cannot control death and its inevitable, inexorable grip on life. I cannot control its timeliness or lack thereof. I cannot control when and where I must deal with loss. And I probably will not be able to choose how I will die. But I now know how to control my reaction to death, both that of others and my own. I learned about what it is to die with dignity and this has softened the blow.

With respect to our own death, we can choose to cower in the face of it or to look at it squarely. This is my own end, and I can confront it and accept it. Thus an overpowering fear of death will not have defined my life.

3

Where Angels Fear to Tread

Rita V. Rogan

Pools of low light warmed the campus walk as I looked out from my darkened office. My best friend had just left after telling me of his father's suicide. I sat stunned and saddened, but what frightened me was the return of the intense anxiety, verging on panic, that I had always struggled with when someone close had died.

The ring of the phone was jarring. When I answered it, a stranger's voice filled the darkness. "I am dying," he told me, "and I want to be hypnotized so that I can go back to my last life, to the moment when the soul leaves the body and the meaning of that life is known. Then I believe I can know what the task of this life is and do that work in the 3 to 4 months I have left." I imagined the negative shake of my supervisor's head at the idea of such an unorthodox use of hypnosis. I said, "I'm sorry. I don't use hypnosis to do past-life regressions." We talked for a while about his situation. My heart went out to this man. He had a wife, a 7-year-old son, and a 5-year-old diagnosis of Stage IV Non-Hodgkin's Lymphoma. He was only 27.

As we spoke, I shared with him the three things that Kubler-Ross (1975) found made facing one's death easier: a strong belief system, a good marriage or relationship, and the experience of having watched someone die with acceptance. He said he had one of the three: faith. We ended the call with my offer that, although I could not meet his request, I would be glad to talk through his feelings about dying with him.

As I returned my gaze to the quiet campus evening, the phone rang again. This time it was my clinical supervisor. I mentioned the last call to him, expecting his seasoned endorsement of my having declined the case. Instead, to my surprise, he stated his regret. "When people are facing death, we must work within their beliefs." He would be happy to supervise.

I regretted that I did not have the young man's phone number. So, when 30 minutes later he called again to ask me to reconsider my earlier decision, I scheduled an appointment. This time, when I hung up the phone I felt the full rush of an anxiety that harkened back to earlier years when I worked medically with dying people. Now I would be watching the illness and deterioration from a much closer position. I was grateful for the excellent supervision I had because I realized I was going to need it. I began to feel the effect of the night's events. "This must be my year to learn about death" I thought.

As the first appointment drew near, my apprehension grew. It was his physical condition that I feared. During those earlier years, I was exposed to the horrors that the human body can endure. I never quite got used to it. I always believed that it would be easier for patients and for me if I could relate to the person inside. Yet, here was my chance to do just that, and I was becoming anxious. Did I really want to know what went on in the mind of the dying? At the appointed hour I went to the waiting room and found it empty save one healthy looking, handsome, young man with finely chiseled features. He was dressed in a fashionable business suit. "You're not Mr. C. are you?" I said. To my amazement, he was.

In the first hour I learned a number of things: the long five years that John (as I will call him) struggled with his illness, how his parents had divorced, and his mother remarried, that he had earned a Bachelors Degree, worked as a Sales Manager, and that he was frustrated with his marriage. I also learned that his wish that he die in the arms of a beautiful woman was quite likely to come true. He was maintaining five separate affairs up to that moment. This was not what I expected.

His relationship with his wife began when he saw her on a beach in California. "There was this gorgeous blonde in a bikini." He had left his girlfriend of more than 1 year behind on a blanket on that same beach and had neither seen her again nor taken her calls.

He described his current frustration over his wife's lessened interest in sex. And he seemed to take personally the 20 pounds she put on since the birth of their son. He had affairs over nearly the entire course of their marriage. Among other things, I learned that he had a strong belief in Reincarnation and in himself. One of my supervisors who saw him in the hall after this session summed it up, "He looks very healthy, narcissistically healthy!"

After this first session I felt disbelief that he was as ill as he reported, that he had only 3 to 4 months to live. Although he carried a cane and walked with a pronounced limp, I had the distinct feeling that I was being fooled. But why, I thought, would someone adopt such a charade? This blunted response to the man's predicament was soon diluted by two things. The first was information. Records forwarded to my office from his medical care team confirmed the story he had given me. This opened the way to the second: my awareness of my own anger. Although I found his narcissistic disregard for others disturbing, I was really angry because he was so different from what I expected. I was embarrassed to realize that I held a stereotype: a belief that someone who was terminally ill would be vulnerable, humble, pitiable, deserving, and in need of rescue: my brand of rescue. At this realization I felt lighter and better able to consider the issues involved.

After a few more sessions and a great deal more information, John began to make subtle references to how his taste in women was changing from blondes to brunettes (I am a brunette), to dream material of the two of us dancing and, finally, to more explicit seduction fantasies about me. When I found myself squirming in my chair, I was both surprised and troubled. Although I knew how to deal with a client's seductive behavior, I never before had sexual feelings of my own for a client. Didn't I know enough about this man's issues to see what this was about? Why was I responding to him?

I asked a former supervisor for help. His counsel was equally daunting. He instructed me to imagine that I had just spent the night with this man and that it was wonderful. I protested and became increasingly uncomfortable. "Your best protection against acting on something is acknowledging it, understanding it, and bringing it under conscious control," he counseled. I imagined what he suggested. This led me to a feeling of privacy in which there were no secrets between John and me, and time seemed to stop. "It's like we are inside of a bubble. The world stops for a while." "That's what you, and perhaps he, are seeking—that feeling. What is important is that you did not have to sleep with him to get it." Armed with this new insight, I asked John to imagine as I had done. "I can't do that!" he protested. Then he realized that he feared losing the therapy that had become the one place where he could speak about his unpleasant feelings and his depression without concern about how he felt the other person might react.

This realization led to his understanding not only his sexualizing of relationships but also the price he paid for it: the need to be only attractive, upbeat, and charming. The feeling he sought was of oneness and safety. He realized he had developed no ways, other than sex, for getting that feeling. This made him aware of how tired he was of trying to keep up appearances for co-workers, friends, and mistresses. He began to speak of how depressed he felt and for the first time I could feel a consistency between his life situation and the emotions in the room—both mine and his. His seduction ideas fell away.

We were now ready to focus on his initial request to be regressed via hypnosis to his past life and the moment when the soul left the body. He felt by knowing the meaning of his past life, he would be able to better use the time he had left in this life.

During the next session, we did an age regression. Although John was a good subject, I doubted we would reach a point that felt to him like his goal. After about 20 minutes, John reported that he was "rocking—rocking in the hull of a ship." (My last name at that time was Hull.) I asked how old he was and he said "7." He described a large, dark room with many sick people. He had no idea how he got there. I asked him to go back further in time to the point of understanding how he got on the boat. He did, and described walking down a dusty road with a man who was taking him somewhere "to go away." He said the man was not his father but some kind of fathering person who had responsibility for his well being. He described buildings, smoke-filled streets, horse-drawn wagons and pungent odors in the air.

He said he was not sure what year it was, but perhaps it was sometime in the 1800s. He looked up at the worn sleeve of the man's coat and felt his small hand wrapped in the man's large, hard one. He saw money change hands and knew that he was being sent somewhere. He sensed that he was an orphan. He had somehow lost his family.

When asked to move forward to the trip's destination, he described being on a beach watching the boat disappear into the horizon. He had been forgotten, left behind. He felt desperate, terribly alone and frightened as he sat huddled on the beach long after the boat had gone.

He was able to move forward in time to the moment at which he died, the moment at which he believed the soul would leave the body and the meaning of that life would be revealed. He described being strapped to a stake, smoke filling his nose, making his eyes burn and tear (they actually did). Realizing that he was being burned at the stake, he was able to hover in a neutral place where he felt no pain, but could look back over that life. He was 16 when he died and had lived 9 excruciatingly lonely years alone on this island. There was a hostile native tribe on the island that he had spent his time eluding. They found him, nonetheless, and sacrificed him. He saw that in the life prior to this island one, he had a family whom he had taken for granted, whom he had not loved. The lesson in the island life, where he had no one to love, was to learn the importance of loved ones. The task he carried in his current life, then, was to love and appreciate his loved ones—something he was not doing. He wept openly during this narrative and spoke with deep conviction.

After this session, he ended four of the affairs and focused his attention on his wife and his family. He also reduced the amount of time, energy, and attention he was devoting to his business, where he was treated as something of a hero. He preferred instead to spend that time with his family. There was a fundamental shift in his view of his wife after this point. He saw not only his own viewpoint but hers as well. He did not end one affair. It was with a woman for whom he realized he cared both deeply and genuinely.

The therapy continued on a twice weekly basis. His "expected time of departure," as he called it, came and went. Spring blossomed into summer. He participated with his wife in a canoe trip with other couples, although his nausea and weakness were constant and his lower body was seriously weakened. He managed these difficulties quietly and enjoyed knowing he was welcome and wanted despite his ill health. These people, his friends, had become increasingly dear.

During this time, hypnosis was used to facilitate his imagery to strengthen his immune system in its battle with the cancer and also for pain management. One method transferred a glove anesthesia to his wife's hands for massages. This deepened their significantly improved relationship. His wife throughout was supportive and honest about her feelings.

Paralysis was his worst fear. "I know I won't be striving to win the wheelchair Olympics. I pray I do not have to face that humiliation." The major site of the disease was his spine, however, where a large tumor was growing rapidly. Several times, he went through gradual loss of feeling and function in his legs and his bladder, then spinal surgery, and then rehabilitation to regain function. He worked hard using self-hypnosis to increase his endurance in rehabilitation and to manage pain. Using hypnotic time distortion, he was able to compress time to exercise longer and also to expand it to sustain pain-free times and moments of peace.

As the therapy continued John spoke of his anger, depression, and sadness, as well as of the joy he found in simple pleasures. Yet he felt a growing isolation from his extended family with whom he could not speak of.

He was recovering from the second spinal surgery as the Christmas holidays approached. His extended family was not planning to get together as had been their custom in prior years. They were a family whose meeting ground was set in parties and whose relationships ran smoothly only when lubricated by alcohol. He felt they were avoiding him and each other now that his deteriorated condition pointed so undeniably to his dying. He was concerned about the impact of his dying on his family and their future relationships with each other.

He asked if I would do some family work with them. A number of concerns crossed my mind, all revolving around time. The development of an ongoing family therapy was not possible. What could be done with a family so historically reliant on alcohol and parties to manage their relationships and emotions? Could we learn enough about the things that stood in this family's way to enable them to draw on, rather than avoid, each other? Was trying to do so now a help, or an intrusion? Could they even come together as a group?

John suggested a single daylong marathon session. His brother's home, a place where the family normally had their gatherings, seemed the warmest and safest setting.

It was not until the time of crafting the invitations that I learned that the number of family members was more than 20. I was taken aback. I felt overwhelmed and wanted to withdraw from the whole thing. At the same time, I still believed there was a strong and reasonable need for what John was asking. I also knew it meant a lot to other members of the family.

We turned our attention to framing the invitations as permissibly as possible. One of the most awkward of these was to his father, Norm. Norm was a proud salesman whose postdivorce lifestyle revealed a lonely, shy man who had never remarried. John was concerned about his father's difficulty dealing with his feelings and his tendency to isolate himself from his family in times of need. He also knew that his father had avoided any situation that would have put him in the presence of his ex-wife Bernice and her current husband, Eddie. Bernice and Eddie were currently in early retirement. They had left their home state temporarily to help out as John's condition deteriorated, and they planned to live in John's community through the balance of his life. Since their arrival Norm had not been seen. John wanted especially his father to be at this family session and framed Norm's invitation to reflect his feelings and to define the situation. He wanted Norm to assume his position as the father of the family, not only for John himself, but for his brothers and sister, as well. Yet, he would respect his father's decision about whether to attend the gathering. John said he missed seeing Norm, understood his absence and wanted them to have more time together. Without pressuring, his brothers and sister also called Norm and reiterated their desire for his presence.

I had only 1½ weeks to prepare. My list of planned activities was not lost on my supervisor. In his reliably calm presence, I found my attention gently redirected to my own obvious anxiety. Realizing it had taken this form helped me to reclaim the more appropriate role of facilitator and thereby feel less responsible for the outcome of the event. My supervisor advocated having no structure at all, thereby allowing the group to establish its own level of work. I was willing to try that but wanted a backup "Plan B." In it I would recommend that we have three full group sessions, three quiet times, that we break bread together and that there be music. John's concern about the family's reliance on alcohol and partying as a way of being together produced my only nonnegotiable requirement. There would be no alcohol.

The marathon session was scheduled to begin at 9:00 a.m. We would work until our lunch together and continue until 5:00 p.m. or 6:00 p.m. I slept fitfully the night before and was quite nervous as I left my home that morning. On my way, I impulsively and uncharacteristically stopped and entered the church I was passing, aware of my constant anxiety. A Mass was in progress, and I slowly began to derive some comfort.

As I moved up the aisle with other communicants, I tried to focus my thoughts. "Everybody has to die, and this is just one person. It's no more important, this death, than any other. It's no more important, this death, than your own!" This thought pushed through the anxiety in my chest, leaving a clean-washed calm in its place. I realized that about John's death I could do nothing. About each person's death, I could do nothing. About my own death, I could do nothing. I could however, be there. I could be with these people as they each did what they could do. I could do what was needed so we could come closer to the person who was dying—as I would want people to be with me when I died. And each of us in our own ways could exercise the healing that would enable as John's death rehearsed our own. I left the church quieted in a way I had not been in months.

When I arrived I learned that the group coming in from Ohio was going to be about 1 hour late. John's wife said, "they are so resistant." I hoped at that point that John had been honest with me about how he had presented the invitation to them. Their presence as choice rather than duress was important. Finally, all arrived.

I looked around the room at his mother, stepfather, his father, two brothers (one with a wife), his sister, her fiancé, his mother's sister, Hannah, who had flown in from Arizona, John's wife, his mother's other sister from Ohio, who had just arrived with her husband and two adult children, and his mother's brother. As I looked at the pairs of wide anxious eyes staring back at me, it seemed quite a formidable group.

The question of structure was decided by the near panic of the group in response to the idea of proceeding spontaneously. I suggested my Plan B for the sessions: working as a group in three sessions, each followed by a quiet period. We would break bread together and enjoy some music. After a lively discussion, the format was adopted with one point of departure. They could not tolerate 15 minutes of silence and settled on 10 for the quiet period. They were a raucous group and their genuine humor was infectious and inviting.

We began the first group meeting. I borrowed the method of the Native American "talking stone" to define the process and order of speaking. The person who held the stone held the floor. The others would not interrupt. There would be no criticism of anyone's input. All had the option of passing the stone to the next person if they preferred not to speak. I pulled a seashell from a collection at my elbow and began.

"I guess each of us had some reluctance to coming to this gathering and yet, since we're here, we must each have had stronger reasons to participate," I said, and invited people to talk about these personal dilemmas as I handed the shell to John. He began:

> I look around and see each of your faces. It is sobering to realize that if I have had an effect on anyone in my life it has been on each of you. Right now I don't know what, if anything, that has been. But each of you has affected me. You are the people who are most important to me. I want to tell you how, and what, you mean to me. If I have harmed, offended, or hurt you, I want to know. I want us to finish our business together. My fear is that this day will pass without our opening our hearts to one another, that you won't let me in, or that I won't be able to hear what you have to say. All I know is that I don't want my life to end without trying.

He passed the shell to his wife. She expressed her worry that people would be angry with each other with no resolution, but her commitment to support her husband overrode that fear. John's father acknowledged what had been known by all but never before spoken, that it was very hard for him to be in the presence of the whole family, especially Eddie, his ex-wife's husband. Only his love for his son and a wish to make the remaining time worthwhile was enough to make it worth doing. Eddie said he felt fearful about this day but could not name the fear, only that he knew he could manage it. John's mother said she felt anxious but willing. She too could not identify the source of her anxiety. The patriarch of the Ohio contingent spoke about the forecasted, but not yet real snow, that had caused their delay and said he was "here because I was asked." Several persons passed. John's aunt from Arizona, pondered the shell, then said simply that she had no fears and was grateful to be there. We broke for our first quiet time.

When we returned, we began the second group session with no prescribed agenda. This time more people passed the talking shell. Those who spoke did so with less content than before. The Patriarch from the Ohio contingent finally broke through the vacuum. Arms folded across his chest and foot bobbing, he said, "I don't know what all the fuss is about. No offense, John, but people get sick and die every day without all of this. I'm here, but I don't see the point." There were audible gasps as he passed the shell.

When the shell reached me, I said that like several of the others I, too, had been anxious and had not known why. I reported my strange journey to the church that morning to this Catholic family. Then I described the way my own thoughts had mirrored Ohio's. His posture relaxed as did that of others. When I spoke of my realization, that the big deal was no more than my own death, he sobered. Leaning forward with elbows on his knees, he indicated his wish to speak. When I passed him the shell, he asked John how he felt about his comments. Then John confessed that his own thoughts had often taken the same form, back and forth. This was a good time for our second quiet time.

From here we stepped into the deeper, darker realm of emotions. Anger, fear, and frustration filled the room throughout much of the afternoon. Back and forth we cycled between feelings of wanting to hold on to life and time, and impatience with the prolonged nature of the dying process. People broke off into smaller groups when the need for privacy warranted it. Old hurts surfaced and people listened.

We broke for our meal and worked together in warm companionship to set up the tables and prepare the food. Hannah told of the legend of the sand dollar, the shell I had pulled for the talking stone. It had a mythic association to the holiday season and contained within five "doves of peace" that, if the shell is broken, fly free. The lore added to the holiday mood.

Christmas carols followed our meal as Eddie distributed the song sheets. After the obvious missed attempts of some voices to find their notes, the group moved to harmonizing. We laughed our way through Frosty the Snowman, with good-natured booing of flat notes and arguments about misspoken lyrics. An easiness and warmth merged with the lingering smell of cinnamon in the air. Then I noticed the three voices of John, Norm, and Eddie, baritone, tenor, and bass, grow stronger. I looked at them as I heard the direction the lyrics were taking. John's father and Eddie were holding the same song sheet. Their eyes were locked with John's across the room so that the three pulled the rest of our voices into the single strong ribbon. "Here we are as in olden days … faithful friends who are dear to us gather near to us once more.… Through the years we all will be together … if the fates allow … so have yourself a merry little Christmas, now." Tears rolled freely down every face in the room.

By 6:00 p.m., the tableau of the last group session found John on his father's lap, (adult) children grouped at the feet of their parents and most people's arms around each other. The group that did not want to begin did not want to end. Every emotion had filled the room that day. Old rifts had been healed. New issues were opened and work begun. Contentment, satisfaction, and humor were expressed. As John passed the sand dollar for the last time to his uncle, it broke between their hands. We all watched the "doves" fly free of their cage. The two men embraced, and we ended our day together.

Four months passed and a third spinal surgery was completed before the tumor won. John was paralyzed in both legs and one arm. The tumor was growing and there were metastases in his brain. The vision in his right eye was blurring, and we knew it would soon be gone. His hearing was already lost in his right ear. His body was bloated to three times its size, unrecognizable from its earlier form.

We all knew he was going home from the hospital this time to die. He asked me to be present to bring him home. Although there was a shortage of lifting help that day, this trip would not be made by ambulance. Eddie,

John's mother Sarah, and I coordinated the transfers from the chair to the car and from the car to the house. When John was settled in the hospital bed that was brought to a downstairs room, I left. Later that evening I got a call. Eddie, John's stepfather, suffered a sudden massive stroke. He was dead. We were all stunned. His children were called and arrangements were made. Although John wanted to attend the services, it was impossible.

They asked if I would stay with him, "baby sit me" was John's way of putting it. Everyone else, including John's father, would be at the funeral. After they left, I sat next to the bed. John had the use of one eye, one ear, and one hand. The rest was dead weight. I read a soul-deep fatigue on his face.

An idea occurred to me. "How would you like a vacation?" To his puzzled response I said, "Let's change places." His face brightened and although I had never done such a thing before, we both closed our eyes into a deep simultaneous trance. We agreed on 20 minutes. Time seemed to stop.

When his eyes opened, he looked very refreshed. "You look exhausted," he said. He asked me to speak of it: "First I noticed the difference in my hands. Only one had feeling, it was warmer but it felt rough, like after raking the yard. It hurt to tighten it. Then I noticed how important my left eye had become. Although it really was closed, I experienced it as opened. It became extremely important *not* to close it. It was my only connection to *everything, everyone, life!* The feeling could get close to panic." John nodded gently. "At the same time, I felt increasingly tired of the effort, as though nothing would relieve me more than to just let it close." I paused as I reviewed the experience. "And there was something else, I'm sorry, you'll probably think I'm crazy, but I was bored!"

"Yes," he said in a near gasp as a tear spilled over his lower lid. "My last moments and I'm watching brain-rot TV soap operas! You really did do it. Thank you."

After a moment of quiet, he smiled, his face regaining color. "Now, I'll tell you." He looked at me lovingly as he said, "You're gonna have a wonderful life. I loved the seasons, even the rain and slush. It felt so good to walk again. I could feel cold, wet feet. You really love to dance, don't you? Thank you for letting me get behind your eyes for even this little time." There was not much more we needed to say.

A few nights later I was reading in bed when John called. "My temp went up, so I'm having my alcohol bath." The odd question and lateness of the hour alerted me. He had been spiking temperatures for several days. "Sarah's going to make some homemade ice cream. It's so good. I thought maybe you could come over and have some with me. And while you're at it maybe you could, uh, help folks around here know what happens if we can't get my temp to go down." There it was. This was his way of getting help for his family, while protecting them at the same time. "The ice cream sounds great," I said, "I'll be right over." When I arrived, he was asleep. The family welcomed me warmly to the social center—the kitchen table. We talked for a few minutes. Then his mother asked, "what does happen if we can't get his temperature down?" I knew they had Home Health Care nurses and Hospice visits intermittently, yet no one had prepared them.

We wrapped tongue depressors with adhesive tape as we talked then about seizures and how to protect John from hurting himself. The pile grew to well over a dozen—more than would likely be needed.

A little later, John woke and the house came alive again with activity. His temperature was remaining stable and Sarah's ice cream was ready. Although others declined, John and I each had a big bowl. It was, as promised, delicious. As we sat together enjoying our ice cream, we talked and laughed. After we finished, things seemed calm enough that I could take my leave. At about 3:30 a.m. I arrived home and fell into a deep sleep.

I was awakened at 8:30 a.m. by the phone. It was Sarah. Everyone had gone home. I could hear the fear in her voice. "He's not responding. It sounds like it will be soon now, from what I've read. I was just wondering, uh, if you would be able to come and … make coffee."

The front door was ajar when I arrived. The women's voices guided me to John's room. I stopped at the door, disoriented by what I saw. Sarah was on the left side of the bed and his mother the right. They were speaking to him in calm voices, as if unaware that the whole bed was moving wildly. John had the control button of the hospital bed gripped in his one good hand, directing it through its full range of gyrating motions. I could see the sense of stark panic in John's one eye—opened wide—looking straight at me as I approached the foot of the bed. Although not a sound issued from his body, the eye screamed, "Help! HELP!"

Time seemed to stand still. Although his movements looked intentional, in all likelihood he was having a seizure. In the confusion, each of us fumbled and bumped into each other. Someone said, "Poor John, at a time like this you have the Three Stooges trying to help you."

On his right Sarah was repeating, "Please don't leave me, John. Don't leave me. Please." On his left his mother was saying, "I brought you into this world and I'm telling you it's all right. It's time to leave it now. You can go." I was saying, "Go to the peaceful place," where so many times in self-hypnotic preparation for this he had gone. Only when I saw the morning light from the window illuminate the tears that poured from his mother's face, did I realize that mine were spilling with hers onto our hands as we worked. In all of this panic, his eye kept pulling us to do something that we could not. We fumbled trying to help until he finally died. It was anything but peaceful.

Later, after the others left, I returned to the room that was now so quiet. The well-intentioned tongue depressors sat on the night table. Sarah had gone to bring their son home to see John. John had chewed his tongue. I washed his face and neck of those things that had issued forth from his mouth and cleaned his mouth so that nothing more would spill and frighten his son. And I thanked him. Nothing more needed to be said or done.

The body would stay in the house until everyone could get there. At the family's request I stayed and was able to witness the quite extraordinary events that occurred in the healing process of this family over the course of that day.

John's son, who initially approached timidly and sadly, was allowed to be with his father as his comfort and curiosity permitted. He began the little tests of an 8-year-old to determine how Daddy's body was different. He asked questions and explained to others in the room the things his father had told him he could expect. By the end of the day, he went freely into the room, crawled onto the bed, sat there as other people talked, held his father's hand and nestled into the crook of his arm, no longer showing any signs of fearfulness of his father's dead body.

At one point during the day, John's brothers, his sister, his mother, and his father spent time together with John. They reminisced about times they had spent together, laughing, joking, his brothers punching him in the arm in goodnatured camaraderie. They vowed to get even when they caught up with him later for all of his card cheating during family vacations. Mother sat on Father's lap, as had been their family posture years before. They cried together as they reviewed the time in their life with the child they were now to bury. It was nearly 6:00 p.m. when John's body left his home.

By the next evening at the funeral home, however, comments by John's wife began to take on an ominous tone. She was feeling spooked by an angry presence in the home. His mother, too, seemed unsettled whenever she had time to herself. By the day of the funeral, each of these reactions was more intense and extreme. All who were present at his death were having nightmares. I felt bothered also by the image of his eye expecting me to do something I could not.

The four of us met before the funeral and, when asked if they felt we should meet again to ease these problems, all eagerly agreed. Later that evening we gathered in one of the bedrooms of the home we had met in that first time we had done the marathon almost 6 months before. Bernice's sister joined us. I suggested that, uninterrupted, we each tell our story of that event in as much detail as possible, as though none of the others had been present. John's sister began, rendering her perspective. Then, John's wife described how suddenly panic stricken and desperate she had felt as she was trying to keep him from leaving. She spoke of her frustration and anger at his mother telling him to go.

His mother described hearing Sharon ask him to stay and the conflict this caused within her—being angry at the request that he stay while in such pain, yet at the same time understanding that, having just lost her own husband, she had had those same feelings. And then, describing the chaos near the end, she included something about John that the others of us had each omitted. "There was so much contorting in his face, then suddenly the tension stopped. It was as though his eye caught something and he turned his head to follow it out the window and he said, 'Oh, Wo-o-ow!'" As she said the last words his wife said them with her. His mother—with tears in her eyes said, "You heard him say that too?" "Yes, I was afraid to say that—people would say I was crazy"

I, of course had seen and heard it as well and, equally inhibited had not reported it. With the joy of this validation mother and wife held each other, and, one was saying, "I can forgive you for telling him to go, if you'll forgive me for asking him to stay," as the other was making the reciprocal plea.

As we all settled back, we could ponder what each of us had seen and heard. What was it that broke the chaos? What was it that he saw that he followed out of the room with awe? Each of us left that night having our own view, along with a prescription for our own well being: to tell the story at least five more times to someone. To tell it until it was just the story.

REFLECTIONS

I changed more, both professionally and personally, over the course of this therapy than any other. These changes have been not only significant but lasting. As I review the ways this therapy worked its changes on me, I think of the process of sculpting. The clay must be soft and the sculptor strong. At the beginning, adapted to its environment, the clay is cold. The hands are rough. One pounds, strokes, caresses, and struggles to make the other into its image. The clay resists and when warmed, responds. Each must give up control. They warm and blend. The result is different from what each had intended.

The changes in me that are the easiest to define are the professional ones. Over the course of the therapy, learning consolidated. My "kit bag" of techniques increased. I learned their value: to prompt me to question why when they worked. More important, however, I learned their limitations. Therapeutic techniques and formulas are not a substitute for clinical competence, a capacity for mutuality and for *being with* another.

My understanding deepened. After the hard work of learning to assess, label, define, study, and classify (which is never fully done), I learned to depathologize—to strive to see the world from the other person's point of view, to validate it and from there to join the search for other solutions. And I relaxed. I learned to see the lessened significance of my role in making things happen, or fixing things. With this came a deep respect for the force of the human spirit and its natural tendency toward healing which sometimes needs only a well placed word to take hold.

Some of the most important insights came from John's process rather than a therapeutic interpretation. He therefore became one of the best opportunities for me to learn that the client makes the best interpretations. When we as therapists make them, we are at risk of working to reduce our own anxiety, not the client's. I learned, therefore, how to stop making interpretations when my own need to do so pressed, but instead to learn the well-placed questions that "facilitate the emergence" (Reyher, 1978) of insights. The first of these questions is always asked of myself, "what would it mean to me *not* to make this statement?" I continue to devote time to building expertise in developing and asking these questions, of both myself and my client.

This case also enabled me to reach my current understanding of the place of hypnosis in psychotherapy. When used appropriately, hypnosis can carry the process through an impasse, and provide some of the most interesting paths to follow. But, the thing that I like most about hypnosis is that when used to facilitate healing, it discourages rigidity. What would have been the outcome of John's goals in approaching his death if I had adhered to my initial rejection of the presenting request for treatment? Or, if I had felt a need to interpret the past life experience?

Of these professional changes, I suspect the "how" was multidetermined. The support and encouragement of my supervisors taught me the importance of trusting myself. This was often, as they said, a situation in which there were no established paths. There were several significant times when my fears were great. In each, my internal evolution or shift resulted in a relief of the fear and this preceded or coincided with a parallel shift in the clinical situation. For instance, the working through of my early response to the erotic transference and countertransference preceded John's; the relaxation of my defenses around my own death anxiety preceding the marathon facilitated theirs.

The personal changes I experienced over the course of this therapy are more broad based and therefore, less amenable to definition. First, the grieving has been resolved. Prior to this case I did not deal well with losses. John's death was different. I have had no disturbing dreams as I had in prior instances, only an occasional pleasant one of Sarah in her new home. I have felt no anxiety, tearfulness, or depression. What remains within me is a sense of poignancy. The haunting images of John's eye and the feelings of helplessness associated with it have been laid to rest. I attribute this, in part, to the therapeutic effect of the postfuneral session with the family. To gain that benefit, I had to acknowledge my own symptoms to accept that I too had been affected by the chaos of his actual death, and I also had to actively engage in the group process.

However, the confrontation with my own death anxiety marked the largest change for me. When I began this case I had just heard the news of my friend's father's suicide. I felt the intense anxiety, and dread that was the same response I had to the few deaths of loved ones I had experienced up to that point. Although over the first half of John's treatment my anxiety varied in intensity, from near primal panic, to free-floating unease, I could not find relief from it. My reading in recent years explains it best to me. Yalom (1998), in discussing death as a primary source of anxiety, posited that "death is of such momentous importance that it can, if properly confronted, alter one's life perspective and promote a truly authentic immersion in life" (p. 249). He further distinguished underlying death anxiety from fear. He explained that anxiety is eased by its attaching to a specific object or situation, thereby transforming to fear. Anxiety, then, is fear of something specific which has a location in time and space. And because it can be located, it can be tolerated and even managed.

This describes my experience. At the outset of the therapy I encountered my anxieties regarding deterioration, helplessness, and death (my own and others.) This often attached to something else. Fear regarding the clinical tasks at hand, for instance, which I then tried to manage by overpreparation in the face of not having enough time. Facing, rather than acting on, this concious fear allowed me to become aware of the deeper anxiety. Each time this happened I was left with the true, underlying issue until, in that moment in the church, I saw and felt what it was: the fear of my own death. Once named, I could deal with this fact of my mortality. About it nothing could be done. My awareness of mortality, a fact of my humanity, enabled me to feel my kinship with others. I am not alone. To face it is to be at one with others. We all must struggle with it. This kinship, I believe, is the greatest source of comfort we have in dealing with knowing we are mortal. Thus, there was something that could be done. Being with another in his or her struggle helps us both to feel less alone. I now know I can handle far more than I would have believed. This resulted in a more pervasive self-confidence and a reverence for each moment of this life, be it pleasure or pain. I simply do not fear death—mine, or others'—as I once did.

It does, however, still give me pause to ponder the how of my own dying. In that respect, I share my father's wish, when he says with his Irish humor, "I wanna just wake up dead some morning." John, however, was a wonderful model for dealing with a debilitating progressive death and its physical pain. His underutilization of medication to preserve every conscious moment, his perseverance to work out whenever possible for the process, not the product, were inspiring. I admire most his profound consideration for others. After Eddie's funeral the family returned to the home. John's grandfather, a man in his 80s wanted to make a contribution with his Polaroid camera. John encouraged us past our discomfort, smiled and posed with each one of us, his one eye rolled upward in his misshapen face. Afterward, he privately requested each of us to return the photos to him. He did not want us to be left remembering him only in that condition. His grandfather left with his prized photo and John's compliments on his talent. I could only pray for as much grace under fire. This was the same man whose initial disregard for others was so troubling to me.

He could change; I can change. He could die; I can die. He continues to live in my memory; I will continue to live in the memory of those I have loved. Since this death there have been other deaths, most dearly, my mother's. My relationship with mortality had been changed so much that by the time of her death, I could work with the funeral director to prepare her body. When I had worked the flesh of her face into the familiar smile, I felt it again: You can die; I can die. Each death has continued to prepare me for the next.

I hope that I can bring as much dignity to my own dying as each has shown me. I have learned to live more mindfully, flexibly, and serendipitously and to welcome the mystery that, when allowed, releases its surprises. One thing that has not changed in me, except to have become stronger, is the curiosity that continues to take me along paths where angels fear to tread.

REFERENCES

Kubler-Ross, E. (1975). *Death: the final stage of growth.* Englewood Cliffs, NJ: Prentice-Hall.
Kubler-Ross, E. (1982). *Working it through.* New York: Macmillan.
Reyher, J. (1978). Emergent uncovering psychotherapy: The use of imagioc and linguistic vehicles in objectifying psychodynamic processes. In J. L. Singer & K. S. Pope (Eds.), *The power of human imagination* (pp. 51–93). New York: Plenum.
Yalom, I. D. (1998). *The Yalom Reader.* New York: Basic Books.

4

Hearing the Unspoken: From Hypnotherapist to Comatherapist

Erika Wick

INTRODUCTION

Growth and change is what psychotherapy is all about. And because the therapeutic exchange is more intense than the average human interaction, the changes that take place are more powerful, affecting both the client and the therapist. When both individuals are truly involved in the therapeutic interaction then "the encounter between the two personalities is like the mixing of two chemical elements; if any reaction occurs, both are transformed" (Jacobi, 1964, p. 67, summarizing Jung's thoughts).

Therapist change is neither a favorite topic in the current literature, nor was there a need to address it in the older authoritarian therapy literature. On the other hand, therapists with an egalitarian outlook discussed the topic years ago. Karl Jaspers (1956, 1959) pointed out that both client and therapist will emerge changed from a genuine and successful therapeutic situation. He took a stand "against the alienating one-sidedness of treatment" emphasizing the mutuality of the therapeutic process: "There is the danger to see in the client something different than [what we see] in ourselves.... But psychologically, man has to find himself in the other one. Only then can he help from within" (p. 685, my translation). Jaspers contrasted regular medical practice with psychotherapy: In medical practice the doctor is the subject treating the object, the patient and his or her illness being the focus of treatment. In psychotherapy the psychotherapist has to understand the seriousness of his or her encompassing engagement: "In this type of practice which is oriented towards the totality of being human, the therapist [doctor] is called upon to be more than a therapist [doctor]" (p. 679, my translation). He is called to engage himself as a full human being, open to be changed in the process. However, as Jung (1931) stated "the demand that the therapist change himself, in order to become able to change the patient, is an unpopular demand" (p. 31, my translation). But change is not merely required, it is also a natural outcome of the dialectical nature of the therapeutic and analytical dialogue, because "the psychologist ... does not analyze an object theoretically, from a distance; rather he himself is just as much in analysis as is the patient" (Jacobi, 1964, p. 66). Jung repeatedly made clear that change in the therapist had to be an outcome of the mutuality of the therapeutic process: "The treatment is the product of mutual influence.... If a connection is made, both will be changed" (p. 31, my translation).

Therapist change is the natural outgrowth of a therapeutic involvement, a chance to grow and broaden horizons. I perceive it as a bonus for genuinely caring, for walking with another person in that person's shoes. I have felt growth when sharing in human experiences not close to my own field of awareness, as they activated my access to deeper layers of the collectively human realm in which I am participating.

Therapists also change as persons. All our experiences affect and influence us. Often the effects and ensuing changes are so subtle that we may not notice them as they occur. We only become aware of them when the cumulative effect of the received input expresses itself in new thoughts, feelings, attitudes, or behaviors. In the encounter with a client, the attention is not merely focused on the client but on the interaction as well. This permits therapists to experience themselves as being in process as much as they want the client to be. Their own openness to change sets the stage and creates the atmosphere that encourages change. As we struggle with the clients to help them make the change to which they aspire, we feel the chords that are struck in our own psyche and become retuned in the process, receiving unexpected interest on the personal investment of ourselves in each client involved in therapeutic interaction. Change and growth are the essence and the goal of therapy.

Sometimes growth comes at an unexpected time leading in an unexpected direction. An unpredicted event in one of my client's life, brought change for me, in three phases and in three very different directions, all unexpected: The first experience was brought on by a challenge to venture into unmarked territory. It provoked the courage to explore new options that I had not sought, namely, to set aside what I knew about the comatose state and impelled by intuition, inspiration, or instinct to engage in the absurd task of communicating with an unconscious patient. The second phase demanded that I sidestep the scientific definition of and theories about coma in favor of experiential data that seemed to indicate that comatose individuals may not be as inaccessible and incommunicado as formerly believed. And finally, I had to balance my belief in an imperative to rescue lives against the rights of comatose patients who had no desire to return to our conscious reality.

GREG'S STORY

The landmark case of Gregory McGregor established the intervention approach I call *comatherapy*. This patient was nearing age 40 and had by consensus of his therapy team a promising future ahead of him. However, he considered himself a failure. Never having completed his doctorate and devastated by a failed marriage he tried to drown his depression in alcohol, which predictably took him downhill faster and destroyed what he had left: his career. Greg was treated by a therapeutic team. I saw him for individual therapy, including hypnosis and was a cotherapist of his therapy group. We got to know Gregory as a caring, sensitive person whom everybody liked. After Greg had held a highly responsible job with a prestigious international company for over 6 months, the team evaluation became optimistic and we began discussing a shift to the weaning phase of therapy.

The critical event occurred the day Greg picked up some of his belongings his exwife had left for him outside the family home. On the way back that evening, Greg's car, after missing a curve at high speed, rolled down a steep embankment and wrapped itself around a tree where the state police found it, completely demolished.

In a comatose state, Greg was rushed to the intensive care unit (ICU) of a nearby hospital, about 30 miles from our clinic. He was in critical condition and not expected to live. The next morning, he was removed from the small ICU, which lacked beds for maintaining a patient who had no chance for recovery.

Our social worker suggested to Greg's wife that she provide him with private nursing care but was told that as his exwife, she had no more responsibility toward him. The social worker then suggested that the team, the psychiatrist, and I, pay for two shifts of special nursing care per day, as we all shared the same professional opinion: that Gregory had a good future, despite his psychiatric history. We could not allow him to die without making an attempt to rescue him. After the hospital was informed about the private nursing arrangements, the attending physician cautioned us not to harbor false hope, as nothing short of a miracle could save him.

The day after Greg's near fatal car accident, I went to visit him, expecting to spend 5 to 10 minutes there. I knew he was in a comatose state but without special nursing care in the afternoon. The nurse at the station reiterated that this patient was in extremely critical condition, having merely hours to live. And as if to seal the case, she added that the chaplain had already visited him. A sign saying "family visits only" marked the door of the room in which Greg lay all by himself. The door was semiclosed. The patient, ostensibly, had been left to die. What followed was an unplanned, spontaneously emerging effort, empowered by the shared hopes of three professionals who wanted Greg's life to continue. It was in that little room, reserved for patients about to die that comatherapy was born.

Greg, badly battered, hooked up to the usual tubes and contraptions, was still breathing, labored, and rasping. Each breath he managed to take seemed to be a miracle but could not inspire hope that he would live. I touched Greg's arm. There was no response from him. I stood by the bed, sensing the overwhelming odds.

Change occurred unexpectedly. Greg's breathing turned shallow and then unnoticeable. He appeared to have stopped breathing. "Breathe, Greg, breathe!" I said loudly, while ringing for the nurse. Then I touched Greg's shoulders and told him to keep breathing. I ordered, I commanded Greg to breathe: "Keep breathing, Greg, breathe. You have to keep breathing. Take a breath right now. In and out," over and over again. Finally, Greg's chest moved a tiny bit. I could not be sure it meant anything. The nurse had not come, yet. The one thing I knew was that I could not leave Greg now, even to get help. I was not thinking; I merely took action, automatically, instinctively and continued to push him to breathe. As I did this I slipped back to my old, repetitive hypnosis routine, as if working with a client in hypnosis, except my patient was in a coma.

I had never worked with a comatose patient before. From a scientific viewpoint, it was clear that my intervention attempt was absurd: I was talking to someone who could not hear me. Fortunately, I had no time to think about it, for established knowledge tends to prevent us from exploring the actual facts. I was absorbed in doing what was familiar to me and familiar to Greg, if he was at all able to hear me. My talking was fairly automatic while I watched for the slightest movements of his chest. All I was concerned about was Greg's breathing. I was not concerned that Greg might die. I felt intense determination to get him back. Finally, Gregory resumed breathing, barely visibly, at first. Over the next few minutes breathing became slightly more active, and the chest movements became discernable again. It took more than 5 minutes for the nurse to come. I reported the breathing incident and asked for a bigger and warmer blanket.

Communications seemed important if I did not want Greg to slip away again. Greg had resumed breathing either spontaneously or possibly in response to being told to do so. My working hypothesis now was that Greg was reachable. Knowing that auditory input is supposed to be the last sensory input we can receive when close to death, I kept talking to Gregory as if he were in a hypnotic trance state. Although the emphasis was still on deep and regular breathing, I began to include powerful suggestions of healing and messages to strengthen Greg's will to live. I made no mention of death. Survival was presented as a must, not as an option. My efforts were based on the conviction that Greg's life was eminently worth living.

I do, however, remember a twinge of uncertainty gripping me for a moment. I questioned whether I were intervening on behalf of this patient or whether I were transgressing beyond normal intervention, maybe treading on forbidden grounds. Was I interfering in Greg's life, engaging in a struggle with forces beyond my known reality? I realized Greg had no say in either living or dying. Looking at his ailing body, I was fully aware of the uphill battle he was facing. I knew it would be so much easier for this patient to abandon all struggles, mental and physical, and to give in to the lure of death with its promise of peace. I deliberately left no room for uncertainty. Why should Greg die now, after he had made such remarkable progress in therapy and after his life had finally entered a truly constructive phase? I kept on working.

I had arrived at the hospital reconciled to saying good bye to Gregory. About 6 hours later, I left the hospital with Greg in the care of the private night nurse we had hired. Although I remained impressed with the physicians' verdict that Greg's accident had imposed a death sentence on him, I felt that I had come upon a way to appeal the sentence. I was no longer resigned to the fact that there was no hope.

The next morning, Greg was still in critical condition but showing slight improvement. Later that day, I returned to the hospital to spend 4 hours with him. My approach remained essentially the same, except that I now incorporated something I had learned from the ICU nurse: I consistently added touch to the sound input.

On the third day, Greg's status was changed from *critical* to *serious*. For 4 to 6 hours every day, I kept working with Greg. On my day off, it amounted to 10 hours. Although exhausting, the work felt worthwhile and became ever more fascinating, as there were indications that Greg was slipping in and out of short periods of consciousness, albeit clouded. Eventually, Greg's periods of consciousness grew longer and clearer. Before a week was up, Greg was discharged from the hospital and eventually saw me again at the clinic. Greg's prominent memory of being in a coma was an experience of total, all encompassing peace, matching the "feelings of peace as well as a transcendent sense of well being" (Ring, 1982, p. 121) reported by Ring after near death experiences. It slowly dawned on Greg how close he had come to death. Having missed death seemed to concern him more than the possibility of almost having missed out on life.

Why had Greg returned to our reality? He never stated that his come-back had been voluntary. He remembered feeling as if he were being pulled, very powerfully to go somewhere, whereas at other times, it felt more as if he needed to return to somewhere. The pull was strong, but he was totally without any understanding as to where this pull came from or where it was leading. Eventually, he could hear a voice, sometimes voices. Felt messages were received more often than specific words or sentences. The pull remained strong and would not let go. Zigzagging for a while be-tween not wanting to but feeling the pressure of having to, the pull was ulti-mately strong enough for Greg to return to consciousness. I wondered how much of the delay in Greg's return was attributable to wake-up resistance, a phenomenon well reported in hypnotized subjects.

Greg responded to being back with a measured amount of gratitude and without any enthusiasm. It was sobering to learn how Greg, stuck in his mis-erably hurting body, really felt about his survival. It was considerably later, after his body had healed that he slowly came to appreciate being alive. At that time he cited his brush with death as the wakeup call to the challenge of making a difference in this world: "These new vaccines I am working on will save many lives." It looked like he had found his mission in life.

About 10 years later I heard from Jim, who had been a member of Greg's therapy group. Jim had unexpectedly met Gregory while on a busi-ness trip. At a red light, Greg came up to his car barely recognizable beg-ging for money. Jim invited Greg for dinner. Greg was homeless, living primarily on cheap alcohol. How could this have happened? Greg ex-plained: "You remember my car accident? While in the hospital, I came to a Y fork. I took the right way, choosing peace. But my [curse] therapist pulled me back from the right path and pushed me onto the left path of de-struction. That's why my whole life fell apart." Jim suggested that he speak to me, but he refused. During dinner, Jim coaxed him to write me a note. "You've got to get this off your chest, or you'll never get over it." Jim called to forewarn me. The letter stated: "Why did you have to ruin my life? I was at peace with myself and with God. Everything was OK. My children would have been proud of me. Now, they have to be ashamed of their father. I will never find peace again. Why did you have to ruin my life? Why?"

Actually, Greg was not my only comatose patient who survived and lived to regret it. Although I am disappointed that Greg could not sustain a productive life, it was the fact that there were more individuals who—albeit for different reasons—opposed rescue efforts they had not asked for. The comatherapists' dilemma is: Does the therapists' or the relatives' desire for life overstep the boundaries of another person's freedom. I was forced to look at what I had done.

THERAPIST CHANGE

My comatherapy experiences changed me as a psychotherapist, broadening my therapeutic approach, allowing both patient and therapist to expand beyond the realm of consciousness. The challenge to my scientific and philosophical thinking additionally altered my viewpoint, by opening up a new way of perceiving of the limits of consciousness. Three areas of change are identifiable: First of all, Gregory McGregor, my first comatose patient, became the catalyst that turned my hypnosis skills into unexpected comatherapy skills, helping me to work intensively with such patients.

Second, Greg's successful recovery validated for me that my intuition may have access to knowledge beyond the secure confines of science. The attempt to reach a comatose person may sound absurd to the scientifically trained brain. Venturing into the "scientifically incorrect" can access a more complex reality, one still waiting for scientific verification. Finally, I had to learn to accept that rescue attempts may not be appreciated by all coma survivors. Greg's rejection of his postcoma life forced me to revise my philosophy concerning coma patients' rights and comatherapists' professional ethics.

From Hypnotherapist to Comatherapist

Coaching the comatose patient back to consciousness brought new growth and an expansion of my therapy horizon. I truly fell into a new field of work, without intending to. Prior to the mind-opening experience with Greg, comatherapy would have appeared to be absurd and a successful outcome impossible. Less than a week after the accident, Greg was discharged from the hospital, defying all medical prognoses. I had to accept that more happened than could ever have been predicted. Greg's improvement stimulated my interest, and I continued exploring the possibilities. This case is particularly remarkable because the recovery cannot be explained in terms of a client's powerful desire to live. Here, the patient did not want to return to consciousness. Yet he did and survived.

Comatherapy came to me as a surprise, as a gift. The impossible became possible. What was not supposed to happen, happened. To see the results was captivating, fascinating, and exhilarating. There was new hope for hopeless cases. And I felt obligated to help whenever I was called.

Scientifically Incorrect

Facts that appear to be obvious or are known to be scientifically established are not necessarily based on factual reality, and established scientific facts may be the greatest impediment to further inquiry and scientific progress. This meant striving to keep my direction as I left the safe harbor of established reality. Jung (1963) stated that psychotherapy and medical psychology taught him to

> behave towards such things in a pragmatic way.... Maybe nowhere do we have to take into account so much of the unknown as exactly in this realm, and nowhere do we get accustomed to applying what is effective, even when, for some time, we do not catch on to why it works. Unexpected healings take place with questionable methods and unexpected failures occur when supposedly proven methods are employed. In researching the unconscious we stumble upon the strangest things, from which a rationalist would distance himself in disgust.... The abundance of the irrational in life has taught me, never to reject or scrap anything, even though it contradicts all our, alas, so short lived, theories or otherwise appears to remain inexplicable for the time being. Granted, such experiences are disquieting; it is uncertain whether the compass points in the right direction. But discoveries are not made in the quiet place of safe certainty. (pp. 639–640, my translation)

I have grown to keep myself open to data that are not scientifically verified, to facts that belie the secure confines of reason and logic. I do believe that we are called to explore what professionals, especially those trained in hypnosis, can do for patients in a comatose state. I have become aware of what it means to leave the safe haven of the scientifically established realm and move into uncharted territory. We still do not know how comatherapy works, but we do know that it can work. And for now that is enough reason to keep doing it.

Hearing the Unspoken, Heeding the Unspoken: Honoring the Client's Choice

Much to my amazement, instead of rejoicing over returning to consciousness and escaping a presumably wrongful death Greg (and others) decried their wrongful life and denigrated their survival.

My first reaction to such a negative response to recovery was disbelief. But I had to learn to accept that my life-supporting effort was not measured in terms of the intensity of my investment in the comatose patient's survival or in terms of my belief in the value of conscious life. Instead, recovered clients approved of their return to consciousness depending on the degree to which they rated their personal conscious life as desirable. An equivalent of the increase in valuing life observed in many disaster survivors after events, such as a life-threatening hurricane, did not become apparent in some coma survivors. The comatose state generally seems to be experienced as a peaceful haven. Why should patients welcome my attempt to drag them out of it? Do I have a right to project my belief in the desirability of life onto them? I had to question my position.

To me, the mandate to try to save a life, including the life of a comatose patient, had been nothing short of a categorical imperative. Slowly, the imperative started to turn conditional. Ideally, any patient should have a voice regarding his or her recovery. But realistically considered, can comatose patients form a valid opinion about their rescue? Provided they can, are they able to communicate their wishes to the caregiver? And will the message they attempt to transmit be understood? Mindell (1989) answered my concerns by putting the responsibility for communicating with a comatose patient on the professionals: "We need to learn more about how to unfold the signals of profound states of unconsciousness, so that we can give our clients the ability to make their own decisions about life" (p. 101). He did not seem to share my concern about a comatose patient's ability to weigh pro and con factors or about our obligation to be fair to a client who might enjoy life later, but whose strength is temporarily lacking.

I certainly agree that individuals should make life and death decisions for themselves whenever possible, but I still do not know enough about comatose states to free myself of all responsibility in deciding on the degree of assistance needed by a comatose patient. But I had to question what I was doing. Did my intervention cheat Greg out of his rightful death? Or did I help him to take care of unfinished business and gain a reprieve to advance in his growth? I do not know the answer. Whatever the ultimate reality may be, the truth that emerged for me is that I had to learn to leave more room for the client's own choice. My changing was not easy because I saw no clear parameters emerging that could delineate what is right for which patient. When I come across need, I tend to act spontaneously, able to trust my intuition and instincts to guide me. But I had to learn constraint, to hold back and to listen first for the unspoken.

I no longer pressure comatose patients into returning to consciousness, unless I have a clear mandate from the patient to do so. Patients have to let me know clearly, that they want my support either prior to undergoing an operation or if their comatose state arises unexpectedly, with a signal that cannot be misunderstood. If I cannot get an understandable sign from a patient, I phrase my suggestions for a return to consciousness conditionally, giving two choices. The options are to cooperate with the rescue effort or to ignore it. If the comatose patient cooperates with the coaching effort, this will stand for *permission of treatment*. Disengagement from the life-saving attempt equals *rejection of treatment*. This way, I do not have to elicit signals from patients that may or may not reveal to me what their life or death choice is. Patients simply will go along with the suggestions that fit their goals. Although I have made this change, I maintain some reservations about it. It appears that clear commands to return to consciousness are more effective in this patient population than conditional talk, offering options, which most likely few, if any, comatose patients can sort out. Either way, with directive and with conditional suggestions, the support evidently is felt. The benefit of the conditional suggestions is patients returning to conscious reality can be assured that they were given a choice. The fact that they did come back, means they chose life. Nobody pushed them into it.

SUMMARY

Change came as I was moved in directions I had not sought or even imagined. Being open to the impossible, the impossible became possible: The comatose patient was reached. I have not only learned to talk to comatose patients, I have also learned to listen to them and to accompany them and, above all, guide them to wherever they choose to go. One of the most important insights I have gained from coma survivors is that to those who wish to die, death loses its power as an adversary of life. Life can then be perceived as the adversary of death. It is still sometimes hard to accept that it may not be helpful to insist that a patient return to life.

I have learned much and have changed in the process. I am far from knowing all about the mystery of the many varied altered states of consciousness we simply label *coma*. I remain hesitant to acknowledge coma as a state of ecstasy and as the key to awakening as Mindell (1989) saw it, but after much learning and changing I have awakened to the coma patients' gentler understanding of death. I expect that more changes will be needed as brain research progresses and will enlighten us so that we can improve our communications with comatose patients and can serve them better.

REFERENCES

Jacobi, J., (1964). *The psychology of C. G. Jung*. New Haven, CT: Yale University Press.
Jaspers, K. (1956). *Philosophie* (Vol. 3, 3rd ed.). Berlin: Springer Verlag.
Jaspers, K. (1959). *Allgemeine Psychopathologie* [General psychopathology]. Berlin: Springer Verlag.
Jung, C. G. (1931). *Seelenprobleme der Gegenwart* [Current problems of the psyche]. Zurich: Rascher Verlag.
Jung, C. G. (1963). *Vorwort zum I GING* [Forward to the I Ging]. In C. G. Jung (Ed.), *Zur Psychologie westlicher und östlicher Religion* [Psychology of eastern and western religion]. Zurich: Rascher Verlag.
Mindell, A. (1989). *Coma, key to awakening*. Boston: Shambhala.
Ring, K. (1982). Frequency and stages of the prototypic near-death experience. In C. R. Lundahl (Ed.), *A collection of near-death research readings* (pp. 110–147). Chicago: Nelson Hall.

II

CHANGES IN ABILITY
TO MOURN PARENTS

5

Finding a Fatherly Self

David A. Soskis

CASE SUMMARY

Malcolm, a 41-year-old bank executive, sought help controlling his two pack per day smoking habit. On his first visit he requested hypnotherapy to make him stop smoking. He was functioning well at work and at home as a spouse and parent, but his wife was troubled by the dangers of his smoking for both himself and his family. After a behavioral and psychodynamic assessment and an evaluation of his hypnotic talent as moderate, I treated him with hypnotherapy. The treatment was initially dramatically successful with a brief period of not smoking. This was followed by a demoralizing relapse that led to a significant change in my approach to Malcolm and in my views on effective psychotherapy. Malcolm was eventually able to achieve partial control of his smoking at a much reduced level of five or six cigarettes per day.

MALCOLM'S LIFE

Our initial sessions covered an exploration of Malcolm's pattern of smoking, his understanding of and talent for hypnosis, and a broader exploration of his personal background. Psychiatrically, he was remarkably healthy and generally satisfied with his life. There was no past or significant family psychiatric history or history of alcohol or other drug abuse, but both his parents were smokers. He was unable to identify any dysphoric feelings of anxiety, depression, or anger that regularly preceded his smoking and were relieved by it and noted that he had little trouble staying within the boundaries set by his wife and his workplace for the timing and location of smoking.

Malcolm had grown up in a suburban home with both parents and one brother 3 years older. He described his birth and early development as normal, and he was an excellent student in elementary school as well as participating in scouting and a number of other activities. Although both of his parents smoked in the house, his father was a much heavier smoker, consuming two to three packs of cigarettes per day. His mother, on the other hand, would take a week to go through one pack of cigarettes. She was concerned about her husband's heavy smoking even before the information on the association between cigarettes smoking and lung cancer appeared and began lecturing him about the need to cut down. He did not respond to these lectures but reduced his smoking sharply after what he described as an "almost heart attack" at age 59. His parents had always told their children to "do what we say not what we do" and warned them that smoking was "a bad habit and a very hard one to break."

In junior high, Malcolm began to spend more time out of the house with a small group of friends, some of whom began smoking. He was curious about this exciting and dangerous habit but having watched his parents smoke for many years did not have an urge at that time to try it. On a scouting overnight, he and his friends sneaked out of the tent and into the woods, finding their way cautiously with partially shielded flashlights. They were being so careful not to make noise and to keep the flashlights shielded that they were unaware until the last minute that they had encountered others from the same troop. This group, which included Malcolm's older brother, were all smoking cigarettes.

Malcolm was shocked and a bit frightened at this discovery. His friend, who also smoked, asked Malcolm's brother to "be a good guy, and give us a cigarette too," and he complied. Malcolm found the odor of the tobacco pleasant, and the experience "exciting … a real adventure," because it was forbidden and because they had been taken into the fellowship of the older boys including his brother. As he described this incident in my office, he spoke with obvious relish and was smiling broadly.

On their return, Malcolm's brother warned him not to tell their parents, making more explicit the nature of their rebellion. Malcolm reassured him, and they colluded in their rebellion, keeping this secret from their parents together. Throughout high school Malcolm did not buy cigarettes for himself but would accept them from his friend and from his older brother when they were alone and away from the house.

At college, Malcolm experienced a whole new way of life; it was the first time he was really on his own. He took some time to get used to the absence of his parents' demands as a regulator of his study time, but after a few bad grades he began to apply himself in a fairly organized manner. Around this period he bought his first pack of cigarettes, which he took back to his dormitory room and smoked alone for the first time. He maintained a one pack per week rate of smoking throughout his college years. After graduation, he began work in the banking field and rose to a responsible position where he supervised loan officers at a number of branches and traveled a good deal to meet with them. His smoking increased during periods of work stress and gradually stabilized at around 2 packs per day.

Malcolm met his wife-to-be when she came to his work site as part of an audit, and their relationship developed quickly. Malcolm admired his wife's intelligence, her "toughness and ability to get to the bottom of things" as an accountant, and found her physically attractive as well. After a year, they became engaged and married within 6 months. Although Malcolm knew that his wife was a nonsmoker and never offered her a cigarette, his smoking, to the best of his memory, was never discussed as a significant issue between them when they were planning their life together.

After they were married, Malcolm's smoking became an issue, one of a group of issues that they had to negotiate as a couple. Malcolm's wife expressed what he experienced as relatively mild disapproval of his smoking and he began to do most of his smoking away from the house. When Malcolm's wife became pregnant with their first child she asked him to stop smoking in the house on a permanent basis, and he readily agreed. He was delighted with the pregnancy and actually shared her concern for the effects of smoke on the fetus. It was at this time that he began smoking under a tree in their backyard, and when his brother and sister-in-law came to visit them they both smoked under this tree, and his brother noted that it was "just like the first time when we were camping." Malcolm chuckled at this but realized that he had made the same association when he began going outside to smoke under the tree.

From that time on he never smoked in the house and tried to conceal his smoking from his children. His wife appreciated his efforts but began to mention occasionally that it was looking as if "smoking really took years off of your life, and I want you around for a long time." Malcolm listened to these comments, but, like his father, did not change his smoking behavior in response to them. He described the period of the birth of his other two children as being a happy time and was gratified by his success at work and by his regular promotions and raises. Smoking, he reported, "was just part of my life." In recounting this period, he did not appear aware of the similarities between his wife's comments and his mother's concerning his father's smoking habit.

Four years before he came to see me, Malcolm went for his first executive physical. His general health was excellent, including physical examination, laboratory values, EKG, and pattern of diet, weight, and exercise. The physician noted, however, that his smoking habit was a real red flag from the health point of view and reviewed with him a number of projections of his longevity with and without smoking. The physician suggested that he stop or at least cut down but did not give any specific suggestions as to how.

Malcolm remembered that a colleague of his had stopped smoking with hypnosis, so he asked him to whom he had gone. Malcolm had little trouble finding this hypnotist but was surprised at how shabby his office was compared to his large color ad in the Yellow Pages. He described the hypnotist as a man in his 60s who "made you feel like he'd been doing this stuff for many years" although Malcolm realized that he was not a professional in the sense that he was used to. He remembered two things most vividly about the hypnotist: a pickled lung from a smoker that he kept in a jar and used to illustrate the terrible effects of smoking, and a spinning disc with a spiral on it that he used as a focal point for his hypnotic induction. Malcolm was not sure whether he had been given any posthypnotic suggestions for amnesia but remembered very little of the hypnotic procedure, except that it involved relaxation and closing his eyes. He was not assigned any homework and the hypnotist made it clear that he had confidence in his procedure. Without offering an explanation, he specified that his was a one-shot treatment and that refresher sessions were not available.

Malcolm initially had no reason to complain considering his resolution to stop smoking appeared much easier and he went cold turkey for about 1½ years. His wife was delighted and praised him lavishly. He resumed smoking after accepting an offered cigarette at a party, smoking at first in secret from his wife but soon resuming his old pattern and locations. His wife was unhappy about this relapse but stopped pestering him about it after it was clear that he was not going to stop right away.

At Malcolm's next company physical, the same doctor saw him. His physical examination and lab tests were still fine, but this time the doctor seemed quite serious about the problem of his smoking. On hearing about Malcolm's previous experience with hypnosis, the doctor suggested trying it again. Otherwise, he would make a strong recommendation for a structured program that included group sessions, something that Malcolm did not particularly like. It was this ultimatum, along with the lay hypnotist's refusal to see him again, that brought him to my office.

MY BACKGROUND IN HYPNOSIS

My interest in hypnosis began in my teens, when the advisor of a magic club I belonged to suggested that I might do better at it than at sleight-of-hand.

Among my mother's college books I found several with sections on hypnosis and I supplemented them with readings at the local public library. I had not encountered any descriptions of hypnosis as being dangerous, and in my naiveté began trying it out with considerable success on my friends. Soon, I demonstrated with them most of the phenomena I had read about, including posthypnotic suggestions and amnesia.

My early hypnotic career came to an abrupt halt when my parents, having been informed by neighbors, forbade me to continue and told me that I was lucky no serious damage had been done. Such an authoritarian approach was unusual for them, and I initially challenged it but eventually obeyed when I saw their resolve, especially because they were both social workers and knew much more about this area than I did. They did offer me some hope, in the form of a group of professions in which hypnosis was legitimately used, and I was immediately drawn to explore them.

During my first week in medical school I posted index cards on hospital bulletin boards with my name and dormitory phone number and the simple description "hypnosis." I got several calls during medical school, but by this time I was psychologically sophisticated enough to stay within my limits and used hypnosis only for purposes of relaxation. I had much more use for it on my various clinical rotations, where I found that hypnotic talk, without a formal hypnotic induction, was extremely useful in calming patients in the emergency room and in clinics. I was developing respect for both the "magic" and the science of hypnosis.

In my psychiatric residency I began to encounter more scholarly references to and descriptions of clinical hypnosis. I was also becoming uneasy with the hypnotic induction methods I was using and felt that they implied or generated a passive, regressed position in the patient that caused problems later in therapy. When I encountered the work of Herbert Spiegel, I sensed that I had finally found what I had been looking for. I was fascinated with Spiegel's approach to self-hypnosis—a matter-of-fact induction that spoke to the adult part of patients. I immediately began using the Hypnotic Induction Profile (Spiegel & Spiegel, 1978) and felt very comfortable with it. This new approach also fit nicely with my growing interest in the area of informed consent and patient participation in medical care. I began focusing on teaching patients self-hypnosis in my clinical work and later, as a faculty member, training advanced psychiatry residents.

My own approach to clinical hypnosis has evolved and eventually formed the basis for my book, *Teaching Self-Hypnosis* (Soskis, 1986). This approach can be summarized as a collaborative, consumer-oriented hypnotherapy in which the therapist models and teaches the patient a self-hypnosis exercise and helps him or her apply it to the clinical problem at hand. It is a relatively permissive approach that provides initial high levels of structure but welcomes the development of what would be called in

Fromm and Kahn's (1990) model self-initiated and self-directed hypnotic processes. My own self-hypnosis exercise (brief hypnotic experience) was indeed brief (about 10 minutes) and used an eyes-closed hand levitation induction, a counting and relaxation deepening phase, and the use of a pleasant relaxing scene coupled with a "key-phrase," which addressed the patient's particular clinical needs.

MY CLINICAL WORK WITH MALCOLM

The first sessions with Malcolm were spent collecting the history described earlier and in assessing Malcolm's hypnotic talent. He scored 18 out of a possible score of 24 on the Brief Hypnotic Experience Evaluation Form (Soskis, 1986), which showed a moderate level of hypnotic responsiveness. He appeared relatively healthy psychologically and open to hypnosis; as he put it himself, "you can't argue with results." In telling his story, he did not see the parallels between his own and his father's situation; both his mother and his wife lectured on the dangers of smoking, and both he and his father decided to stop or cut down because of health concerns. By the third session we began focusing more specifically in both the hypnosis and smoking areas. I went through my usual, permissive induction and helped him devise a pleasant relaxing scene where he was alone, sitting by a small brook in a cool forest. Because the target of our therapy was smoking cessation I chose to use Herbert Spiegel's widely used sequence of statements, which Malcolm modified slightly so that it sounded right for him: "(1) for my body smoking is a poison; (2) I need my body to live; (3) I owe my body and my family this protection and respect" (Spiegel & Spiegel, 1978, pp. 210–219).

The mention of his family made the statement reflect what Malcolm actually experienced as his motivations: pressure from his wife and concern for his children. After we had gone through the exercise, Malcolm was instructed to practice it at home twice daily, 5 days a week, until he had practiced it a total of 20 times before our next session in 2 weeks. At his fourth session Malcolm reported that he had practiced the exercise 15 times; when he did practice, he found the normal problems in getting 10 minutes to himself but appeared to understand and enjoy the exercise.

The remainder of the session was spent planning the behavioral components of Malcolm's actually stopping smoking that he wished to time with his birthday in the coming week. We went through his smoking rituals and paraphernalia and made efforts to find reasonable substitutes and to minimize smoking stimuli in his environment. I acknowledged how difficult it was to stop smoking and that he deserved a great deal of credit.

Malcolm came for his next session a week later reporting that he had indeed stopped smoking as of the night before his birthday. His wife was delighted and impressed. The hardest times for him were driving in his car to work and passing his "smoking buddies" outside the bank's office. He had practiced his exercise twice daily and reported that it was becoming almost automatic. Malcolm's success continued through the sixth session a week later with no dramatic developments. I praised his steadfastness in getting through the most difficult 2 weeks and began to switch my approach to a *relapse prevention* mode. We arranged for a follow-up session in 2 weeks, with a plan of gradually tapering the sessions if Malcolm's smoking cessation held.

Malcolm canceled his next session 3 days in advance because of an unexpected business trip. When I next saw him 3 weeks after our previous appointment, he began the session by announcing "I've got good news and bad news." The bad news was that he had smoked about half a pack of cigarettes while staying in a hotel room. He knew he would smoke when he declined a nonsmoking room but also "knew I was deciding not to think about it a lot" as his series of meetings began. The good news was that he had not resumed smoking when he returned home. At the next session a week later, however, Malcolm reported himself as "partially sliding backward" in that he had smoked several times outside his office. In my cautious efforts to explore his feelings about these developments I encountered considerable resistance and what sometimes bordered on a dismissive tone; he made another appointment with clear ambivalence.

Malcolm began this ninth session by announcing "the news is all bad this time" and described being caught and confronted by his wife, who smelled tobacco on his breath when he came home from work. He confessed to her, and she expressed her disappointment and anger at his failure to stop smoking, his concealing his smoking from her, and his "expensive visits to a psychiatrist." I too was disappointed and annoyed by this clear therapeutic failure, but I did my best to contain the negative spiral by acknowledging the failure and asking Malcolm for his thoughts and feelings about what we should do.

I was about as surprised as I have been in a psychotherapy session by the communication that followed. Malcolm was frank and direct in his expression as he described his feelings that the treatment failed, mostly because it had been ineffective from the start.

THE THERAPIST CHANGES

Malcolm's disappointment in this failure of hypnosis had two components. The first was the undeniable fact that he had resumed smoking; he agreed somewhat with his wife that all these visits to an expensive psychiatrist should have produced something better. My talk about the difficulty of stopping smoking and the expectation of relapses did not seem to have made much of an impression. Second, Malcolm described his growing conviction that the self-hypnosis exercise that I taught him was "not the real thing." It had felt different from the beginning as compared to his initial experience with the lay hypnotist; and the exercise itself had always seemed "like a chore, and I've got plenty of those." I needed all the time left in the session to regain my composure and to explore with Malcolm whether he wanted to continue. In the end, he decided to continue but asked me to try a different approach. I agreed and scheduled another meeting for 2 weeks, not at all sure what the new approach would be.

During the next 2 weeks I reviewed material on hypnosis and smoking cessation as well as my notes and memories from Malcolm's sessions. It seemed likely that Malcolm had experienced the first hypnotist as a benign parental figure who took charge and that he experienced my own more collaborative approach as less effective, perhaps reminding him of his collaboration with his older brother and their joint rebellion that initiated his smoking. With these possible dynamics in mind as I went through my sources, I found the section on smoking in Crasilneck and Hall's (1985) immensely useful textbook *Clinical Hypnosis* (225–226). As I read through the verbatim transcript of one of the hypnotic sessions devoted to smoking cessation I realized that this was about as far from my own approach as one could get in terms of hypnotic style but also that it might be just what Malcolm needed. Here is a sample of the script:

> You will find that through the immense power of your unconscious mind you will be able to overcome this old, outgrown, outworn addiction, which we now know, statistically, robs you of four minutes of life with every cigarette you smoke.… You will be able to give up this dirty and unhealthy habit … as you permit your body to rid itself of this undeserved burden of smoking, your lungs will again become efficient, your red blood cells will carry more oxygen to all your vital organs, you will feel more alert and alive and you will have a justifiable sense of pride for having worked toward and accomplished this important, healthy, worthwhile goal … your craving for tobacco will be minimal and will decline to a zero level at a rapid pace.

I studied the script carefully, trying to figure out why each phrase was being used in the way it was. Over several days I became familiar enough with it to read it without my original hesitation and embarrassment. During this process, I experienced some memories from my own childhood: comforting instructions from my parents for handling tough or dangerous situations when I was about 5 or 6. I tried to reproduce that tone of voice in the way I presented the material.

Malcolm was much calmer than I was when our next session began. I explained to him that I had found an approach to smoking cessation using hypnosis from an admired and respected teacher in our field. Malcolm replied that "I'm willing to try anything," and we began. This time, I used an eye closure induction combined with progressive relaxation. Malcolm responded to this well, and seemed relaxed and receptive as I began the antismoking script. About halfway through, a faint smile flickered across Malcolm's face and I knew I had at least made a different connection. Over the next few weeks I repeated this same script in every session. Malcolm decided to quit smoking again, and this time his success lasted much longer. His behavior in other situations, as he reported it to me, did not show any regression and he remained assertive and skeptical in a constructive way in his interchanges with me.

We began to taper our sessions but resumed when a relapse again occurred during an out-of-town trip. Malcolm enjoyed working with numbers and informed me that he had cut his smoking by more than five sixths; his internist had assured him that this was already having positive health consequences and encouraged him to continue. When I last saw him, Malcolm had settled into a pattern of long periods of no smoking interrupted by brief relapses. He still practiced his self-hypnosis exercise occasionally, but it was clear to both of us that the "real stuff" had occurred during our sessions.

EFFECTS ON THE THERAPIST AND IMPLICATIONS FOR TREATMENT

Malcolm went on with his life as an occasionally relapsing nonsmoker and he, his wife, and his physician appeared satisfied with the change at a 1-year follow-up. For a long time after I stopped seeing him, however, my encounter with Malcolm continued to reverberate. I had to ask myself why I found an authoritative, "parental" approach so distasteful in view of its effectiveness with Malcolm compared to my usual "collaborative" technique. Malcolm's dramatic, positive response to this "new" technique came as a pleasant surprise to him but forced me to reevaluate my own beliefs about how and why people change in psychotherapy.

Gradually, I began to separate being parental from being paternalistic in my interactions with patients; being authoritative from being authoritarian. As this process continued I asked myself "what's wrong with being a good parent?" I had been blessed with good parenting that, like most human interactions, encompassed many dimensions, including unconditional acceptance, protection and guidance, authoritarian elements (as in the prohibition to use hypnosis as a teenager), and modeling of adult relationships in my parents' marriage and in the disciplined caring of their social work careers. Like Malcolm, my reactions to my parenting were complex combinations of identification, rebellion and repetition.

I began to incorporate more awareness of this parental dimension in my psychotherapy with and without hypnosis. I also became more able to acknowledge my identification with Malcolm's secret rebellion—something I had not done in response to my parents' firm limit setting to my teenage hypnotic experiments. When I did this, I could see some of the positive elements in Malcolm's rebelliousness: the social bonding to peers and to his brother fostered by his smoking and its symbolic value as a token of his independence, a step to his being able to adjust to going away to college and to starting a family of his own. My antismoking zeal and my reluctance to face the ways in which Malcolm and I were similar had stood in the way of a really comprehensive understanding of what smoking meant to him.

Although I treated only a minority of patients with psychoanalytically oriented psychotherapy, I began to think in terms of Franz Alexander's (Alexander & French, 1946) corrective emotional experience. I also began watching for the pitfalls of this approach: infantilization of the patient and fantasies of replacing a bad parent. As I reviewed my therapies it became clear that I had strayed in both of these errors with a number of patients without realizing it, lulled into a sense of invulnerability by my supposedly collaborative, adult-to-adult, approach.

Although I was not aware of it at the time, my contact with Malcolm also served as one of a number of catalysts for working through my grief over my parents' deaths about a year before I saw Malcolm. A constructive part of this was my incorporation of many elements of the parenting I received in how I dealt with others. Mourning them and moving on meant my collaborative approach could change to a more authoritative approach. I no longer had to view authority as stifling because I felt the need to avoid squelching a healthy rebelliousness (my own or any one else's). This affected my own parenting of my children, as well as my work with students and supervisees. Most of all, it made it easier for me to be fatherly or motherly when my patient needed it.

REFERENCES

Alexander, F., & French, T. M. (1946). *Psychoanalytic therapy: Principles and applications.* New York: Ronald.

Crasilneck, H. B., & Hall, J. A. (1985). *Clinical hypnosis: Principles and applications* (2nd ed.). Orlando, FL: Grune & Stratton.

Fromm, E., & Kahn, S. (1990). *Self-hypnosis: The Chicago paradigm.* New York: Guilford.

Soskis, D. A. (1986). *Teaching self-hypnosis: An introductory guide for clinicians.* New York: Norton.

Spiegel, H. S., & Spiegel, D. (1978). *Trance and treatment: Clinical uses of hypnosis.* Washington, DC: APA.

6

The Nike Boy and I

Linn LaClave

Our work together began when the Nike Boy was 12 years old. At age 4, while sleeping with an aunt and cousin, his mother rushed into the bedroom pursued by his father who proceeded to shoot both the mother and the aunt and finally turned the gun on himself, committing suicide. The mother recovered, however, the aunt died within 10 minutes of the incident.

Intermittently for 8 years, both this child and his mother experienced symptoms of post-traumatic stress disorder (PTSD). The symptoms were predominantly intrusive in nature, and it appeared that the denial phase that is classically associated with PTSD (Horowitz, 1973) had been only minimally experienced. Previous psychotherapy led to amelioration of symptoms; however, there were frequent exacerbations around stressful situations, particularly events associated with illness and death.

Referral for hypnotherapy came after an increase in the patient's symptoms following the murder of yet another aunt. An impasse occurred with traditional psychotherapy in which no improvement took place, and the patient was eventually referred to me for work with hypnosis. Previous therapists were respected senior colleagues, which lead me to doubt my ability to help this child. If these clinicians had questionable success, how could my efforts produce better results? Furthermore, the referring therapist did not propose that we both treat this patient. An adjunctive role was more familiar to me, and in my experience, an effective one that could preserve the original relationship between the patient and the primary therapist. As I would understand much later, a collaborative approach would have relieved me of some of the burden that I started to feel from this referral. I began to suspect that there was an element of magical expectations about the use of hypnosis on the part of my otherwise sophisticated colleague. It also became apparent that the patient endorsed his therapist's expectations.

Positive expectations, both on the part of the patient and the therapist, play an intricate role in growth through psychotherapy (Frank, 1962). There is also evidence that such attitudes are even more important in hypnotherapy (Sarbin & Coe, 1972). I, however, was feeling a growing sense of tension and reluctance to accept the case, particularly as primary therapist. Performance anxiety was rearing its ugly and immobilizing head. I felt not only pressured but also abandoned by the previous therapist. These were conscious reactions; therefore, I deluded myself to attributing my reluctance to the knowledge regarding the extensiveness of his trauma, thus permitting me to ignore countertransference possibilities. After careful consideration, I agreed to undertake the therapy. It was only much later that these obstructionist reactions were understood and worked through.

In contrast, the Nike Boy began hypnotherapy with enthusiasm. He showed no evidence of anxiety about the use of hypnosis in his treatment and he was optimistic about treatment outcome. Additionally, he told me that a classmate used hypnosis to help control chronic pain associated with an organic illness. After all, he assured me, his classmate used hypnosis successfully; there was no reason that he could not do the same. Gruenewald (1971) pointed out that intensification of the interpersonal process in hypnotherapy increases the importance of self-awareness on the part of the therapist. Problems in aggression, power hunger, and unresolved dependency needs are the most likely countertransference difficulties. Although not strictly a countertransference reaction because I was conscious of the source of the feeling, it would seem that I had fallen victim to unresolved dependency conflicts in feeling abandoned by his previous therapists. Thus, the beginning phase of therapy was characterized by my reluctance and resistance, whereas the patient overtly exhibited only receptivity and confidence in me and in hypnotherapy. I now suspect that my new patient harbored ambivalence about termination with his primary therapist and did not want to undertake a third therapeutic relationship. In addition, his positive presentation may have been related to an unconscious recognition of my ambivalence, thus placing more of the burden of alliance building on him.

His presenting problems included sleep disturbances with frequent episodes of sleepwalking and nightmares. Failing grades due to distractibility and poor concentration, resulted in the Nike Boy being in jeopardy of elimination from a special academic program. He not only was aware of this but was highly motivated to remain with his class. There were also visual hallucinations of his father appearing at school that left him frightened and disoriented. He reported how thoughts of his father and the loss of the aunt, whom he described as a second mother, led to his inability to concentrate both at home and at school. His sense of his inability to cope diminished his self-esteem even further.

The Nike Boy expressed confidence that he would be able to get his symptoms under control and also said that he wished to know more details about the original trauma. He further confided that his family discouraged discussion about what had occurred and that he wanted an opportunity to talk about his losses and to explore what he experienced. Initial examination revealed an intelligent sixth grader who was unusually sensitive to the needs of others. Additional resources included creative abilities, excellent use of visual imagery, and high motivation for mastery of the problems.

The course of hypnotherapy consisted of 12 sessions. The initial session was used for assessing hypnotizability, mental-status exam, and getting acquainted. Although I used no formal hypnotizability scale, I administered the *Apple Technique* (Strauss, 1991), which uses concentration and imagination to help the subject to enter an altered state of consciousness. The Nike Boy was cooperative with this technique, relaxed easily, and engaged in elaborate imagery of the apple. He also experienced arm levitation that was perceived as involuntary, thus experiencing the *classic hypnotic effect* as defined by Weitzenhoffer (1957). The patient's score on the Apple Technique was 3 (score range is 0–3). This was an experience of success for him that not only boosted his diminished self-esteem but assisted him in rapid establishment of a positive therapeutic alliance as well as in consolidating his belief in hypnosis.

I suggested that we initially work on controlling the symptoms that interfered with his functioning, and he readily agreed. At the second session he came in my office wearing new Nike tennis shoes. He proceeded to tell me about his love for basketball and about his hero, Michael Jordan. Although I know very little about spectator sports, I did remember the Nike slogan "Just Do It." I decided to utilize these positive images, and in hypnosis that day I suggested that when the intrusive thoughts occurred, the phrase "Just Do It" would refocus his attention on the task at hand.

A connection was made between success in completing work and Michael Jordan's success on the court, suggesting that basketball, like academic achievement, resulted in part from the ability to focus. During the session I also utilized behavioral rehearsal within the context of hypnosis to give him practice in gaining control over the interfering thoughts and providing reinforcement for his success experiences. In subsequent hypnotherapy sessions, the slogan "Just Do It" was used many times to help him fall asleep easily as well as to improve concentration both at home and at school. Because swimming was a pleasurable experience for him, we also utilized images of deep-sea diving to promote soothing and comforting for him at times of high arousal.

By the fourth session, I had begun to think of him fondly as the Nike Boy because of his treasured sports shoes. He spontaneously reported to me that several of his friends noticed a change in him. They told him that he seemed more friendly and funny and was also louder than he used to be. I felt that this was a highly significant endorsement of improvement as these comments came from 11- and 12-year-old children who generally are not known for paying much attention to the mental state of others. Despite the knowledge that our work was not completed, the Nike Boy and I shared a strong sense of accomplishment at this juncture in the therapy.

It was some weeks later that my patient reported to me that he had been imagining himself as a grandfather. I decided to use age progression to intensify this positive image. I felt that it was important for him to identify with his grandfather, as identification with the father figure was conflictual, if not impossible. In addition, with the family history of violent death in young adults, I wanted to support and strengthen the expectation that he would live to old age.

During hypnosis, I suggested that he picture himself as a grandfather, hearing himself tell about the events that he experienced and his ability to learn successfully to cope with them. This allowed him to see that the many traumas that he experienced had helped him to become a strong, sensitive person, one who can persevere in the face of adversity. After termination of the trance he said simply "this is the best I've ever done." The big smile on his face indicated to me that this was a very positive healing experience, one that helped him own the success and take credit for the changes. This is consistent with the contemporary focus on hypnosis as facilitating mastery (Eisen, 1990). Horowitz (1973), in his cognitive-processing model of PTSD, emphasized that the treatment goal should be one of integration not merely emotional expression. I felt that this particular session facilitated integration of the trauma for this youngster.

In the waking state, the Nike boy increasingly exhibited a strong interest in exploring the details of the original murder and suicide. I undertook this with some trepidation, delaying the use of age regression. In the end, his push to explore the details won. I was suggesting exploration when I proposed the image of deep-sea diving (Brown & Fromm, 1986) for comfort early in our work. I used this imagery again, and he was able to spontaneously recall two pieces of information that had been repressed. The first was a vivid image of being held up high, surrounded by the color blue, feeling sad, fearful, and confused. We later concluded that the memory was associated with being carried into the emergency room by a police officer, a fact that relatives confirmed. The second memory consisted of his aunt's last statement to him. He remembered that she said "don't forget me." This was the first indication that the Nike Boy had memory for verbal content of what took place that fatal night.

Before ending this hypnotherapy session, I suggested that he would feel comfortable and in control and that he would recall only those details that he was ready to remember. At the termination of trance, the Nike Boy indeed reported feeling in control and comfortable and remembered everything that had transpired during the session. The aunt's plea seemed to cause him to remember the trauma. At age 4, my patient would be in Piaget's (1965) preoperational stage of cognitive development and thus take what the aunt had said literally; he was unable to comprehend the abstract aspect of the message. I suggested to him that what she meant was to remember the relationship that the two of them had shared, not the trauma itself. He visibly relaxed at this, feeling relieved of his burden. He ended the session saying, "this is why I came." In subsequent sessions he revealed that he no longer had thoughts of the trauma but could at last think of his aunt with fond memories and the satisfying happy times they had experienced together. With a mixture of sadness and joy, he described a family picnic he remembered occurring shortly before the tragedy.

This course of hypnotherapy ended after 12 sessions when the Nike Boy and I mutually agreed that symptoms were well under control and that he had at last been able to recall those details that he had wished for so long to remember and work through. Tragically, 2 months after the termination of this treatment, another relative, a cousin, was murdered. Grief proceeded in a normal manner without recurrence of PTSD symptoms. At this time I began to understand that another source of my initial resistance to accepting this treatment case was that I was grieving the loss of three relatives whose deaths occurred in the preceding 18 months. All had died from natural causes, yet these deaths made profound changes in my life, as had the violent deaths experienced by my patient. It was the unconscious fear that my own grief would be augmented through an empathic connection with my patient's pain that led to my defensiveness.

The Nike Boy is now in late adolescence and functions well academically and in extracurricular activities. He has normal, satisfying relationships with both his peers as well as his family. Perhaps of equal importance, he has developed coping skills that are effective and are characterized by mature defense mechanisms.

Why was this course of hypnotherapy so successful in such a short time, particularly in light of my initial reluctance? Despite the catastrophic trauma that he experienced, the Nike Boy brought considerable resources to his hypnotherapy. Despite the chronicity of the symptoms that had been present intermittently for 8 years, he presented with simple PTSD defined by Brown and Fromm (1986) as occurring when cognitive processing of a traumatic event is blocked. Resolution can occur if conditions are established to facilitate processing. However, he lived in a family system that blocked this processing and working through of the trauma because it was felt that this was in the best interest of the child. Although the patient's symptoms diminished his functioning and self-esteem, the disorder was not severe. Therefore he did not require long-term therapy for satisfactory resolution to occur. Horowitz (1976) described in his cognitive-processing model of PTSD that treatment should begin with stabilization of presenting symptoms followed by integration of the trauma into the personality structure. The Nike Boy's therapy, facilitated by the use of hypnosis, progressed rapidly and smoothly through these treatment phases. He was able to reframe his experiences as leading to increased strength, ability to cope with the environment, and sensitivity to the needs of others. Additionally, he acquired the ability to identify with healthy role models, further strengthening and expanding adaptation.

The Nike Boy also had considerable innate hypnotic talent. He was able to use hypnosis to obtain relief from frightening images and other memories. Hypnosis also allowed him to relive the trauma that he had long wanted to do. This led to uncovering material that was blocking his coming to terms with his many losses.

Hypnosis was the core intervention in the Nike Boy's therapy, and its importance cannot be underestimated. First, even prior to treatment, the idea of using hypnosis increased the patient's sense of hope and positive expectations about undertaking a third course of treatment. These expectations may have taken on an element of "magical wish" (Eisen, 1990), which possibly was initiated by the referring therapist. However, as therapy progressed, this wish was superseded by a "belief in the self" (Eisen, 1990). The Nike Boy learned to develop self-confidence through success experiences, which quickly diminished his helplessness and allowed him to overcome catastrophic environmental stressors and debilitating symptoms. He increasingly was able to accept his success and mastery over his traumatic history.

The Nike Boy also had considerable innate hypnotic talent. He was able to use hypnosis to obtain relief from frightening images and other memories. Hypnosis also allowed him to relive the trauma that he had long wanted to do. This led to uncovering material that was blocking his coming to terms with his many losses.

My relationship with the Nike Boy influenced me in many personal and professional ways, some of which were immediately apparent whereas others were revealed gradually as the months and years passed since our work together. The success of the case gave me a sense of renewed admiration for the resilience of the human spirit and its drive for overcoming obstacles to growth. The poignancy of this child's history and his resilience facilitated an awareness in me that I, too, had the capacity to survive the pain of separation and loss, hence promoting my ability to accept and adjust to the loss of my family members.

The Nike Boy grieved for his deceased relatives individually. Observing his grief helped me understand that I had not done so for my family members. I began to understand that each of my losses interrupted the mourning for the previous ones. Although grief is never linear, there is healing in feeling the impact of a loss without interference or distraction from this process. I found myself gradually able to focus on the uniqueness of each of my relatives and on the impact they each had on my formation as a person. Also, as time passed, I became able to experience and mourn for the ways the loss of these important attachments changed my life. This promoted acceptance of their absence through internalization of their relationship and their influence on me.

Becoming gradually aware that initial self-doubt is frequently a pattern associated with accepting a difficult therapeutic task, I have become able more quickly to differentiate reality variables from countertransference ones and reduce their interference with the challenge at hand. Specifically, I focus less on content of the presenting problem and more on the process that brings the patient and me together for healing and growth. Freeing the energy I once expended in self-doubt increased my ability to be involved in this growth process. This has significantly increased my sense of self-confidence, thus freeing me for the task of engaging my patients in therapy rather than expecting them to engage me. This particularly has proven to be helpful when object loss through death is the focus of treatment.

One source of my initial concern about this treatment I later came to understand was a fear of possible strong affects the Nike Boy and I might experience, particularly those that could occur during age regression. It was not only his grief that I feared I could not manage but his combined with my own. The combination of our affective states might prove to be synergistic and beyond an easy control. I learned that the process of grieving, although always painful, does not have to be overwhelming or destructive. The intensity of a loss can be modulated through relationships leading to life-affirming experiences. As the grieving process ends, renewed connections to existing attachments and an openness to new affiliations can occur.

The success the Nike Boy achieved helped me to be more aware of my abilities and my defenses. I experienced a sense that I gained as much through being his therapist as he gained from being my patient, an outcome that I had not anticipated. I since often have pondered the question of whether this is an acceptable experience. Should a therapist gain as much benefit from therapy as his or her patient? If therapy is a microcosm of real life where intimate connections define our humanness and where emotional closeness between patient and therapist is part of the healing process, then mutual benefit would enhance that closeness. Under conditions in which the patient's needs are consistently placed first and in which the therapist's needs in no way conflict or jeopardize that of the patient's, perhaps mutual benefit not only is acceptable but facilitating of the therapeutic process. The therapeutic relationship in this respect can be seen as analogous to a healthy parent–child matrix. Although the relationship is a complementary one, growth in one member facilitates growth in the other. Perhaps in a similar manner, the patient and therapist grow together toward increasing mastery and differentiation.

The Nike Boy was able to experience his losses and the subsequent grief as factors making him a strong person who is sensitive to the needs of others. His ability to grieve yet acknowledge the positive sequelae of the trauma appeared to assist him with subsequent loss. My ability to overcome resistance in treating this child and to join him in this work helped me to do the same.

REFERENCES

Brown, D. P., & Fromm, E. (1986). *Hypnotherapy and hypnoanalysis.* Hillsdale, NJ: Lawrence Erlbaum Associates.

Eisen, M. (1990). From magical wish to belief in the self. In M. Fass & D. P. Brown (Eds.), *Creative mastery in hypnosis: A Festschrift for Erika Fromm* (pp. 147–159). Hillsdale, NJ: Lawrence Erlbaum Associates.

Frank, J. (1962). *Persuasion and healing.* New York: Shocken.

Gruenewald, D. (1971). Transference and countertransference in hypnosis. *International Journal of Clinical and Experimental Hypnosis, 19,* 71–82.

Horowitz, M. J. (1973). Phase oriented treatment of stress response syndrome. *American Journal of Psychotherapy, 27,* 506–515.

Horowitz, M. J. (1976). *Stress response syndromes.* New York: Aronson.

Olness, K., & Gardner, G. (1988). Early uses of hypnosis in children. In *Hypnosis and hypnotherapy with children* (pp. 7–19). Philadelphia: Grune & Stratton.

Piaget, J. (1965). *Judgement and reasoning in a child.* Routledge & Kegan Paul Ltd.

Sarbin, T., & Coe, W. C. (1972). *Hypnosis: A social psychological analysis of influence communication.* New York: Holt, Rinehart & Winston.

Strauss, B. S. (1991). The use of a multimodal image, the Apple Technique, to facilitate clinical hypnosis: A brief communication. *The International Journal of Clinical & Experimental Hypnosis, 39*(1), 1–5.

Weitzenhoffer, A.M. (1957) *General techniques of hypnotism.* New York: Grune and Straton.

III

CHANGES IN PERSPECTIVES OF THE SELF

7

Pain: A Story

Brenda Bursch
Lonnie Zeltzer

INTRODUCTION

Jane Watson, a 10-year-old girl, was referred to me (Lonnie Zeltzer) by the chief of pediatric orthopedics because of knee pain. In the orthopedist's telephone referral, he said, "I have this child crying in my clinic. This is a pain problem ... not an orthopedic one. Please help!" Such a direct and personal referral set the stage initially for me to want to relieve this child of her pain, especially when the previous four doctors had not been successful. The assumption I made initially was that this child had neuropathic pain and had just not received the right treatment. We intervened with straightforward approaches to treatment of neuropathic pain, but these were not effective. The distress of this child and her family, including numerous telephone calls for help on a daily basis, eventually led to a hospitalization and a subsequent year of individual hypnotherapy with me for Jane, and family psychotherapy with Brenda Bursch. I present the history and evolution of treatment for the patient, and Dr. Bursch discusses the family treatment. We both explore the feelings and changes that each of us experienced through the process. This was the first patient with whom we worked together. Thus, this story is about not only the development of ourselves as individuals but also the development of our professional relationship.

CASE OVERVIEW

In our first meeting, Jane and her mother, Mrs. Watson, told me their story with strong emotions. The right knee pain began 3 months earlier and had steadily progressed. Jane said that it made her limp until she could no longer walk, and it felt like "something was not right inside." After an MRI showed torn cartilage Jane underwent surgery to repair the cartilage, with only worsening of the pain after surgery. She described with tears the "torture" that she experienced with physical therapy. Subsequently, a rheumatologist intervened with steroids and knee injections. Mrs. Watson, also teary-eyed, reported that, after no improvement and normal tests, the rheumatologist told Jane, "enough pillows, straighten your legs.... I have other patients with real pain ... if you don't start moving your leg, I'll put it in a brace and crank it up at night!" This kind of treatment infuriated both Jane and her mother and made them feel even more helpless.

Jane's family had moved from England 2 years ago because of a job change for Mr. Watson. Her mother was a 40-year-old homemaker who had migraines secondary to stress. Her father, 46-years-old, was an electrical engineer and healthy. Jane, the youngest of two children, was in fifth grade. Her 16-year-old brother, a high school senior, was reportedly very angry about the move for the first year but settled down after the parents told him that he could go back to England to live with relatives. Jane was a straight A student and very active in basketball and swimming before the knee pain. All activities, including school attendance, had come to a halt as the knee pain progressed.

After a failed pharmacologic approach during the first week, Jane was seen by Dr. Smith, a psychologist in our pain clinic, for hypnotherapy. He attempted several hypnotic interventions (e.g., direct pain reduction, change of sensation, distraction) but none was effective. His recommendation was that hypnotherapy not be attempted again because Jane was repeatedly disappointed by promises. He further recommended that I work on reducing the pain first; otherwise there would be "serious emotional consequences" if intervention failed again.

At this point, my belief in hypnotherapy, one of the salient routes to treatment, was shaken. I was only a pediatrician, whereas this eminent psychologist, who taught hypnotherapy at national meetings, believed that hypnotherapy should not be used. I began to question myself and my clinical judgement. I had not formally trained in psychotherapy, and the hypnotherapeutic work that I conducted with these children with pain problems was psychotherapy using hypnosis. At this point, I did not even consider the idea that Jane and her mother might have connected to me so strongly that Jane would be resistant to working individually with anyone else (e.g., the psychologist). My shaken belief in my own judgment led me to avoid further discussion of the dynamics of

Jane's behaviors with the psychologist. I felt like the emperor in his "new clothes." I wanted to reduce her pain so the psychologist could intervene. But, how was I going to reduce her pain if psychotherapy and, in particular, hypnotherapy were not to be used until after Jane's pain was mitigated?

After numerous telephone calls from both parents pleading for me to do something to take away the pain, I admitted Jane to the hospital the next week. At this point, although I felt that my treatment had failed, I had fantasies that surely my anesthesia colleagues could perform an epidural sympathetic nerve block and "turn off" the sensation and thus the pain. I hoped that a direct biological route to treatment would succeed because the hypnotherapeutic strategy that I initially judged to be the best approach was clearly flawed (or so I believed at that point in time). However, despite enough infused anesthetic to produce a dense motor block, there was no change in Jane's pain. I assumed that the problem was likely related to the pediatric anesthesiologist's lack of sufficient technical expertise. I thus asked the senior pain anesthesiologist for help, and he suggested a deeper femoral nerve block.

Following this deeper femoral nerve block, Jane achieved numbness in her leg but no change in her knee pain. Injecting local anesthetic into her knee still produced no change in her pain. The anesthesiologist told me that Jane was "manipulative and faking her pain for attention." Mrs. and Mr. Watson were becoming increasingly angry with the medical staff and complained to me. They also kept begging me to do something. Jane spent increasing amounts of time crying because of her pain that she reported as being unbearable.

Next, and partly out of desperation, I asked the hospital pediatric psychiatry service and the chief of pediatric orthopedics to evaluate Jane. According to Jane, the child psychiatry fellow seemed to accuse her of faking her pain for attention. Then I asked the fellow's supervisor, Dr. Bursch, to see this patient and family. Thankfully, Jane and the family reported that they liked Dr. Bursch a lot (perhaps in part because I spoke so highly of her, hoping that she might be the one with the answers). The orthopedist also saw Jane and recommended serial casting of her leg, leaving a window for her knee because it was so sensitive to touch.

The hospitalization extended longer than originally estimated. Because I was due to leave for Paris the next day to attend a conference for 3 weeks, I obtained the details of the procedure and was told that the leg would remain in its bent position and very gradually recasted as an outpatient and straightened. I spent considerable time the evening before leaving reassuring the family and explaining what was going to happen. My guilt at "abandoning" Jane and her family was calmed by the family's positive response. By this time, I had been giving oral opioids for Jane's pain as a "temporizing" measure. I left feeling reassured.

In my absence, during the casting procedure, the orthopedist decided to fully straighten Jane's leg (for which, later, I assumed responsibility and felt very guilty). It was later reported to me by the family that Jane "went berserk" when she awoke. The orthopedist had explained to the family, to no avail, that this had been the best clinical decision because her leg had naturally straightened under anesthesia. This explanation mattered little to the extremely distressed family, and Dr. Bursch spent considerable time with the family as they tried to cope with this crisis.

I received almost daily phone calls in Paris from the first pediatric anesthesiologist to complain about this "needy, impossible" family that he was "only willing to see as an outpatient until I returned." As if I did not feel guilty enough about abandoning this patient, the idea of leaving this patient in the hands of someone whom I did not trust added to the guilt. Amazing to me now, I even seriously thought about returning earlier than originally planned from Paris in order to assume responsibility of the case. Fortunately, I talked myself out of that idea. However, it is clear to me now that the insecurities about my own skill, knowledge, and clinical judgment, initiated by the recommendation of the pain clinic psychologist that hypnotherapy should not be used until I could reduce the pain, set up a chain reaction of my projections of inadequacy onto the various anesthesiologists and the orthopedist. Furthermore, my guilt about not being able to reduce Jane's pain was mounting and spreading to guilt about my treating other pediatric patients who had chronic pain. The 1 year of weekly individual therapy with Jane, her family therapy with Dr. Bursch, and the impact of these on ourselves and our relationship are detailed in the following section.

CASE PROGRESSION AND RESOLUTION

Both Jane and her parents struggled with the accuracy of the diagnosis and the relevance of the recommendations to her pain. Issues related to adherence to the treatment plan surfaced frequently. As Mr. and Mrs. Watson became aware of their contribution to Jane's dependence, their expectations of Jane's independent functioning increased. During this time, Jane's extreme emotional distress, cognitive distortions, and regressed self-serving behavior became overt. After learning to express herself more directly and to better modulate her emotion, Jane became significantly more motivated in physical therapy. Finally, with her increased functioning and improved physical health, Jane began to feel a sense of mastery over her environment and body that was not dependent on her ability to manipulate her mother.

The challenges presented by the family to us as the treatment team included the family's initial strong belief in medical intervention for the treatment of their daughter, their tendency to externalize blame for Jane's lack of progress, and their inconsistent adherence to behavioral recommendations. We contributed to the difficulty by our desire to please the family, feelings of incompetence, and difficulty sharing responsibility for the case as an interdependent team (i.e., the pre-existing, unresolved trust issues, such as the ones between the pediatric anesthesiologist and me, became magnified, with the help of a family that promoted splitting among the team members). As we learned to refrain from colluding with the family and to share responsibility for the case, our feelings of incompetence lessened, and we found openings for effective intervention as well as growth within ourselves.

After approximately 1 year in physical therapy, hypnotherapy, and family therapy, Jane was able to ambulate without a wheelchair, attend school full-time, and be active in her social and school life. The family psychotherapy focus changed over time from Jane's knee pain to the emotions and dynamics that were central to the family as a whole. At her 2-year follow-up, Jane was an active adolescent with no residual pain-related disability.

LONNIE ZELTZER'S STORY

Initially, I met with Jane and her parents prior to or just after the family's psychotherapy sessions with Dr. Bursch. Considering the recommendation from the first psychologist, I avoided hypnotherapy. The individual sessions with Jane that followed and the multiple phone calls from the family focused on the magnitude of Jane's suffering and the family's anger at each of us (Dr. Bursch, the anesthesiologist, the orthopedist, and me). Again, I began feeling helpless and reconsulted the senior pain anesthesiologist. I was certain that he would have the answers, and I could absolve my guilt for taking on a patient whom I felt I did not have the skills or experience to treat. He said that a spinal block might be effective but only if Jane really wanted to get better. I found myself angry with him. I wanted him to fix her so that I could feel better.

In the meantime, Dr. Bursch and I changed our approach to encourage Jane to increase function before her pain changed. This was a new strategy that was the opposite of what the pain clinic psychologist had previously recommended. In fact, I was not quite sure that I believed that this newer strategy of increasing function with the pain rather than first reducing the pain was going to work. I was feeling that I was rather cruel to suggest this. However, I told the family that I would give Jane opioids to help her to increase her function but that the parents had to reinforce and maintain the behavioral plan. The behavioral plan was initiated by Dr. Bursch. Although the behavioral plan made sense to me cognitively, my guilt for not being able to improve Jane's pain made it difficult for me to hear about Jane's suffering and to have emotional faith in the plan.

The parents would call Dr. Bursch and me, complaining about the other or indicating differing opinions that we were telling the family. Because of this behavior, Dr. Bursch and I agreed to call each other as soon as we received a call from the Watsons so that splitting would be minimized and we could help together to contain the family's anxiety. I was glad for the ongoing support from Dr. Bursch so that I could receive reassurance because I continued to feel inadequate to treat this patient. To add to my guilt, Mr. Watson kept asking if there was anything else we could do or somewhere else in the country where there was more experience and where they could go to get help for Jane. We told the family that the senior pain anesthesiologist who had already seen Jane was one of the national experts on neuropathic pain. In truth, I was still feeling angry with this anesthesiologist for not fixing her pain. He met with the family and recommended that spinal anesthesia was a possibility but only when Jane was ready and really wanted to undergo that treatment. However, he did not believe she was currently ready.

Following this meeting, I received a long letter from Mr. Watson (with copies to Dr. Bursch and to all physicians who had ever been involved in Jane's care), in which he outlined all of the failed treatments and disappointments especially when Jane was "lied to" with the casting and leg straightening. He indicated that I had no plan until we met with the senior anesthesiologist, who was expected to do something. However, he was shocked that the anesthesiologist said that Jane was not ready. I felt overwhelmingly guilty especially when he accused me of forcing Jane to experience incredible pain. I felt I was an imposter. I am not an anesthesiologist, I do not perform nerve blocks. Why did I think that I knew how to treat children with pain? I was believing that I had done a terrible disservice to this family. My confidence in myself was at its lowest point. I found myself dreaming of this patient and her family with disasters befalling Jane, and I would be a helpless bystander. Jane occupied my thoughts when I was awake as well.

My helpless feelings in relation to Jane entered my own psychotherapy sessions. I found childhood feelings of helplessness connected to my inabilities to get my father to stop gambling or to help my mother to do so. My own academic successes had worked at various times to divert my parents' attention from their own problems, but clearly beneath these accomplishments I felt inadequate. Here was this feeling emerging so strongly again.

I needed reassurance and my first reaction was to call Dr. Bursch for emotional support under the guise of needing to develop a plan for how to handle the letter. Somehow, through discussions with each other about our own worries and about feelings of inadequacy, we were each able to encourage each other's belief in our own basic clinical intuitions. We talked about other patients whom we had each treated, we talked about ourselves, and, through this process, we found mutual support for working together with this family. I decided at this point that my clinical judgment in this matter was sound and that I would pursue my initial instincts about the value of hypnotherapy. I also decided that I would no longer need to look to the anesthesiologist for magic. Dr. Bursch and I met with the family to deal with their concerns and to state clearly and resolutely our therapeutic plans. It appeared as if when we began to trust ourselves and each other, the family dysfunction was contained, and Jane began to make progress. Conversely, as the family began to trust us, we began to trust ourselves and to use each other for ongoing support for our own judgments.

Jane's relationship with me was good from the start, despite the father's letter about loss of trust. Our sessions would typically begin with Jane telling me about her frustrations at home, in school, with friends, at the doctors, and, almost always, in family therapy sessions with Dr. Bursch whom she "despised." She would complain bitterly about how Dr. Bursch did not understand her (i.e., like I did) and how Dr. Bursch enjoyed making her suffer. There were times that Jane's complaints created worry about whether Dr. Bursch was doing the right thing in family therapy. However, I was feeling comfortable enough in my relationship with Dr. Bursch that I was able to discuss these worries with her and to feel reassured through these discussions. Soon, Jane's complaints about Dr. Bursch no longer bothered me. In fact, these complaints reassured me that the family therapy was going well. After all, when I first met Jane, she never became or admitted to being angry or distressed about anything.

If my hypnotherapy sessions with Jane had taken place earlier during the course of treatment, when my guilt was high and my confidence and collegial trust low, I easily could have inadvertently colluded with the splitting that Jane was attempting. Instead, I was able to listen to Jane, ask her a few questions and then suggest that she had suffered long enough and worked so hard that she could now enjoy a deep state of relaxation and comfort. After an induction I suggested that she could go to a place where she knew how to feel good, strong, in control, cared for, and happy. Eventually, this became a place where she could run, swim, and do all the things physically that she could not do because of her knee pain. She reported exercising vigorously during the hypnotherapy and that it felt good. However, she always saw her knee as just a knee but not hers. Whenever I suggested a central sensory control station in her brain that controlled the nerve signals for sensory information coming from her body to her brain, she was able to achieve deep anesthetic experiences with all parts of her body except her right knee. Throughout the year, she was unable in her imagination to picture herself touching or bending her knee. Clinically, Jane reported the same amount of pain but that she was able to cope with it better. Her functioning dramatically improved as did her abilities to express anger and to act more independently. Simultaneously, progress was being made in family therapy.

I was feeling increasingly competent; I felt increasing admiration for Dr. Bursch in her clinical skills, judgment, and perseverance with this difficult family. Over time, I felt the same about myself. I also realized how much I had learned from working with Dr. Bursch. I had not previously had an integrated working relationship with the other mental health professionals I knew. The traditional model had been my medical visits and their psychotherapy sessions, as in parallel play. However, with Dr. Bursch, I felt as if we were cotherapists, each with our own role, but working jointly in one coordinated effort. I found that I looked forward to our discussions about each of our sessions with this child and her family afterward. I think that these discussions with Dr. Bursch helped me to feel that I had good clinical skills and judgment. I even began to be amazed, on occasion, at the metaphors that seemed to emerge by themselves during my hypnotherapy sessions with Jane that seemed to be pertinent to her progress.

In summary, my personal experiences with the Watsons and with Dr. Bursch have helped me to trust myself and to feel good about my clinical judgment and skills as a hypnotherapist for children with pain. Additionally, Dr. Bursch and I have developed an ongoing, mutually beneficial and enjoyable professional relationship. Because of the changes we experienced as clinicians and as a team, we have developed a reputation for treating children with chronic pain. These children are now referred to us from many parts of the country. I also have incorporated hypnotherapy in almost all of my therapeutic work with children with chronic pain and am continuously amazed at its effectiveness, not just for symptom control but for the children's own psychological growth as well. Approaching the barriers related to the traditional boundaries and roles for the *pediatrician* versus the *mental health professional* remains difficult. However, my trust in myself is growing as I often become the psychologist–pediatrician for complicated patients and find that I am effective. I can also discuss my differences with psychologists and psychiatrists and trust my own judgment more than previously. Likewise, I believe I have become more adept at recognizing the ways in which health professionals in any discipline can inadvertently contribute to pain-related disability. Consequently, I make more attempts to provide integrated care with the child's other health professionals in order to reduce such barriers to clinical improvement.

BRENDA BURSCH'S STORY

I met the Watsons when Jane was admitted to the hospital for pain treatment with blocks. The medical team was frustrated that nothing seemed to help Jane's pain or satisfy Mrs. Watson. When I entered the hospital room,

Jane was moaning in pain, Mrs. Watson was at her side, and Mr. Watson was sitting in the other available chair across the other side of the room. Jane and Mrs. Watson energetically listed the problems they had encountered during Jane's experience with her knee pain and during the hospitalization. The two of them spoke interchangeably with each other, sharing both vocabulary and emotion. Mr. Watson did not speak. This typified Mrs. Watson's and Jane's enmeshment and the father's lack of involvement. Being relatively new to my psychiatry consultant role at the University of California, Los Angeles (UCLA), and new to the pain team, it was an overwhelming experience. I did my best to remember the basics. If nothing else, I could establish rapport and refer them to an expert.

I was successful at establishing rapport. The Watsons informed me that if they had to be in family therapy, which was a condition of treatment by the pain team, it was me they wanted as their therapist. The family explained that previous mental health providers did not understand Jane's pain like I did. Dr. Zeltzer echoed the family's confidence in me and desire for me to work with them. I decided to see them in family therapy and to rely on a consultant for assistance.

I felt extremely inadequate but viewed this challenge as an important opportunity for transition to the pain team. Consequently, I agreed to work with the Watsons despite my significant misgivings. It was a very uncomfortable feeling. At the time, I was unaware that this challenge of my faith in myself and in the therapeutic process would become a familiar theme in my work with the complicated families I most often see with Dr. Zeltzer. It is also a theme that I now, with the benefits of increased familiarity and success stories, find exhilarating and compelling. It is hard to imagine how I would define such challenges today, had my experience with the Watsons not been successful.

I felt sorry for this family. They were in much distress and quite frightened by a disorder they could not understand. Jane was an intelligent, polite, articulate, and self-righteous girl who seemed to be faking extreme pain. Mrs. Watson was an over-protective and over-reactive mother who could not tolerate seeing her revered daughter in pain. Mr. Watson was polite, reserved, and clear that he did not see the relevance of family therapy to his daughter's pain. Jane's older brother, Mike, was a verbal, direct, and observant teenager. Mrs. Watson sat close to her daughter and held her hand throughout the first session. Her husband sat on the other side of their daughter at some distance. Mike sat opposite them. They were all exceedingly nice. I felt impatient. I wanted to tell Jane to quit moaning, Mrs. Watson to relax, and Mr. Watson to loosen up and trust me. Perhaps I most liked Mike because he expressed his and my impatience.

Questions flooded my mind. How could I challenge this nice family? How could I take Jane's distress seriously when it appeared so dramatized?

How could I figure out how much protectiveness was reasonable being from a very independence encouraging, perhaps detached, family? How could I challenge Mr. Watson when his reserve and skepticism so much reminded me of my father? I even asked: How much could I trust that Dr. Zeltzer did not miss something medically?

Like many people with advanced degrees in helping professions, and like Jane, I had become successful in part by pleasing others and being an overachiever. It was likely the quality that the Watson family initially found attractive about both Dr. Zeltzer and me. Unlike the Watson family, my family background includes my parents' divorce when I was 12 years old and, consequently, much independence in my preadolescent and adolescent years. During these years, I had the type of family that typically did not eat dinner together, take vacations together, discuss private matters with each other, or interfere too much with each other's social plans. Transition to college was exciting and easy. My independence was regularly rewarded in various jobs I held and contributed to my ability to finish my doctoral dissertation in a timely manner. Working in a large, academic setting like UCLA is no different. My first impression of UCLA was not that I was hired to work for the organization, but that I was given permission to have an independent practice within the walls of the University. Independence, both financially and clinically, appeared to be the key to success.

During the beginning family therapy sessions with the Watson family, I relied on Jane's older brother for perspective. He accused his mother of babying Jane and Jane of being manipulative. As the family attempted to paint Mike as the problem in the family, his accusations came to life. Jane adeptly manipulated her mother into defending her. Mrs. Watson spoke for her daughter as if Jane, a very bright and articulate girl, did not have the capacity to verbally respond to her brother's accusations. The family united against Mike. In the initial stages of family therapy, they vigorously questioned the relevancy of family therapy to their daughter's pain. They only remained in therapy because it was a condition of being followed by the pain team. Their resistance was reflected in their extreme difficulty following through with treatment recommendations, blaming of various team members for their daughter's continued pain, and strong adherence to familiar family dynamics. Although small movements forward were noted, such as Jane successfully being prompted to respond to her brother herself, the successes were quickly followed by retreat in strong resistance and multiple telephone calls to Dr. Zeltzer and me.

Over time, my frustration, impatience, and anger toward the family also served to further strengthen my feelings of inadequacy to help them. This resulted in my second guessing the diagnosis and therapeutic plan I had made, fear that I was not providing appropriate care, much thought about what I might have missed, and feelings that I was letting down Dr. Zeltzer. Although the expert I had consulted was extremely helpful, the fact that his style was different than mine contributed to my feelings they would be better off with the expert than with me. Additionally, I began to wonder what it was about me that resulted in me seeing this particular family in therapy.

It soon became clear that the family's high anxiety and attempts at splitting Dr. Zeltzer and me required action. We agreed to immediately call each other when we received a telephone call from one of the Watson family members in order to ensure we each responded to them similarly. This resulted in daily telephone calls in the beginning. Although our plan for high communication initially seemed to be a cumbersome time commitment, and I was initially concerned about bothering Dr. Zeltzer with possibly unimportant information, the effectiveness of the plan was apparent. The excessive telephone calls were contained and resulted in Dr. Zeltzer and I gaining insight into the treatment.

Unexpectedly, I also found great pleasure in this process and received significant emotional support from Dr. Zeltzer. Surprising to me, rather than feeling burdened by our extensive contact, Dr. Zeltzer expressed value in communicating with me also. My treatment of this family required me to work in a much more interdependent fashion with Dr. Zeltzer than my own family model of independence and detachment taught me to do. This model was also contrary to be long-held belief about how to obtain professional success. In retrospect, I believe that I had to move away from a more detached model of relationships to allow the family to feel safe enough to move away from their more enmeshed model and, thus to give me more therapeutic leverage. Representing an enormous change in me, I now find this model of collaboration both indispensable when working with complicated families, and an important feature of my love for my work.

Themes of isolation (and related fears of detachment and independence) were strong in this family. It was common to hear that no one understood the problem, no one can help, and people who try to help, make it worse. The feelings of isolation were only exacerbated by leaving their extended family, friends, and country when they moved to the United States. Even Jane's reports in hypnotherapy with Dr. Zeltzer that her knee was not a part of her body and her experiences that medical interventions impacted other parts of her body but not her knee, suggested a dissociation, something out of place. Jane had become her knee and was screaming out her family's pain. Jane, and her family, actively struggled with the perceived trap of enmeshment (not feeling unique, special or self-efficacious) versus isolation and detachment. Jane was intensely fearful that she would feel abandoned by her parents if she improved. Rather than feeling sorry for the Watson family as I did in the beginning, I started to admire them and learn from them as they courageously endured such painful fears. Although, from my family model, it was always clear to me how their enmeshment created problems for them, what I began to observe was how the strength of their close relationships was also a strong support for them. It was especially helpful for me to appreciate the benefits of their closeness as I was developing a more interdependent relationship with Dr. Zeltzer. The Watsons accommodations to each other, together with Dr. Zeltzer's active respect for my skills, provided me with a conceptual framework for interdependence I had not previously experienced. A door was open for me to enter.

Another theme for the family was not knowing how hard to push for change. Fear was literally paralyzing Jane and her family. Their desperation for change was matched by their fear, and resulted in vigorous campaigning and complaining regarding the ability of others to achieve change in them. As if that request was not difficult enough, they also demanded painless change. The parallel process in my own role was more than obvious. One of my primary struggles was knowing how hard to push for change. Jane already despised me and was at times hysterical during therapy sessions, yet it was also clear that her parents needed to push her harder. It seemed to me that I had to push them harder. Yet, they had successfully solidified my fears that they (and I) would be unable to tolerate it, and that fear paralyzed me.

As time progressed, Dr. Zeltzer's comments that she wanted us to do more for the family strengthened my feelings of inadequacy and cowardice. Slowly, however, I began to be aware of the problems created by our common desire to help this family. Over time, it occurred to me that Dr. Zeltzer and I were well liked by this family because we initially colluded with them in their belief that we would fix Jane. We did not challenge them but promised that help was forthcoming. Although we were very effective in engaging them in treatment, we both had difficulty giving up or even sharing the responsibility for fixing Jane. As the family continued to demand more of us, we responded by feeling we were not providing enough or appropriate care. It was easy to engage this family, but difficult to identify our roles in maintaining them in their familiar pattern by trying to have the answers for them. We finally started to see the problem, however. The key was not doing more, it was doing less. How could it have taken us so long to do what we had been asking the parents to do for so long?

As I understood our roles as obstacles in Jane's progress, I also came to understand that our collusion helped the family stay in treatment with us. Since the first week of treatment, the expert I had consulted had been encouraging me to push the family harder. Although the family probably could have been pushed a bit harder, I began to trust that my sense about how hard to push them (or not push them) was valuable. If I had pushed them too hard in the beginning, they would not have remained in treatment.

I began to change in small ways. First, Jane had an emotional crisis when it was decided to remove her leg from the cast. I got an emergency call from the family immediately following the removal of the cast because Jane was in extreme distress. Rather than immediately provide recommendations about how to change the situation as my familiar pattern would dictate, I decided to evaluate the situation after 1 week to allow time for her to figure out how to manage the problem. Jane adapted to the brace within 24 hours.

When the parents lamented that they had been following treatment recommendations but that nothing had improved, rather than defending treatment I pointed out that Mrs. Watson pushed Jane in her wheelchair into therapy that day rather than have her wheel herself. Mrs. Watson began to recognize the ways she subtlety fostered her daughter's dependence on her. I could see that Mrs. Watson could be pushed harder than I gave her credit for—the very point I was attempting to make regarding her expectations of Jane. Mrs. Watson's emerging perspective change became apparent one day when, after I gently physically restrained Mrs. Watson to prevent her from helping her daughter, Mrs. Watson was able to laugh at herself. At this point, I started to feel the deep and genuine trust forming between us. My ability to demonstrate how I had come to care about this family, despite my frustrations, strengthened. My trust in myself and in the therapeutic process was also being restored.

Despite such successes, the family's familiar state of confusion and impatience continued to surface on a regular basis, usually voiced by Mr. Watson. Additionally, Jane became increasingly anxious, depressed, and medically compromised with many physical complaints. Although theoretically I believed that the family's increase in overt distress represented progress, my feelings of responsibility continually haunted me and intermittently threatened my trust of the therapeutic process. I could not help sharing their concern that I was unnecessarily creating distress in the family. I feared that Dr. Zeltzer agreed, especially because I knew Jane was complaining about me to her.

My feelings of responsibility emerged even more strongly when Mr. Watson again wanted to discontinue therapy. Instead of defending treatment, I requested that Mr. and Mrs. Watson discuss and resolve the problem, thereby giving them the responsibility for the family's progress. The ensuing argument resulted in the first display of anger I had witnessed by Mrs. Watson toward her husband. She eloquently summarized what she had learned in therapy and forcefully expressed her request that they continue. They made a decision together to remain in family therapy. During the same session, Mr. Watson requested literature about chronic pain (for about the third time). I suggested that he go to the library and conduct his own literature search. The tide was changing. Seven months had passed.

Jane, too, began to take charge of her pain and gained leverage against it. Once this shift occurred, her progress was steady. I started meeting more with Mr. and Mrs. Watson without Jane to reinforce her independent efforts at rehabilitating herself. Her parents became more adept at identifying how her pain was extremely sensitive to their marital tension and other family and social stressors.

I was enormously relieved that our approach was successful and that our credibility was being restored. In addition a significant portion of my relief was related to my slow release of personal responsibility for fixing Jane. The high expectations and complementary feelings of personal responsibility experienced in both the parental system and in the medical system had been misplaced. Once we successfully charged the parents to charge Jane with the responsibility to improve her functioning, we all became unstuck.

One of the most significant changes that occurred in me as a result of my experiences with the Watson family and with Dr. Zeltzer is the development of a much stronger trust in the therapeutic process for such complicated problems. Although each new family represents a new challenge and triggers my concerns of responsibility and skill, my trust of the process and excitement at the prospect of participating in such an intimate challenge contains my fears and propels me forward. Since this experience, I have come to understand the importance of entering the family system in a respectful and caring manner in order to achieve change.

On the personal side, I have expanded my relationships to include more interdependent relationships. This shift has allowed me to increase my options and enjoyment of relationship with others. Before, I was much less likely to share responsibility with others. I had been strongly independent, and that had always worked for me. Now, I enjoy and seek out the team approach—one that is collaborative and clearly more effective for this type of patient. Further, my confidence in myself in this interdependent mode grew as I was closely observed by Dr. Zeltzer and ultimately validated for my work. Interdependence does not mean a loss of freedom. I had felt that Jane and her family needed more independence and individual responsibility. Interestingly, they learned these skills through the same therapy process that taught me the value of interdependence. I am grateful to them for this memorable experience.

EPILOGUE

The Watson family continues to call us on occasion for updates. Jane has changed from being a compliant, "nice" girl to being a normal adolescent with the usual problems. The family has agreed to serve as supports for other families whose child has a chronic pain problem, to encourage them that things can get better and to describe the value of hypnotherapy and family therapy for a chronic pain problem.

We continue to see patients independently of each other as well as jointly. Our feelings of competence have grown and we continue to learn from each other, as well as from our best teachers, the families with whom we work. Perhaps the most obvious evidence of our internal changes in understanding how we fit into the treatment plan is that we have changed the way we approach severely disabled chronic pain patients who require inpatient rehabilitation. Rather than conducting the initial inpatient evaluation and then sending the patients to another treatment team for inpatient rehabilitation (and consequently, instilling in the treatment team the responsibility of fixing the child), we now attempt whenever possible to capitalize on the relationships we form during the diagnostic process by remaining the treatment team once the child is transferred for rehabilitation. With this approach, we are now able to accelerate the shift in responsibility resulting in more timely clinical improvements. This small innovation in how we deliver our services has vastly improved our success with severely debilitated chronic pain patients. We continue to be surprised and pleased by the effectiveness of the skills we developed during our work with the Watsons and with the wealth of direction we have at our disposal if only we stop to consider our personal involvement and reactions to a family and to each other.

8

Gently Wiping Her Tears Away

Phyllis A. Alden

The process of change is ongoing in all of us. It is not possible to interact with one's environment, family, friends, and patients without there being some impact. To identify a patient–therapist situation that produced a particular change in the therapist, and to examine the process of that change has, therefore, required considerable soul-searching and analysis. To understand the impact the patient had on me requires me to set this in the context of my life. Self-disclosure, however, is not easy and it is with some trepidation that I share my history with you.

BACKGROUND

I was born virtually blind as a consequence of my mother having had German Measles during pregnancy. Thanks to her astuteness it was treated fairly quickly, with the result that I grew up with some vision. In fact, my mother told me she had not realized she contracted German Measles, but had a dream in which her baby—a girl—was born wearing glasses, which the nurse informed her, were to help the baby to see. My mother was greatly distressed by the dream, and from then on was convinced I would be born with eye trouble. She was right. She insisted that I should be referred to a specialist. The general practitioner, although he could see nothing wrong, sent us to the hospital to humor my mother. He later admitted he had thought she was "crackers." I believe that at that time one did not normally operate on children under age 2. My mother, driven by the determination that her child should have the best insisted on seeing the top specialist. As a result, I was operated on at the age of 6 months, the first of many unpleasant hospital experiences. It is thanks to that early intervention that I have as much sight now as I do.

As I reached school age, my parents were faced with a dilemma of either sending me to a special school for visually impaired children, where I would have received a terrible education (and no chance of a decent career), or sending me to private school. They chose the latter, and from an early age on I was told "you have to be something."

I did push myself and studied hard. In fact, at age 11, when it was time to go on to the senior school, I insisted on going to an ordinary school—enough private education. I wanted to be the same as everyone else. It was not easy, but I prevailed and went on to the university. I then went onward to become what I am now, a clinical psychologist.

It is a strange thing growing up with limited vision; because it has always been there, you take it for granted. Until the world started to impinge on me and say "you can't do this or that because you can't see well enough," and so forth, I don't think I ever realized that it would make any difference, or indeed, that it set me apart in any way from other people. I know I could not read the blackboard or play sports. However, I did have lots of friends to play with, and I was quite a tomboy. I enjoyed climbing trees and getting very dirty crawling through the mud to secret "hidey holes."

In addition, I always had to be perfect for my mother. She demanded that I do better than everyone else. As I grew up, I had to dress well, wear makeup, keep my hair nice, get good exam marks, and so on. I also sang, and that had to be perfect too. Heaven help me if Mother did not like a note.

It really was only when I went to university that I started to realize that I was regarded as a second-class citizen. Early on I decided that I wanted to be a clinical psychologist. But one day, close to the exams at the university, one of the lecturers took me aside and carefully—as if to a 2-year old—explained that with my sight I could not possibly be a clinician. He said you needed good sight to do the job, and indeed, that even if I got a first-class degree, I would be lucky if I got a job that someone with a low-level degree might get.

You cannot begin to imagine the devastation that followed. My performance deteriorated significantly. I felt miserable. My world collapsed around me and it took a lot of support and encouragement from family, and a guardian angel in the form of a local child psychiatrist to help start to build it up again. Thanks to him I did get into training as a psychologist. But the damage had been done. Looking back, I realize now that my mother's drive for my perfection had included a message to hide my problem. I was being told to disguise it with eye makeup (impossible). I was expected to achieve so highly that my visual difficulties would not matter, and—most importantly—I was never to admit to them. The effect of the lecturer's well-meaning advice about my future was to solidify that message even more. I wasted great energy pretending my visual difficulties did not exist.

After completing my degree (a miracle) I did meet my guardian angel and thanks to him, got hired as a clinical psychology trainee. This wonderful man gave me letters of introduction to a couple of hospitals, one of which offered me a training post. But even after this acceptance, the problems and the nightmares only continued with increased intensity. Now that I was there, I must never be found out. I did not dare go in for the British Psychological Society Diploma exams as they might respond negatively to my condition. Instead, I became credentialed through in-service training and upgrading my position.

Initially I did not have a lot of confidence in myself. I lived in terror that one day, I would be found out, and worse, found wanting. Despite promotions, the support of a wonderful husband, and my professional and personal achievements, the confidence I painstakingly built up was only surface deep and was easily shaken. A substrate of terror continued, always ready to undermine my self-confidence, perhaps rather like the San Andreas Fault. Part of the defense was the concerted effort to hide my eye condition to the extent of refusing to acknowledge it or to ask for appropriate help. I was always upset and deflated when someone commented on it, demonstrating that yet again my strategy had failed.

THE BEGINNINGS OF CHANGE

The process of change started with the traumatic loss of my mother following a short illness. After her death I began to realize to what extent she had been projecting her own inability to cope with my eye problem on me. I had to be perfect so she could feel better and so that she could pretend I did not have a problem. Her relentless criticism made me feel I was never good enough at anything. It was the comments of others telling me how proud she had been of my achievements that really struck home. Why did she not tell me that? Perhaps she feared that if she overpraised me I would become conceited or stop achieving. I had thus helped her to cope with my problems, but what about the problems I had developed in my service to her needs? Although this realization helped me to acknowledge that visual impairment does not make one less of a person, it did not shift the terror of being discovered. During the next few years, various events helped me progress toward registering myself as legally blind, and being able to take advantage of all the available help—I wished I'd done it years before. I also started to learn to be able to ask for help. But the fear remained. Then I met Barbara, the patient who changed me.

THE SESSION

I was working as a psychologist on a spinal injuries unit, a place where one cannot help but encounter issues of disability. One day, I was asked to speak with Barbara, a woman in her early 50s who had broken her neck when she accidentally fell out of a window while cleaning, leaving her paralyzed. Barbara was a single parent with a 15-year-old son.

Prior to this fateful day, I had not spent much time with Barbara. There had been no formal sessions. When patients were admitted to our unit, usually in the early stages of their injury, I would make a point of going to see them to introduce myself and to let them know I was there for them whenever they wanted me. I would spend time just getting to know them, building rapport and checking if they would like help with anything. Many patients would politely send me away at that point, some would share fears and feelings. It varied a lot, but the important contact was always made. Barbara and I had chatted and she had talked about her fears over her son's care and her distress at being injured. All fairly normal, but that was as far as it had gone.

As we talked further, Barbara told me that she was feeling very depressed and needed to discuss her overwhelming sense of guilt. She grew up in Southern Ireland in a staunchly Catholic community. She was educated by nuns and intended to become one herself. Tragically, the nuns did not provide sex education, and she got pregnant, the worst sin she could have committed. Barbara wept as she described her shame and the way in which she was ostracized. She had to leave her village and move away to where no-one knew her. Although she put her child up for adoption, she could not go back to her community as she was forever branded as a *harlot*. She felt compelled to come to England as her only means of escaping her past. Through her tears she told me she believed that her spinal cord injury was God's punishment for her unforgivable sin.

She was completely paralyzed from the neck down. She could not even wipe her own tears away. As she cried, and I gently wiped away her tears with my finger—a tissue would have been too cold and impersonal, I found myself incredibly moved and humbled and deeply felt the tragedy of this woman. I can still feel my own tears now, so many years later, flowing just as they did when I sat with her. I do not know what was going through my mind at the time, other than the desperate need of this woman and my own sense of humility and inadequacy. After all, her tragedy was so much worse than mine. I shall never forget the feel of her skin, so fragile that the least roughness would inflict pain or a bruise. I can never forget her so complete helplessness, so dependent on me to do as simple a thing as wipe those tears away, and my privileged position in being permitted to do so.

I stayed with her just stroking her hair and wiping away her tears. I offered no trite words of comfort; I was not God or even his priest. I just let her know I was there with her. You did not need to see to do that. And I cannot describe to you just how it felt to be there, wiping these tears away with my finger. I can only say that there was a kind of wrenching feeling in me, like an intense feeling of grief combined with something that defies identification.

When she stopped crying, and became calm, she thanked me for listening, and said that she had needed to talk about it for years. She felt better, and with her agreement, I arranged for a priest to visit her.

Following that session, I saw Barbara fairly regularly, but there was never another session like that one. We spent time working through the normal issues of coping with such a devastating disability. The only reference made to that day was Barbara thanking me for getting her a priest, and telling me how she found herself feeling less guilty, less punished, and more able to face dealing with her situation. Her depression became more a normal response to an abnormal set of circumstances. After all, she had to deal with paralysis, never being able to return to her apartment that was upstairs with no elevator, and so forth. She also had to come to terms with all the things she could not do and learn to place a new value on the things she could do.

Every time I saw her, I felt again an echo of that powerful wrenching feeling I had felt in that session. As she slowly learned to deal with her guilt and her life, I found myself experiencing that sense of humility and became very aware of our relative disabilities. I might have trouble seeing, but I could do so many things she could not do. On a 10-point scale of limitations, I was at about 2, and Barbara, 9.

THE PROCESS OF CHANGE

At the time I could not say that the change process was like a light going on or some magical transformation. With hindsight, it does seem that way. For me, it was a turning point. I only know that at the time I felt something turn and click. I also know that in some way I did not recognize at the time that I felt different.

At first I did not realize what was happening. It started gradually. There was an increased confidence in meetings. Instead of being quiet, I started to speak up but not loudly. I was amazed when the manager of the unit commented one day: "You don't raise your voice, but there is something about it that makes it impossible to ignore." Then I started to feel more confident about fellow professionals sitting in on my therapy sessions, a prospect hitherto regarded with dread. I could not understand it. I also found myself feeling much more relaxed about telling people I had visual difficulties. I went through a period where I made a point of doing so.

I had always enjoyed doing a certain amount of teaching both my fellow psychologists and other professional groups and was able to credit myself with knowing something, so I had always had reasonable self-confidence. But despite my confidence here, there was an additional change. Before this, my speaking had always been tinged with nervousness: Just suppose I did not really know what I was doing, or the dreaded someone spoke up and said, "How can you do this, you can't see properly." These fears, too, fell by the wayside, and teaching has become a real pleasure. I also find I can accept constructive criticism of my presentation style much more easily without experiencing it as a personal injury.

The process of transformation has not always been easy. I wish I could say that the road has been smooth and filled with sunlight. There have been storms, times when I felt things were just as before. Fortunately, these have been short-lived and the sun has always come out again.

The session with Barbara took place early in 1990. Since then I have changed jobs and now have reached the top band of my profession as a consultant psychologist. I love my job and feel confident in what I do. I believe in myself as a good clinician and also accept, as we all should, that I do have limitations both professionally and personally. But my visual limitations are, I believe, now much more realistic. I accept that I cannot drive a car, or cross busy roads that don't have *Walk* signals. I also accept that there are certain client groups that I do not have the expertise to treat—not because I cannot see, but because I have not had appropriate training and experience.

I have published papers in respectable journals and have even made it to international conferences, something that at one time would have been beyond my wildest dreams. And finally, I have overcome a longstanding problem with performance anxiety that had turned my enjoyment of singing in public into a nightmare. Now (remembering my mother) if a note is not perfect, I do not give a toss!

ANALYZING THE PROCESS

What actually did happen inside me? I think that I grew up with a rather negative set of beliefs both about myself and the rest of the world. Looking back, I saw myself not only as imperfect but also saw imperfection as meaning a lack of worth. I might even be unlovable unless I could make myself worthwhile and perfect. I also think I believed that the rest of the world did not accept imperfection and that my lack of vision rendered me unacceptable unless I could hide it. This explains my terror and dread, my need to hide, and my lack of confidence.

As I said earlier, the change had already started when I sat with Barbara (and is still going on). My loving husband was clear evidence that I could be lovable. I had already gone partway to acknowledging my difficulties by becoming registered as legally blind. But although I had achieved some change, I believe much of it was, at the time of my encounter with Barbara, only superficial, no more than a dent in my negativity about myself.

Somehow through Barbara, the long-held negative beliefs in which I equated being whole with being worthwhile, started to dissolve. They were profoundly challenged on that day with the realization of how unimportant my poor sight was compared to the suffering of this haunted woman. I believe that at some point, either during or after our session, I did a double take. I vaguely recall having thought, "How can I get so upset over a little thing like limited vision. Look at Barbara."

Over the sessions with Barbara, watching her deal with her guilt and grapple with the problems of learning to live as a quadriplegic, that initial realization was continuously reinforced. She had to learn to use her very limited hand function to operate an electric wheelchair. She had to learn to direct her care. She had to move and learn to accept dependence on others. I guess in parallel, I learned that to survive intact, one must learn to accept and operate within limitations. To fight against them will only maximize them.

As Barbara learned that as a quadriplegic freed of much of her guilt she was a worthwhile individual, perhaps I was also learning the same lesson. Despite being visually impaired, I was also worthwhile and worthy of respect. Looking back, however, I think it took me a lot longer than it took her.

It has long been recognized that therapy is not an intellectual exercise and that the process must encompass an affective response. I certainly experienced a profound emotional reaction on that day with Barbara that I now recognize as having been crucial. As well as my very real response to Barbara's heartbreaking history, there was also the realization of what it meant to me. There was a shifting of perspective that was not superficial but penetrated deeply to the core of my own being and gave these negative beliefs a long overdue and much-needed shaking.

Since 1990, these long-held beliefs have undergone quite a transformation. As I said, this has not always been smooth. At one point, I was forced to realize that I did not like myself very much and that I personally was as much to blame for these negative feelings as anybody else. I also had to come to terms with the fact that I had gone from feeling so negative about myself to blaming myself for feeling this way and to being angry for having taken so long to learn to change. What I felt can be compared to the feelings of the needle-phobic patient who, once having become better, castigates himself or herself for having had such fears in the first place.

But I did work through my self-depreciation thanks to the help, support, and understanding of colleagues who were prepared to spend some time with me, not being therapists exactly, but certainly by being therapeutic. Most important here was the profound insight I received that day with Barbara, into the value of life. I remember thinking as I listened to her, "what a terrible and tragic waste of a life." Here she was, paralyzed for life, having spent her life haunted by guilt. She had few pleasures. The birth of her son had only heaped hot coals on the ashes. It was, in some ways a powerful emotive flash of realization, also accompanied by the thought, "you are stupid to bother so much about trivia." Was that part of the challenge to my beliefs? I believe it was.

Life is precious, and many of us spend far too much of it wishing for what we are not, rather than valuing what is. The sunlight that warms the earth, the rain that ensures the growth of crops and flowers, winter snows, all are precious and important. The sight of the first leaves and flowers of spring should fill us with delight. Who we are and how we live our lives, with or without any disability, that is precious too. And who we are is dependent on how we are inside and not on the trappings. I thought I had learned that lesson years ago, but I do not believe I really learned it until that day with Barbara.

CONCLUSION

So do I like myself better now? There has been a real transformation, and can I really attribute it to that day with Barbara. Without being conceited about it, I believe that I am a worthwhile person for who I am and that I can be lovable (but like all of us, not always). I have accepted imperfection as part of being human and can enjoy it in myself. Do I believe I have finished changing? No I do not, and I hope it will never stop because I love it.

Although the transformation process had started, and I might indeed have progressed to where I am today, I do believe that the one session with Barbara was profoundly influential, the key that unlocked the process of change and caused the dramatic turning point in my life. I will always remember that day, the sun shining softly through the window, the quietness of the ward, and as my own eyes fill yet again with tears, gently wiping her tears away with my finger.

9

Empathic Interactive Therapy: Feeling and Learning With the Patient

Joan Murray-Jöbsis[1]

OVERVIEW

Sarah first came to see me in 1988, when she was 33 years old. At the time, she was a professional woman working in research after having dropped out of the nursing field because of obsessive-compulsive anxieties over the possibility of making a mistake that might injure someone. She has continued in therapy with me now for several years and was diagnosed as having post-traumatic stress disorder and avoidant personality disorder (DSM IV, 1994).

Sarah initially came to therapy complaining of excessive social anxiety and shyness. Her few attempts at social interaction included group dance lessons and a few group Sunday brunches. She had great difficulty talking to people and felt extremely anxious when dancing. If someone held her when dancing she felt physically hurt by their touch. When things did not go well socially she would conclude that she had done something wrong, give up, and retreat once again to social isolation.

---

[1]Joan Murray-Jöbsis has previously published under the name, Joan Scagnelli.

Because of these presenting complaints, our initial focus in therapy centered around reducing stress and social anxiety and helping her have more positive social behavior. The hope was that Sarah's social behaviors might elicit positive social interaction from others that would in turn reinforce Sarah's social growth. During this phase of therapy, hypnosis was used to desensitize Sarah to some of her social anxieties and to rehearse new social skills and behaviors.

Although we did indeed make some progress, it soon became clear that Sarah's comfort level in social situations did not significantly improve because significant stress from the past was interfering with her ability to function socially. She was the child of a hostile, dysfunctional family with an alcoholic father. Therefore, a second phase of therapy focused on uncovering her childhood experiences and on determining how they might be continuing to interfere with her present life.

During this second phase of therapy, hypnosis was again utilized and proved helpful in accessing childhood memories. Initially Sarah returned to memories that she could consciously recall from her childhood. Later she was able to recall less conscious and more repressed material. Both Sarah and I realized her parents had not only been neglectful but also extremely physically abusive to her and to each other. She had good reason to fear and distrust emotional closeness and physical contact.

Sarah again attempted to get closer to others. However, memories of sexual abuse began to spontaneously surface. Her therapy then moved to a third phase in which the focus centered on uncovering sexual abuse and dealing with the resulting feelings. After these emotions emerged, we focused on containing the trauma and helping her to not become overwhelmed by her memories. We also concentrated on corrective thinking, redoing, and empowerment issues. In all these areas, hypnosis was an integral and a valuable tool.

Currently, much of the emotional trauma of the past has been resolved. However, we continue to work on improving positive social interaction and working through feelings of anger.

SPECIFICS OF TREATMENT

We both experienced the most important changes when Sarah began remembering her past in the second phase of therapy. She described a childhood with an alcoholic father who was intermittently violent when he was drunk. Her father frequently hit her mother. Once, in a drunken argument, he shot the mother in the foot. Another time he broke one of her ribs. Nevertheless, Sarah's mother stayed in the marriage, claiming that she stayed only because of the children.

Initially Sarah felt that it was her father who primarily had been the hostile, destructive member of the family and that her mother had been mostly supportive. However, in one of our early hypnosis sessions she recalled her mother hurting her. She started to become agitated, upset, and tearful. I moved close to her chair intending to comfort her with a touch on the hand. However, before I could touch her, she moved her hand up to protect her face. I was startled by this sudden self-protective movement and by the unexpected realization that she feared me. I realized that our apparent positive transference relationship clearly had significant negative undertones. In waking discussions, she made it clear she did not want me to move anywhere near her during her hypnotic trance. She needed to be reassured that I would stay at a safe distance across the room in my chair and never touch her. She said she experienced intense fear and then anger "like I would like to hurt my mother back."

Gradually Sarah became aware of the fact that perhaps her mother had not been a good and nurturing parent, that there was some fear and anger toward her. In ongoing hypnotic work she began to recall some of her mother's anger. Her mother not only told her she was a bad, ungrateful child, but was frequently grabbing and squeezing her arm. She tried to tell her mother that she was hurting her, but her mother did not care. Sarah specifically remembered her mother raging at her for accidentally ripping her slacks. She then had a flashback of her mother choking her dad and found herself thinking, "I don't want to die." Throughout these early, confusing memories there was much fear, hurt, and anger.

In addition to the uncovering work done during this early phase of therapy, much of the initial therapy focused on renurturing work with Sarah. The technique of renurturing with hypnotic imagery, of creating positive healing scripts, and of providing restitution for the patient's missing, positive developmental environment of the past, is a therapy technique that I have developed over the past 20 years of clinical work with more severely disturbed patients (Murray-Jöbsis, 1984, 1992, 1993, 1995, 1996).

Hypnotic renurturing in Sarah's case involved the creation of imaginary scenes in hypnosis in which the patient's *child-self* was cared for and nurtured by an imaginary composite *mother* (i.e., a composite of the therapist and the adult patient). Because infant and preschool renurturing did not initially feel safe to her, we began our renurturing work at an older child level. During one session she explained her fear of renurturing at the infant level. Instead of seeing herself or the therapist as Mother, her real mother's face would superimpose on the scene, and she would be afraid to be an infant in her mother's arms. Sarah gradually recalled some of her childhood pain, remembering not only her hurt arm but also the fear that her mother might totally lose control and try to kill her. She also accessed her own anger at her mother for not being fair and understanding. My acceptance and understanding of her feelings in these sessions gave her a great deal of relief. She also began to connect her own feelings of anger with her earlier obsessive-compulsive dysfunction as a nurse, seeing that her fears of accidentally hurting someone might have been connected with her repressed anger. She also began to understand her need to withdraw from people. Because her caretakers had hurt her irrationally and unpredictably, it seemed safer to put distance between herself and people who might help her, safer not to need them, and ultimately safer to distance herself from all people.

Sarah's lack of a sense of safety was dramatized when she recently had tripped on some stairs, and a woman near her reached out to help her. Sarah's reaction was not to expect help, but criticism and hurt instead. When the woman actually tried to touch her, she automatically felt fear and anger.

In later hypnosis sessions, she began to recall earlier years when her mom and dad were fighting. She remembered being very afraid. She saw herself cringing against a wall in the living room as far away as possible from the actual fighting. Her parents would be hitting each other, throwing things at each other, and sometimes choking each other. Her feeling was: "I don't want to get hurt;" "I don't want to die." Sometimes she wished that her mother and father would just die or kill each other, and she then felt guilty and feared their retribution. Sometimes she wished that she could just die and end it all. Frequently, she felt responsible for her mother's problems because her mother claimed that she "wouldn't be in this marriage if it weren't for you kids."

My natural reaction was a wish to immediately clarify things for Sarah, to let her know that she was not responsible for her mother. However, I also knew that I had to let Sarah discover that understanding. At a later time in therapy, when she began to imagine herself as the mother and to imagine how she would have treated her child-self, she was able to see the fallacy in her mother's message.

From time to time during hypnosis my chair would squeak as I moved slightly, and Sarah would panic, fearing that I was moving closer to her. She knew intellectually that I was respecting her wishes to keep my distance and to never touch her, but nevertheless she would feel quite terrified.

Given the intensely traumatic childhood she was reporting, I felt a strong sense of her need for nurturance, yet her corresponding and conflicting need to keep her distance and to keep me at a distance. My natural inclination was to respond to the need for nurturance and to give her nurturing words and messages. However, I had to consciously remind myself of her need for distance and restrain some of my natural reactions.

As the therapeutic process continued, Sarah remembered her feeling that her mother hated her and wanted her dead. Her mother never really wanted her (the second baby). Although her mother had given much rocking and attention to the first child, she vowed that she would never do it again. Her mother gave her little or no attention and was angry at her for needing anything at all. Sarah gradually began to realize that although she had always feared and hated her father's drunkenness, thinking of him as the cause of the fighting, she also feared and hated her mother's viciousness and anger. In addition, she began to realize that her mother was also a good part of the cause of the fighting. Sarah gradually understood that she had been severely hurt by her mother, and that she was afraid of, and angry at her. In addition she realized that she had feared that she might be accidentally hurt during these awful fights or when helping her mother escape from her dad. There were many ways of getting hurt in that family. Getting connected and close to anyone was very dangerous.

In several hypnosis sessions she recalled a particularly violent fight in which her father shot her mother in the foot. She felt both guilty and rageful about that experience. The fight started in the kitchen when her father wanted money for beer, and her mother refused him. He took the mother's newly baked pie and dumped it in the soapsuds in the kitchen sink. The mother started screaming at him, and he made a move to hit her. She grabbed a knife and threatened him. He then stomped off to the bedroom and lay down on the bed. She then followed him in and dumped the salad on his head. He followed her back to the kitchen, grabbed a pistol, and shot her in the foot. Sarah felt that she somehow should have helped her mother calm down by cleaning up the kitchen and thus avoided the shooting. In hypnosis we reframed that scene and did some corrective interpretation, letting Sarah know that she could not possibly help protect her mother from all of the violence and anger that both her mother and her father were creating for themselves. She was not responsible for their well-being; she was only a child.

Gradually, in hypnosis, Sarah began to retrieve some of her early preschool memories. During a fight, Sarah was frightened and crying in a corner of the room, but her mom picked her up and used her as a shield between the two raging parents. Sarah remembered that her dad's eyes were red and bulging and scary. Her dad grabbed at her mom but got Sarah's arm by mistake, which "hurt real bad." Her head was hurting and she was crying in pain. She remembered believing "Ma hated me and wanted me dead." Sarah squirmed and kicked trying to get out of her mother's arms, but her mother just became angrier and would not let go.

We later utilized hypnotic imagery to *redo* these early painful experiences. In reworking this early material, we could finally introduce renurturing and reparenting for "little" Sarah. We consoled her. We helped, protected, and soothed her.

During scenes like these, I would feel a tremendous empathy for Sarah. Utilizing these empathic feelings, I would create the healing scripts in our hypnotic sessions that I would hope could provide some restitution and *re-doing* for Sarah. I would feel much of her pain and loss and fear, when sharing her recalled experiences with her. At other times I would experience my own feeling response (i.e., my countertransference) to her recalled experiences. At those moments, a part of me would want to save her, to protect her from her hurtful past. This interplay of empathic and responsive feelings is important for the therapist to acknowledge and understand. It is integral to the healing process. A patient cannot heal in a vacuum. There needs to be another feeling human being with whom to interact.

Sarah initially believed that her recurring thought that "I don't want to die" had to do with her father not loving her. Because of his alcohol he became unreliable and unavailable; the loss of love was like dying. She later became aware that she felt that they wanted her to die and that her death would make them happy in some strange way. Finally she understood why she obsessively replayed the same message, "I don't want to die." Sarah could now enter a period of therapy when she could access early abuse memories. We would use hypnosis to redo these scenes, recreating them as safe and nurturing. Sarah would be tucked into bed and kissed goodnight and protected. No one would interrupt her sleep. Little Sarah could at last feel safe and loved.

Over many months of therapy, she repeatedly reassessed three early fight scenes with hypnosis, as if desensitizing herself to the affect. One fight scene was in the bedroom where her mother and dad were fighting on the floor. Her dad was choking her mother, and her dad's genitals and amputated leg were exposed. In the second fight scene Sarah's mother was holding little Sarah in her arms like a shield in front of her against the father, and Sarah was getting hit in their fight. The third fight scene was the fight in the kitchen where Sarah's mom got shot in the foot. We repeatedly used hypnosis to redo these early scenes with nurturing, protective parenting.

As we continued to redo the fight scenes, Sarah gradually dealt with some of her feelings of grief and loss at not being loved. She said she "didn't want it to turn out this way." She did not want to have to know that she was not loved: "sometimes I'm not sure I believe it." But she gradually dealt with the grief, the sadness, and the anxiety of feeling unloved by both parents.

During the fall months, Sarah integrated many of her abuse memories. She remembered that her head and her arm were hurt repeatedly and that her mother neglected her and emotionally hurt her. She recalled that her mother would give her "that message with her eyes that she wanted me to die." Even today, the message "I don't want to die," is repeated whenever she fears she has offended or irritated others, feeling threatened by their power and possible retribution. However, the inner voice was gradually going away. "I hear it very seldom now. It used to be several times a day." The inner child was feeling safer.

In December, Sarah reported two dreams. In the first dream she stabbed a man to death. There was no resistance and she was not afraid. This dream symbolized her overcoming some of her fear of her father. In the second dream she was left alone by her mother, this clearly affirming her mother's wish to abandon her.

Sarah also reported that a man at a Christmas party had touched shoulders with her and put his arm around her chair back. She had become very anxious and left the party. Later, on the way home in her car, she reported thinking, "How could he do that to me? It hurts!" Although acknowledging that his physical contact was not physically hurtful, she felt it as hurtful. We agreed that this needed exploration.

In hypnotic work, Sarah returned to the scene at the party. Using the *affect bridge* (Watkins, 1971) associative technique, she focused on the hurt and anxiety aroused by the man touching her shoulder and followed those feelings back to earlier, similar ones in childhood. She then stated that "my arm hurts … it is trapped between my body and a man's body … the man is on top … can't breathe … hurting me … could kill him … he shouldn't be doing this … I didn't do anything!" Sarah became visibly distressed and needed to retreat from the hypnotic scene. We then "redid" the frightening scene in imagery. The adult Sarah and I stopped the man and told him, "You must never do this again. No one may touch Sarah's body unless she says it is all right. No one can hurt her. We will protect her."

In a subsequent hypnotic session we again used the affect bridge, and Sarah returned to the childhood assault. "He is pulling my pants down … I see his hands pulling them down. I see his penis and hair. He is a big man. He shouldn't do this." She experienced fear, pain, and anger. Gradually in subsequent hypnosis sessions she saw that the man molesting her was clearly her father. She said that her dad put his hands in her panties and felt her. She felt "so bad." She knew she should not be doing this, and she blamed herself. In still later sessions Sarah recalled that her dad inserted fingers into her and then attempted to insert his penis. She felt a tremendous tearing pain and thought he was cutting into her with a knife. Although she was crying, he would not stop. In hypnosis, we redid this abuse scene many times, creating a caring, protecting mother (a composite of adult Sarah and myself) who could give love without using or abusing little Sarah. And, we acknowledged that the adult Sarah now had power of her own to protect herself.

Sarah continued for many sessions to explore the sexual assault. She shed tears for the little girl who lost her innocence and trust and who was so vulnerable. She was sad for all the losses of a lifetime and especially for the loss of her own potential marriage and children that she felt were no longer possible.

As an empathic therapist through this process of recovery of past trauma, I shared much of Sarah's feelings: her pain, despair, terror, loss, and degradation. It is a difficult journey for both the patient and the therapist, this journey through a traumatic past. It is also, perhaps, the greatest gift a therapist can give to a patient.

CHANGES IN THE THERAPIST

During the therapy with Sarah, I encountered many challenges that caused me to rethink both my own emotional responses to the therapy process and my therapy techniques.

Sarah's therapy was a long, slow process that continued for several years. A therapy process that is so slow in evolving required great patience from me as therapist. There were no rapid insights or break-throughs, but rather a long, slow, tortuous progress and gradual understanding of a very painful life history. Even the individual sessions, were agonizingly slow, punctuated by long pauses of silence. Although I had been previously aware of the need to allow the patient to set the pace of the therapy process, Sarah's therapy highlighted that importance and required exceptional patience from me. My few early attempts to promote more rapid communication with Sarah, by filling in some of the pauses and hesitations in her speech, met with a negative response and continued pauses. Adaptation to the many silences and delayed speech required conscious effort on my part to stay attentive and focused during some of these very labored communications.

Sarah's therapy also demanded that I respect the patient's need for dis-tance. Again I had been aware previously of the need to allow the patient to set the parameters for closeness or distance in the therapy relationship. However, Sarah's acute sensitivity to this issue and her need not to be touched at all brought this issue into sharp focus. My natural inclination is to console and support a patient who is in emotional distress. In working with Sarah I became more acutely aware of my own needs as a therapist to be able to give help to patients and of my need for patients to be able to re-ceive support and consolation. With Sarah and a few other similar patients, I learned to limit the support and consolation I gave in order to adapt to the patients' needs. I restrained my care-taking impulses to give Sarah the physical and emotional distance she needed to feel safe with me and with the therapy.

Through Sarah I also became more aware than I had been before of the fact that new and unexpected material can emerge in the therapy process at unexpected times. In December of 1992, I thought that Sarah's therapy was winding down. We had uncovered much physical abuse and neglect in Sarah's childhood, which would have been enough in themselves to explain her tendency to withdraw from human, social interaction. Hypnotic restructuring helped heal the childhood abuse and loss with hypnotic renurturing. She also had joined several group activities and had begun to practice some positive social behaviors. She even began a romantic relationship that despite its failure showed that Sarah had been moving steadily toward more satisfying and more extensive social interaction.

However, in late December, memories of sexual abuse began to emerge quite unexpectedly and suddenly, triggered by the incidental touch of the man at the Christmas party. A new phase of therapy began, centered around uncovering experiences of the sexual abuse, absorbing the intense affect without becoming overwhelmed by it, and dealing with the resulting issues of self-esteem and empowerment.

In exploring past traumatic material, it is important to maintain a position of suspended judgment and open-mindedness, neither confirming nor refuting the material that the patient presents and, above all, avoiding the suggestion of trauma material to the patient. Patient memories are important information for understanding the patient's emotional problems. I follow the patient's feelings and validate the patient's own sense of belief in the significance of the emotional meaning of the memories (if not the actual details of the memories). It was very difficult for Sarah to accept her own material that was emerging. These unbidden imagery memories felt different to Sarah than the more usual cognitive, verbal memories she was accustomed to. They felt unfamiliar and somewhat alien and therefore not to be trusted. Because of the independent and unsolicited origin of these memories and because of the detail and intensity of the emotions attached to them, both Sarah and I came to trust them as representing aspects of her childhood experience, emotions that needed working through.

This phase of therapy was extremely painful for Sarah as she reassessed feelings of physical pain, terror, despair, killing rage, and guilt. As therapist, this phase of therapy was also often painful for me. To empathize with Sarah and stay with her during her hypnotic experiences took stamina and a willingness to feel some of the pain. This willingness and capacity of the therapist to feel some of the patient's feelings is an essential part of the healing process. Patients need not only to feel their own intense feelings from the past (i.e., to experience a catharsis) but also need to receive validation of their feelings and experiences from another human being.

During this painful process of reaccessing abuse memories, I also learned to trust my intuition more fully. As a result of this heightened empathy and intuition, I created a series of images for redoing or reshaping the abuse imagery memories that Sarah was reporting. I began by creating a mother who was a composite of adult Sarah and myself who would stop the abusing father and protect little Sarah. This mother would listen to little Sarah and validate her, console her, and protect her. Later on, Sarah chose for her adult-self to play the mother role alone, without my image joining in the hypnotic healing recreation of the past. In this way Sarah provided her own renurturing, healing, acceptance, and empowerment.

Although our initial relationship felt extremely positive and our working alliance appeared to be very strong, Sarah also harbored fear and distrust of getting too close to me. In working with Sarah I learned that a patient can appear to have a positive transference with me but also be extremely distrustful and angry with me. Although I was initially surprised by Sarah's defensive hand movement, as I came to understand her past abuse, her response and her mixed feelings toward me made complete sense. In later therapy, Sarah would suddenly be furious with me for imperfectly understanding her feelings or "forgetting something I had told you." Her feelings that I was not caring enough or attentive enough would take me by surprise until I remembered that her real mother had failed her in the same way.

It was Sarah's anger that created the greatest difficulty for me, largely because of my own personal difficulty with this emotion. Although Sarah's anger was relatively minimal and although she could understand how past abuse could distort feelings about me, she would become incensed over my empathic failures. I would feel unjustly accused or criticized, feeling that I had given so much and still she was not satisfied. In addition, I feared that she might abort the therapy, end the relationship, and throw away everything that she and I had worked for. The feelings of helplessness, pain, and rejection can often be intense. I can acknowledge my helplessness and know that each patient must ultimately be able to carry their part of the therapy relationship, that I can be with them but cannot do their therapy work for them. I can acknowledge my pain and know that I can bear the pain of getting close to patients and giving much of myself to them and then losing them. And finally I can analyze my feelings of rejection and know that most of the patient's anger comes from their past and that most of my feeling of rejection comes from my past. Nevertheless these are difficult feelings for me to cope with and, I suspect, for most therapists. In Sarah's case, her ability to maintain our therapy relationship while working through her anger and other transference issues strengthened my belief in the therapy process and my commitment and willingness to share patients' painful feelings. This has helped considerably with patients I saw after Sarah.

In working with Sarah, I also learned that the strength of the human spirit is beyond belief. Sarah's resilience and her courage in working through all the painful feelings of her past in her therapy relationship with me renewed my trust in the healing process. Sarah opened my eyes to this special kind of courage, which I am now able to see more clearly in other patients as well.

In dealing with the trauma uncovered in Sarah's therapy, I extensively utilized the empathic skills and the capacity for nurturance that I had developed throughout my years as a practicing therapist. However, because of my work with Sarah, I learned to be more aware of the limits of empathy and nurturance. I came to understand more clearly that patients may at times be unable to accept my nurturance and that they may occasionally even vilify me. Although this is painful, I have, as a result, learned to nurture with moderation and restraint, and with careful attention to a person's capacity to receive this kind of caring. In some situations, I have learned to nurture by not nurturing; by continuing to care, I help my patients to heal and grow beyond their past trauma. Participating in this process allows me to grow as well.

REFERENCES

American Psychiatric Association. (1994). *Diagnostic and Statistical Manual of Mental Disorders* (4th ed.). Washington, DC: Author.

Murray-Jöbsis, J. (1984). Hypnosis with severely disturbed patients. In W. C. Wester & A. H. Smith (Eds.), *Clinical hypnosis: A multidisciplinary approach* (pp. 368–404). New York: Lippincott.

Murray-Jöbsis, J. (1992). *Hypnotherapy with severely disturbed patients: Presentation of case studies.* In W. Bongartz (Ed.) Hypnosis: 175 years after Mesmer: Recent developments in theory and application. Proceedings of the 5th European Congress of Hypnosis in Psychotherapy and Psychosomatic Medicine (pp. 301-307). Konstanz, Germany.

Murray-Jöbsis, J. (1993). The borderline patient and the psychotic patient. In J. W. Rhue, S. J. Lynn, & I. Kirsh (Eds.), *Handbook of clinical hypnosis* (pp. 425–452). Washington, DC: American Psychological Association.

Murray-Jöbsis, J. (1995). Hypnosis and psychotherapy in the treatment of survivors of trauma. In G. D. Burrows & R. Stanley (Eds.), *Contemporary international hypnosis* (pp. 159–167). Chichester, England: Wiley.

Murray-Jöbsis, J. (1996). Hypnosis with a borderline patient. In S. J. Lynn, I. Kirsch, & J. W. Rhue (Eds.), *Casebook of clinical hypnosis* (pp. 173–192). Washington, DC: American Psychological Association.

Watkins, J. (1971). The affect bridge: A hypnoanalytic technique. *International Journal of Clinical and Experimental Hypnosis, 19,* 21–27.

Death, Bereavement, and the Therapist

Judith W. Rhue

PRESENTING PROBLEM

Susan H., a 16-year-old girl, was referred to me by her family physician when her mother expressed concerns about Susan's response to the death of her younger sister some 6 months earlier. Susan was very close to her 5-year-old sister, Denise, despite the 10 year difference in their ages. Since the time of her sister's accidental death, Susan suffered from a variety of depressive symptoms that had not abated. Susan's mother felt that Susan was becoming increasingly depressed and withdrawn, and she was anxious about Susan's condition. Susan had lost interest in all of the things she used to enjoy, particularly painting. She dropped out of school activities and spent most of her time at home in her room. She lost about 10 pounds from not eating, and she took virtually no interest in her appearance.

FAMILY HISTORY

I interviewed Susan and her mother separately during the first session. The following history is a combination of both Susan and her mother's respective reviews of Susan's relationship with Denise, the accident, and Susan's resulting depression.

After being an only child for the first 10 years of her life, Susan was delighted that she was going to have a sibling when her mother became pregnant. Susan's enthusiasm on hearing that the new sibling was a girl was expressed through cheering, hand clapping, and a good bit of jumping around. From the day of Denise's arrival home from the hospital, Susan assumed the role of a second mother. She carefully watched how her mother handled the new baby, bathed it, and prepared bottles for feeding. Whenever she had the opportunity, Susan helped care for Denise.

Susan's parents expected this honeymoon period with a new sibling to wane and anticipated the appearance of some evidence of jealousy or sibling rivalry as Denise grew. Much to everyone's surprise, Susan's relationship with her young sister remained positive and nurturant. Indeed, Susan sometimes challenged her mother's decisions regarding Denise's care and was not shy about offering her opinion of what was in the infant's best interest. Despite her deep involvement with her little sister, Susan maintained her own circle of friends. During her parents' divorce (when Susan was 14 and Denise was 4), Susan handled the changes well. She was a cheerleader in high school and excelled in art classes. Prior to Denise's death, Susan had completed several paintings, one of which took third place in an East Coast competition of high school age artists.

THE ACCIDENT

Susan often babysat for Denise when their mother had errands to run or grocery shopping to do. Susan was conscientious, and the two siblings generally got along well. Their mother had tried bringing in other babysitters, but both Susan and Denise objected and were so difficult that few babysitters wanted to return. The Saturday of Denise's accident began uneventfully. Denise was up early and had breakfast with her mother, while Susan slept late, as was her habit on the weekends. Although the girls usually spent Saturdays with their father, he was out of town on this Saturday. With grocery shopping to do and a list of errands to run, Susan's mother urged the girls to accompany her. Both girls were admanant in their decline of the opportunity, and Susan offered to babysit.

After their mother left, Susan worked on sandwiches and soup for lunch while Denise played on the swing set in the back yard. The weather was windy, overcast, and unusually cool for October, so that Denise was probably cold in her lightweight shirt. A peer of Susan's called and she talked on the phone in the kitchen, still working on lunch. As she talked, Denise came in from outside and said she wanted to get her skates from the garage. Then she headed through the door and to the long hallway leading to the attached garage. Susan's telephone conversation lasted another 10 minutes.

She remembered hearing a bang but figured that Denise broke something in the garage. After she hung up, she called for Denise to come to lunch but received no response.

When she opened the door to the garage, she saw Denise by the garage door. She was badly burned and seemed to be in shock. As Susan rushed toward her, Denise stretched out her arms. Susan remembered saying to Denise, "It will be all right. I'll get help." Susan ran back to the kitchen and phoned 911. She got through immediately and, despite her crying and intense fear, managed to give their address and explain that her sister was seriously hurt and no one else was home. The operator told her that help would be dispatched immediately and Susan returned to Denise's side. In the few minutes that it took for emergency help to arrive, Susan carefully knelt beside Denise. Susan remembered crouching close, and saying over and over that help was on the way.

The ride to the hospital was done at high speed, and Susan sensed the urgency that the emergency technicians seemed to feel. However, once they were on the way to the hospital, Susan was sure that everything was going to be all right. After all, there were doctors there, and they would take care of Denise. Once in the emergency room waiting area and separated from Denise, Susan began to think of their mother and wondered if she had gotten home yet or if the hospital had been able to contact her.

When her mother arrived, Susan could not remember ever seeing her so upset. With hardly a word to Susan, her mother disappeared to the acute care area where Susan had not been allowed. When her mother emerged some 20 minutes later, her face was tear stained and grim. She hugged Susan and said, "They're doing everything they can. I talked to her." "But, she'll be all right, won't she?" Susan asked. Her mother's next words were the last thing she clearly remembered until after Denise's funeral. "They don't think she's going to make it. She's too badly hurt."

Denise died a week later. Her mother and father asked what she knew about the accident, but Susan could only say, "I don't know how she got hurt." It was later learned that a small camping heater exploded as Denise attempted to light it, probably to warm the garage. Susan's distress was so clear and so acute her parents hardly knew what to do to support her. Susan remembered crying only at the funeral. Thereafter she did not cry and would not visit the cemetery. She reported feeling numb.

REFLECTIONS OF THE THERAPIST

I had been in practice about 10 years at the time I met Susan and her mother. My clinical work is largely, although not exclusively with children. My therapeutic orientation is primarily cognitive behavioral, although I like to integrate hypnotic procedures into the therapeutic process where it may be beneficial.

After the first session with Susan and her mother, I felt somewhat uneasy about agreeing to take this case. Such a response is unusual for me, and I needed to examine it and make a judgment as to whether I would be able to work effectively with Susan and her mother. As I thought through what they had told me, I realized that the depth of loss and emotion surrounding Denise's death struck a vulnerability that parents do not like to give voice to, or perhaps even think about, as if avoidance of the topic wards off such a traumatic event. Being a parent of young children myself, I felt torn by wanting to help and, at the same time, not wanting to get to close to the pain of such a loss.

I also wondered if I could remain objective and therapeutic. Suppose I wanted to give in to a maternal urge to simply hug this poor child and tell her that it would be alright. Worse even, suppose I wanted to blame her for not watching her little sister more closely. I knew that I needed to reconcile my concerns, or refer Susan and her mother before more relationship building occurred. Counterbalancing my concerns, was my sense of being able to help this family. Although I do not see myself as an exceptionally brilliant or gifted therapist, I have developed a sense for my ability to work with and help others during my time in clinical practice. I believed that I had something to offer Susan and her mother. I also wondered if I was using my fears and concerns as a rationalization for not taking a potentially difficult and painful case.

Being careful to avoid any identifying information about this case, I consulted a colleague, who was also a parent, about my concerns that countertransference issues might arise and whether I should refer the case. Despite her encouragement, I felt uncertain. Following a night of troubled sleep, I arose early and looked at my own sleeping children. I kept the case.

THERAPY

I had agreed to work with Susan on a weekly basis to try to help her resolve some of her grief and depression. I also asked to meet with Susan's mother for a few minutes at least once a month to gain input from her. Both Susan and her mother were comfortable with this arrangement. On consultation with Susan's physician, it was decided that antidepressant medication would not be used until I had an opportunity to work with Susan. This decision was agreeable to all in view of the fact that Susan was not actively suicidal and seemed to be suffering a reactive depression. Unless Susan's mental status deteriorated rapidly or she became seriously suicidal, I felt that 3 months represented a reasonable time frame for therapeutic changes to be evident. If it was not, we would reevaluate the need for medication.

Therapy was largely cognitive behavioral in nature, with hypnotic techniques used adjunctively. I felt that Susan needed to process the events surrounding Denise's death and her feelings about it. In view of the trauma involved, I also felt that hypnosis would be helpful in a variety of ways including relaxation, distancing, reviewing the traumatic events, and reformulating inappropriate cognitions through metaphor.

The initial stage of therapy centered on grief work and the retelling of the story of Denise's life and death from Susan's point of view. Before moving to an active stage of reshaping cognitions and helping Susan to make behavior changes, I felt that a period of supportive, accepting, relationship-building therapy based on Rogers (1951) client-centered approach would be helpful to this very distressed girl. In keeping with this approach, I focused the first six sessions on the story of Denise's life as told by Susan. Beginning during this initial phase of therapy, and continuing through the therapy, I employed indirect suggestions (Erickson, Rossi, & Rossi, 1976) to impart to Susan the idea that she could and would successfully work through this intense loss.

Excerpt From Session 1: The Interview With Susan

Susan was relatively reticent during this session, and it was clearly very difficult for her to talk about her sister. My goal was to build rapport with Susan, to gauge her coping skills, and to introduce her to the process of psychotherapy.

Therapist:	I understand your sister died recently.
Susan:	(nodding, her face set)
Therapist:	Can you tell me a bit about her?
Susan:	(sitting silently, looking at the floor)
Therapist:	It must be very hard for you to talk about her.
Susan:	(nodding affirmatively) She was little, only 5, and she died in the hospital. She loved me a lot.
Therapist:	It sounds like you loved her a lot too. Your memories of that time sound pretty painful.
Susan:	(nodding, but silent)
Therapist:	Do you ever cry?
Susan:	No.
Therapist:	How are you handling all of this?
Susan:	(lost in thought, appearing not to hear the therapist's last question) I used to braid her hair, except sometimes

	I wouldn't when I was mad at her. I don't want to talk about it anymore today.
Therapist:	Your family is very concerned about you, and you are clearly very important to them. I can see that you loved your sister and that you miss her very much.
Susan:	(looking almost teary) I loved her so much, but there isn't anything anyone can do. She's dead.
Therapist:	You're right, nothing can bring her back, but I would like to try to hear more about her. OK? Then we'll make some decisions about therapy and about what will be the most helpful for you.
Susan:	OK.
Therapist:	Next week, will you tell me more about her?
Susan:	I can't talk about her too much. I just don't think about her. It's too awful.
Therapist:	But you think about her anyway, don't you. And yet, you're afraid of those thoughts, so you have to work very hard to keep them away. Still, a part of you wants to think about her and miss her and grieve for her. So I want to help you do what you're already doing a little, without being afraid of it. Maybe we can even make a "life story" book for Denise. I can teach you some techniques that may help you to talk about her without it hurting so much.
Susan:	How?
Therapist:	By teaching you self-hypnosis. It will help you to control some of the pain you feel when you talk about her. Tell me what you know about hypnosis.
Susan:	People quack like ducks and do stupid things. No thanks.
Therapist:	I have no ducks in my office. Only people with real pain who will help me help them. In fact, some people ask me to teach them self-hypnosis and I refuse.
Susan:	Why?
Therapist:	Because I don't think they are serious, or I don't think it's right for them. I thought you would be a good person to teach, but maybe you're right. It's a great skill, but not if you're afraid of it. It's important to think about it more and we can talk more about it next week. Also, I would have to ask you not to teach your friends or misuse it.
Susan:	I wouldn't do that.

For me, with three young children of my own, seeing Susan's pain first-hand and realizing what it must be like to lose a child under such tragic circumstances was even more difficult than I had anticipated. At first I fought back my tears, fearful that they would perhaps frighten Susan or even worse, create more guilt. At times, it took all of my concentration and self-discipline not to allow my thoughts to wander, but to stay with the content of what Susan was saying. I again consulted with my colleague over the topic of therapist tears. Was it better to appear strong and dry-eyed, or was that simply an accepted stereotype of strength? Could I cry without shifting the focus of the therapy? I have always taught my students that the client must not be in the position of comforting the therapist. My colleague and I worked on this issue at length but could not agree. She felt that tears were appropriate for therapists in difficult cases. I agreed intellectually with what she said, but not emotionally. Although I cannot say that I had not been moved to tears in therapy sessions prior to this, this case seemed different. Perhaps I was afraid of my own tears in this case, but whatever the reason, I struggled to remain dry-eyed during therapy sessions.

Finally, as my therapeutic relationship with Susan grew, I allowed some of my own tears, telling myself that the fight to withhold them was a losing one and presented an unreal lack of emotion on my part. I asked Susan how she felt about my tears and was surprised to hear that she believed that it meant that I was really listening to her.

I taught Susan self-hypnotic techniques for relaxation and distancing to use when the emotions of these sessions became too powerful. Susan often elected to simultaneously tell and view Denise's story using a split-screen technique and a remote control that allowed her to *diminish affect*, freeze the scene, or replay some aspect of the story. Our progressive retelling seemed to help Susan realize that she could successfully think and talk about Denise and reduce her phobic avoidance of dealing with the trauma.

As therapy progressed, it became increasingly apparent that in addition to experiencing intense grief over the death of her young sister, Susan was also experiencing significant guilt and anger over the occurrence of the accident. As her self-blame and sense of responsibility for the accident emerged, Susan altered the story of Denise's death to depict herself as careless and unreliable. If she had been more vigilant, if she had not wasted time on the phone, the accident would never have happened; or if she had found Denise sooner, she would not have died. In line with blaming herself, Susan also revealed that she felt that her parents blamed her, although they had repeatedly told her that the accident was not her fault and that she had handled the situation as well as possible.

Excerpt From Session 5: The Story of Denise's Death

During this session, Susan's guilt and anger over Denise's accident surfaced.

Therapist: When we ended the last session, you were telling me about Denise's fifth birthday and her party.

Susan: Yes, it was the last party in our family before the accident.

Therapist: We've shared many of your memories of Denise's life. What shall we add to it today?

Susan: The accident.

Therapist: OK. It sounds as if you're ready to talk about it as part of Denise's life. Do you want to take a few minutes and draw on your inner reserves of strength by using self-hypnosis techniques before we begin to review the accident?

Susan: Yes. (At this point Susan closed her eyes and began to describe riding down a long escalator into a deep subterranean room where she felt secure and at peace. When she arrived at the bottom of the staircase, she raised her right index finger to indicate that she was ready to begin. Over the preceding three sessions, Susan and I had utilized this self-hypnosis technique together to help buffer Susan from the anxiety engendered by discussions of Denise's life. Susan rapidly accepted self-hypnosis techniques and adapted them for herself.)

Susan: That day seemed to start alright. Nothing seemed different. Mom wanted to go grocery shopping and Denise and I didn't want to go. So, I said I would babysit Denise. I was a great babysitter, huh.

Therapist: What do you mean?

Susan: Well, I killed her. My mom left me to babysit, and I killed Denise. (Susan begins to cry).

Therapist: Do you really believe you killed her?

Susan: Well, she'd be alive if I'd been more careful. I couldn't get off the phone to check on her. I talked and talked and talked. I was so busy talking that I wasn't listening for her, and I didn't go and look for her. I just cared about myself and my friends. If I hadn't let her out of my sight, she'd be just fine (sobbing). I hate myself, I hate myself (shouting).

Therapist: It was an accident. But, I think it's important for us to talk about your guilty feelings so that we set them straight and put them in perspective.

Susan:	I am so angry at myself. I let my sister die (sobbing). I can still see her walking down the hall toward the garage.
Therapist:	Can you project that on a TV screen in front of you and freeze it, so that we can talk about your feelings more before we go on?
Susan:	Yes, the picture is frozen with her hand on the door to the garage.
Therapist:	Good. You know, in some ways it helps you to blame yourself.
Susan:	What do you mean it helps me? (Susan seems taken aback and angry at me)
Therapist:	Because it makes things that are uncontrollable, controllable. It's a way of trying to make sense out of a horrible, senseless accident.
Susan:	But, if I had just stayed with her, it wouldn't have happened.
Therapist:	Maybe, but maybe not. You only know what happened. You can't predict what might have happened if you had done things differently.
Susan:	But, if I'd been there, it wouldn't have happened.
Therapist:	Maybe you could have stopped her, but maybe it could have happened in front of you.
Susan:	But then I could have saved her!
Therapist:	The burn was instantaneous when the gas ignited. It would have been just as bad. You couldn't have saved her, could you?
Susan:	But, I shouldn't have let her play alone.
Therapist:	If you need this guilt, I won't try to take it away from you. I think you'll let go of it when you're ready, but if you still need it, it's OK.
Susan:	I wish my mother hadn't gone out. It's too awful! She loved me so much (sobbing).
Therapist:	And you loved her too. She knew that.

While supporting her in her feelings, it was important to give her another view of what happened. Giving her a different experience of that awful time would allow her an opportunity to heal. I felt good about helping her, although I knew it would take a number of times repeating such things before it would take.

In retrospect, the review of Denise's life and death was the most difficult phase of the therapy for everyone involved. For Susan, this retelling of Denise's life was the first time she had allowed herself to really think and talk about Denise since her death. The first retracing of that eventful day was painful and frightening. Her fear of thinking about what had occurred had taken on nearly phobic proportions and required dismantling, relaxation, distancing, and support. Once having revisited the memory, Susan seemed strengthened by its retelling. For me, this phase was one in which I experienced many uneasy feelings; occasionally I would imagine what such a loss would be for me and felt the depths of guilt and despair.

After a phase of listening to Susan's story and supporting her telling and retelling, I began to gently challenge Susan with "what-if" questions (i.e., possibly different viewpoints) about various aspects of the story of Denise's accident. At first, Susan vigorously resisted any questioning or implication of change to her version, on occasion growing angry with me. I responded by interpreting her anger as a defense against her own pain and the uncontrollability of the accident and Denise's death.

Finally, over a period of weeks, she began to use the self-hypnotic techniques I taught her to achieve a sense of control or peace or both that enabled her to think through the "what-if" questions I offered. Through the use of a visualized TV screen with a remote for fading the scene, many tears, and much kleenex, Susan played and replayed various scenarios and outcomes of Denise's accident. I shared many of these tears and some of the kleenex.

The goal of this phase of the therapy was to help Susan construct a more realistic view of her role in the accident, one that would enable her go on with her life and her grieving. Susan's belief that she could have controlled everything that happened and prevented the accident represented a significant cognitive distortion. Thus, the cognitive restructuring of Susan's role in the accident was a pivotal one for the therapy. Gradually, Susan began to relinquish her view that she could have controlled Denise's accident if she had only been faster, more observant, or a better person.

I felt that we had achieved a a real breakthrough as I saw her letting go of her need to blame herself and the anger and defense that compounded it. I also realized that during this phase of the therapy, I had been able to let go of my fear of blaming this child. Despite having grappled with thoughts of blame and wondering if I, as a parent, could see her as blame free, I truly took pleasure in helping Susan free herself of guilt. I felt that I had been able to support her in confronting her fears and doubts.

At the agreed on 3-month marker in therapy, the medication question was re-evaluated. Susan was adamant that she did not want medication. At this point her family and her physician agreed. Susan was eating more adequately and her weight had stabilized. Although certainly not her old self, Susan seemed to have a purpose in her life that motivated her to get up each day, to work in school, and to attend therapy. Susan had become invested in trying to make some sense out of the accident.

During the fifth month of therapy, Susan experienced a crisis when her mother decided that the time had come to began donating some of Denise's things to charity. Until this time, Denise's room had been untouched and unused, with the door kept shut. With Susan so upset, her mother agreed to wait an additional month before she removed anything from Denise's room. However, this event propelled the therapy to a phase in which Susan was confronted with some of the tangible items of Denise's life and she was confronted with issues of what to keep and how to move forward.

Excerpt From Session 12

Susan: You need to talk to my mother and stop her. She wants to give away some of Denise's things. You can't let this happen.

Therapist: Can you tell me more?

Susan: Yesterday, when I got home from school, the door to Denise's room was open. It hasn't been open since she died. When I looked in, my Mom was going through her dresser and some of her clothes were out on the bed. When I asked her what she was doing, she said that she thought it might be time to give some of Denise's things to other children who could use them. I yelled at her. I told her to stop and leave them alone, that they didn't belong to her. They belonged to Denise and that she had no right to be in them!

Therapist: What did your Mom say?

Susan: Nothing at first. She stopped and looked at me, and I thought she was going to cry. But then she said, "I won't do it today, but we must do it soon." Then she put back the things and left the room. I didn't go down for supper and I didn't speak to her this morning. She can't take Denise's things! You need to talk to her and explain!

Therapist: Some of Denise's things must mean a great deal to you.

Susan: Yeah, she always played with her Barbies. And her favorite dresses and her little jewelry box. She loved junky little earrings and necklaces. She would wear them with her sweatshirts and jeans, and it looked pretty weird, but nobody ever told her that. She would stand in front of her mirror and put them on and then pretend she was putting on makeup. Nobody else should have that stuff. (Susan began crying).

Therapist: It sounds like there are some things you want to keep, but are there some things that could be donated?

Susan: Maybe. Maybe a few things, but not now. Besides, I need to be sure that the important things don't go.

Therapist:	Maybe you could go in and take out some of the special things. Then you could be there when your mother sorts the others so you can be sure what you want to donate.
Susan:	But, it's wrong to disturb her things. It was her room and it should be left alone.
Therapist:	Have you considered that she might want you to have those special things that she no longer needs. If they were special to her, she would probably be happy that they were special to you also. She might also want others to have the less important things that she can't use.
Susan:	I guess so. Will you talk to my mother with me? I'm not ready yet. I haven't been in her room at all. I just stood in the doorway when my mom was in there. I'm not sure I can go back in.
Therapist:	OK. Let's think about what you want to say to your mom. This must be very hard for her too. Perhaps we can give it some time and help you get ready to go in. How can you and your mom help each other?

Susan's mother readily agreed to let Susan have some time to get used to the idea of visiting Denise's room, and stressed to Susan that they would go together when Susan was ready. Her mother said that she had been afraid it would be too much for Susan to go through Denise's things, and she was relieved that Susan actually wanted to be a part of the process. The meeting with Susan's mother was a tearful one for everyone, including me. At this point, I was not fighting the tears but allowing them to flow.

We used the therapy to rehearse what it would be like to be in Denise's room and to look at, handle, and possibly give away some of her things. First, in imagination, Susan allowed herself to enter Denise's room. It seemed easiest for her to factually describe the room and where things were. Thinking about sitting down on Denise's bed and touching the covers led to a hasty imaginative retreat with the door firmly closed behind her. We processed how all of this felt and made a plan to revisit in imagination for short periods until Susan was ready to try a real visit.

Several sessions later, when Susan said that she was ready to actually go into Denise's room at home, both of her parents agreed to go with her. The following weekend, Susan's father visited, and he and Susan's mother accompanied Susan into Denise's room. All of them felt that although it was a difficult time, everyone benefited from the support they gave each other in Denise's room. Susan reported that at first she sat quietly on the bed and looked around the room. Then she gathered several of Denise's favorite Barbies, and cried while she clutched them tightly. When she left the room, she took the Barbies with her.

Several days later Susan told her mother that it was OK with her to give some of Denise's things away, if she could be in the room with her mother when she went through things, and if she could help make decisions. Her mother readily agreed. Thereafter, the door of Denise's room remained open.

During the final month of therapy, Susan felt strong enough to begin going to the cemetery to visit Denise's grave. At my urging, she accompanied her parents on one of their weekly visits but wanted time alone at the gravesite. There she read a letter to Denise that she had constructed during the prior three sessions of therapy. It was a letter that told her sister how much she missed her and loved her, how she was taking care of the Barbie dolls, and how their parents were doing. Absent from the letter was any reference to guilt and anger which had so characterized the early sessions of her therapy.

Session 22: The Visit to Denise's Grave

> *Susan:*   I went yesterday.
> *Therapist:* Will you share it with me?
> *Susan:*   I did what you suggested. I read the letter to her and tried to visualize her. I told her that I was taking good care of her Barbie and what each one was wearing. I cried a lot, but I was glad I went. I couldn't visualize her, but it seemed OK.
> *Therapist:* I'm glad you were ready to go.
> *Susan:*   My mom asked me if I wanted her to go with me. I told her no, that I wanted to talk to Denise alone. She can go with me next time. Do you want to go there with me? If you really want to hear about it, close your eyes and I'll describe the cemetery to you and you will know what it was like. But, I'm warning you, it's so hard, and I know you, you'll cry too.
> *Therapist:* Go ahead.
> *Susan:*   Ok, close your eyes. You park in this lot and walk to get to where she is. It's real green.... (A lengthy description followed. Both Susan and I wept.) [The session closed as follows.]
> *Therapist:* Thanks for sharing that. How are you feeling now?
> *Susan:*   I am OK, but I don't want to talk about it any more today. Oh, I started a new painting last night ...

Susan's willingness to take me there, to even reversing our roles in guiding the imagery and warning me that it would be emotional, helped her to gain a strength that continued to grow over time. At a 1 year follow-up, Susan was making plans for college and seemed to be doing well.

MY RESPONSE TO SUSAN

This was perhaps the most challenging case I have ever experienced, and several years later, it remains indelibly printed in my memory. In our society, the untimely death of a child is not in keeping with the laws of nature. That is, it is expected that after a full life (or at least in adulthood), individuals die. Further, it is the natural progression of events for parents to die before their children. For parents, the death of their child is the unthinkable. I continue to believe that most parents and therapists maintain an emotional distance from the loss of a child. We read of other's loss or view it on television but maintain the defense of, "them, but not to me." However, when I was faced with helping an older child work through the traumatic death of a well-loved younger sibling, it took all of my professional training, my personal resources, colleagueal input, and many tissues to get through it.

The traumatic nature of Denise's death and the innocence and goodness of those most intimately involved in it were troubling. It is easier for everyone if there is someone to blame in a tragedy. At least then there is a focus and an outlet for the emotions engendered by an untimely death. This case offered no such buffering outlet for anyone involved in it. At times, I could palpably feel the wish to blame someone. I learned to tolerate these feelings while continuing to empathize with Susan. There was no one to blame. As I learned to live with that, so did Susan. She did not need to blame herself or anyone else any longer. We both learned to tolerate the loss of a sense of control over what happens in life.

I learned some things about myself during this case and I value it for the insights it offered. I learned that I could face such an unfathomable tragedy in an innocent victim's life and could allow myself to be vulnerable, deeply involved and affected. I was heartened by and admired Susan's capacity to recover, to go into and experience fully feelings that were so unspeakable. As a result, I feel that I am more able to face such issues with future patients. However, I realize that I would not elect to work in a setting where I handled such cases frequently, although I much admire those therapists who do.

I cannot say that I had not been as tearful in a therapy setting before this case, or since. Like most therapists, I have heard some heart-rending stories and have been privy to the painful adversities of my clients. However, I can say that no case has been a more moving experience or brought me closer to my own personal vulnerabilities. I realize now that there is little that separates us in our daily lives from such incomprehensible tragedy. The fragility of the that thin veil means we are all vulnerable. Whenever Susan was in the room, I could feel this in both of us. But we can and do recover from the unspeakable and, like Susan, go on to be vulnerable again. This case also deepened my appreciation of the role of colleagues in case consultation. The colleagueal relationship provided me with professional feedback so that I could better gauge the accuracy of my own feelings and avoid the pitfalls of professional isolation. It also helped me define and separate my maternal feelings from my skills, to the degree that such a clean separation is possible, and we explored our feelings about therapist tears in the therapy setting. I felt that we gained from our consultation with each other, and our discussions of the issues confronting us as professional women and as mothers.

Overall, when I reflect on this case, I am glad that I took it. I am pleased that I was able to help Susan heal. She has been able to go on and seems to be doing well. I learned the real value of consulting with colleagues on issues that can affect therapy. I faced some of my own personal and professional vulnerabilities and was able to deal with them while remaining effective in therapy.

REFERENCES

Erickson, M., Rossi, E., & Rossi, S. (1976). *Hypnotic realities.* New York: Irvington.
Rogers, C. (1951). *Client-centered therapy.* Boston: Houghton Mifflin.

The Little Engine That Could

Mary Jo Peebles-Kleiger

Writing about growth and change as a therapist necessitates explaining what views were held about the work, about life, and about oneself before the process of change began. Formally, I was trained as a psychoanalytic psychotherapist and, later, as a psychoanalyst, with some specialized training in family-systems theory, psychoanalytic psychological testing, neuropsychological testing, and hypnosis. I always considered my reactions, my feelings, my limitations, and my personality an inevitable influence on the work. For example, in graduate school, I was taught to get to know my *stimulus pull* on patients. My supervision processes always included examination of my thoughts and feelings as data in the job of understanding and helping my patients. The idea that patient and therapist mutually affected each other was a given; both from my psychological and my psychotherapeutic training, I understood that the observer is always a participant in what he or she observes (Heisenberg, 1930).

Nothing that I can remember was said during my training, however, of my patients' potentially changing me. Such a concept lay outside the usual discussions of countertransference. Supervisors described learning from patients, but learning and change seem two different things. One might learn a new technique without changing internally. Searles (1979) addressed the idea briefly, and stated, "the existing literature concerning it is scanty indeed" (p. 440).

Quietly, however, I considered the treatment of several of my patients as having changed me. Some of my patients exposed me to aspects of myself that I might never have clearly known or attempted to master had it not been for the work with them.

In a more personal vein, my views and work prior to the change processes described in this chapter were heavily influenced by my religious (Catholic) upbringing and my mother's unflagging, insistent, optimistic determination. As a child, I believed deeply in the mystical aspects of my religion. I read the lives of saints; our family visited shrines, collected relics, and had holy-water fonts in the house. My mother would anoint us with blessed holy water or holy oil if we were suffering from a prolongation of a childhood illness. I believed deeply in my guardian angel as a child, as someone who was with me always, watching and protecting and keeping me from harm. Thus, for me, at a deep, unnoticed level, protectors existed who were truly all good and quite powerful. If we only gave ourselves over to this all-powerful, all-perfect protection, we would be perfectly cared for. If one were good, good things happened. If bad things were done to us, we were supposed to turn the other cheek. Love was the greatest of virtues (Corinthians, chap. 13:13), and all humans were connected to each other spiritually. Each of us had a bit of God within us; therefore, what we chose to do to each other was what we were choosing to do to God.

Added to this religious influence, was the remarkable influence of my mother. She was often heard saying to herself, "I think I can, I think I can" emulating the Little Blue Engine who was facing a mountain mighty compared to its little size. My mother would have made Dale Carnegie proud. Her own philosophy of life was built on the premise that a positive attitude could make anything possible. For her, one did not give up, and, as she always said, "where there's a will, there's a way."

Looking back on my early years as a therapist, it is no wonder that I chose to do intensive training at an institution that specialized in not giving up on people, who had long ago been given up on by others. This institution also had woven into its philosophy of treatment and care strong religious influences, with a consequent history of dedicating itself to the humane care of the person with the illness, not the illness disembodied and distanced from the person (Shectman, 1979). Jargon was frowned on (Pruyser & Menninger, 1976); the relationship with the treater was central; instilling hope was essential (Menninger, Mayman, & Pruyser, 1963); and the satisfaction of the work was finding which treatment, with which type of person, and at what point in their life would make a difference. As a Little Blue Engine, who (unconsciously at the time) believed that enough love and enough effort could cure anything—I had found my niche.

Working with Mr. Martin collided disturbingly with my idealism. I was unsteadied by the seductiveness of Mr. Martin's idealization, the seductiveness of Mr. Martin's longings for gratification within the treatment, and by the rawness and sheer force of Mr. Martin's ultimate abusiveness toward me. Wrestling with these challenges forced me to discover the complements of those challenges within myself: (a) a secret idealization of myself as a powerful rescuer or guardian angel, (b) the world view that love can cure all, and (c) a life philosophy of "turn the other cheek," underneath which lay a dismaying-to-discover darker side of unintegrated (unwanted) sadism. The treatment work "shattered" (Janoff-Bulman, 1985) some foundations of my world view and professional view and forced me to hold a mirror up to myself as well. I suppose I could have blamed Mr. Martin for his psychopathology and the distasteful effect it had on others. Following this route would have ended in the termination of treatment, but I could not hold that perception for long with any honesty. Nor could this "blue engine" give up on the mountain. Instead, I had to admit, as Winnicott (1949) stated, "The answer to many obscure problems of psycho-analytic practice lies in further analysis of the analyst" (p. 70). It came to pass that only after Mr. Martin indirectly healed (changed) the therapist, could the work progress and reach some sort of satisfactory resolution.

OVERVIEW OF TREATMENT CASE

Mr. Martin was a bright, 28-year-old attorney. He was unmarried, but had been living with his current girlfriend off and on for 2½ years. He came to consult me because he was suffering from depression (restlessness, intermittent hopelessness, low self-esteem, periodic lethargy, sleep disturbance, appetite disturbance, and ruminations about suicide) and conflicts in relationships (with his girlfriend and on the job). The man was articulate and appropriate in affect and self-other boundaries within the initial consultation hours. However, psychological testing (requested as part of the consultation work-up) revealed that Mr. Martin suffered some circumscribed but notable ego weaknesses. More specifically, under the press of affect, Mr. Martin easily became flooded, confused, and confabulatory, reading meaning into perceptions that went beyond the facts of the situation. There was also an immaturity to his relatedness with people. Testing revealed a vulnerability to *fusion* with others, characterized by a longed-for, but problematic, intense closeness in which it was felt as if one knew the thoughts of the other. These circumscribed ego weaknesses existed within the context of someone with a superior intelligence, excellent academic achievements, and respectable vocational achievements. In different words, Mr. Martin was capable of sliding from a character disturbance to borderline ego organization and even to momentary psychotic-like disorganization and back again, depending on the intensity of affect, the degree of intimacy or need, and the crispness of role expectations in a given situation.

We began psychotherapy with the goals of Mr. Martin's attaining relief from his depression and satisfaction with his accomplishments in life. The psychotherapy took place over 6 years. The frequency in the beginning was twice per week; this was interrupted 2 months into therapy by a brief (10-day) hospitalization necessitated by a suicidal crisis. Pharmacotherapy was instituted, and treatment continued on an outpatient basis. About 2 years into therapy, Mr. Martin began a year-long regression, both within and outside the treatment hours. He was abusive to me, had few external contacts, and created increasingly frequent suicidal crises requiring massive outpatient interventions. I requested special case consultation. The consultant recommended actively setting limits on Mr. Martin's abusiveness, re-examining issues around patient gratification (letters, phone calls, and gift-giving to the therapist) with respect to their impact on intensifying a regressive transference, and focusing on rebuilding Mr. Martin's outside life contacts. Following 6 months of acute turmoil in the psychotherapy as these changes were instituted, Mr. Martin stabilized, made progress over the following 2 years, and eventually terminated by mutual consent. Hypnosis was not a part of this treatment process. I used psychoanalytically oriented psychotherapy. In the following, I describe these changes—in Mr. Martin, the treatment, and me—in greater detail.

TREATMENT PHASE I: THE SEDUCTION OF IDEALIZATION ("BECOMING A GUARDIAN ANGEL")

The first phase of the psychotherapy spanned 4 months. Mr. Martin was intelligent, verbal, and warily needy. Reserved, he spoke in highly intellectualized terms and with somewhat muted affect. He described a difficult early childhood, in which his mother was simultaneously indulgent and unpredictable. Despite an intense early emotional closeness with her, he was sent to boarding school at the age of 10 for reasons he did not understand. While he was there, his mother abandoned the family. His account of that abandonment (he never saw her again) was devoid of feeling, yet precise in detail. He felt that perhaps something about the relationship with his mother was interfering with his being able to feel much joy in life, much relief from a gnawing anxiety, and much satisfaction in his relationship with his girlfriend. I remember feeling a mild anxiety about seeing a fellow professional, who was not much younger than I (e.g., "Would I have anything to offer him?" … "Would he expose and ridicule my inexperience, making me ashamed of how little I had to give him, or would he validate my ability to know and help by respecting me as a healer?"). However, it was appealing to talk to someone whose ideas were so crisply delivered instead of buried within clouds of confusingly intense emotion. And I felt a kinship with his drive for more insight. Perhaps I could help him, much like an older sister guiding a brother along a path. Perhaps I could remain steady, as his mother had not been able to do. Perhaps together, with our intellects, we could carefully untangle the confused lines to the past, and thus set him free to live the present.

Mr. Martin was not clear why he was so depressed. He had a law degree; he had gone through a respectable clerkship; he was being considered for employment by several law firms in town; he even had a relationship with a woman who was loyal to a fault and who tried to provide what he needed. However, somehow, over the past year, a gnawing sense of anxiety had slowly intensified into daily dread. He felt alone in the relationship with his girlfriend. He felt burdened by his work. Thoughts of suicide haunted him. Although he was articulate and free of flagrant thought disorder, he showed some overly inferential thinking about others' views of him and motivations toward him. His judgment and impulse control were generally good; however, there had been times when he became impulsive (e.g., suddenly leaving college midsemester to hitchhike through Canada; suddenly moving in and then moving out with his current girlfriend). Because of these inconsistencies, I referred Mr. Martin for psychological testing. Despite Mr. Martin's precise intellectualization within the interview, testing revealed his reality testing could teeter on the brink of psychosis, particularly when intimacy and emotions were high.

For this reason, I explained to him that psychoanalysis would not be a treatment of choice. I explained that a more modulated treatment experience would be indicated, one that could help strengthen his ability to manage strong feelings, and titrate his closeness to others in a controlled fashion. Mr. Martin felt anxious about and irritated by the test findings; however, with some work, he was able to accept the wisdom of the treatment plan. I let Mr. Martin know that I would be leaving on a 4-week vacation in 2 months. Mindful (from his history) of his potential vulnerability to separations, I gave him the option of waiting until I returned to begin our work. However, Mr. Martin was adamant about beginning before my vacation, stating that he could do an important piece of work between now and the time I left. Moreover, he pointed out that the 2 months of not seeing me now, would be far more difficult than 1 month of absence later, with an interim therapist to assist him if need be. His arguments were convincing and well focused. We agreed to begin our twice-weekly psychotherapy process.

Simply agreeing to see me in psychotherapy marked a dramatic change within Mr. Martin. He described beginning to feel alive, for the first time in a long time. This aliveness created an intense preoccupation with me outside the hours. He found the length of time between sessions to be unexpectedly difficult to tolerate. He began writing down his thoughts over the weekend and bringing in lengthy, detailed letters. Occasionally, he hand carried letters to my office between sessions. He felt me to be kind, sensitive, and empathic. He described how long he had waited for someone like me, to whom he could open his soul. I, in turn, felt a confusing mixture of anxiety (that the intensity of attachment was developing so fast) and gratification (that I was able to fill someone with good feelings).

After a few weeks, Mr. Martin phoned, asking for an extra session that afternoon. He rapidly explained that a lot had come up at work, and he was not sure he could make it through the weekend containing so much. I hesitated for a split second. Something did not feel right. The testing had described his loss of boundaries and escalating intensity in intimate encounters. Certainly, it was becoming a struggle for Mr. Martin to contain all that was being stirred by our relationship. However, denying him a session when he was in such need felt cruel. I rationalized to myself that 1 extra hour would not harm him and, thus, arranged to see him. The following week, Mr. Martin phoned between sessions and talked for 30 minutes. Ten days later, he asked for another special session. I continued to agree to these requests, having convinced myself that what he was telling me was true: He had never met anyone like me; I offered him a unique capacity to contain his turmoil, tolerate his upset, and provide words for his turbulent feelings; my psychotherapy with him created a special holding environment (Modell, 1978; Winnicott, 1965) that he needed to be cured.

In short, I was losing sight of my own treatment recommendations. Despite what the testing had said about the dangers of intensifying emotion combined with intensifying intimacy, I was intensifying the treatment process. And I did so more and more as the time for my month-long vacation drew near. I had myself convinced that Mr. Martin was doing important, productive work. I paid attention to his intellectualization, intelligence, and preserved logic. I ignored the increasing pressure of his speech, rawness of emotion, and inability to sustain functioning outside of contact with me. Two weeks before I was to leave, he crashed. His girlfriend called, stating desperately that she "had never seen him like this before." He was unable to sleep, spending long hours into the night writing profusely. She was not sure how much he was eating. He had been hinting cryptically to her of suicide.

I managed to get Mr. Martin in immediately and, following a rapid consultation, hospitalized him on an acute crisis unit. Mr. Martin had been nursing a secret, detailed suicide plan of overdosing in a remote, isolated area. The date he had chosen was the eve of my intended trip.

We were able to stabilize Mr. Martin and begin him on appropriate medication while he was still safe in the hospital. This crisis was resolved. Psychotherapy resumed when I returned from vacation, with the usual, expectable upheaval following a long absence. However, I remained shaken. What had happened within me that I had so lost my clinical centering? A specialist in psychological testing, I had acted in ways that denied the importance of those findings. Why?

I sought help from supervision. An awareness, vague at first and later more fully understood, began to tickle the edges of my consciousness. Mr. Martin had stated that he had never met anyone like me, and … I had believed that to be true. Without being fully conscious of it, I had accepted his idealization of me as fact, unquestioned overtly with him or silently in my mind. As I explored this awareness further, I began to realize that a part of me must have felt I could rescue him (single handedly) from his angst and confusion. I somehow believed that merely talking to *me* would indeed be enough to organize and calm him. Gone was the understanding that no other relationship in his past had withstood the intensity of his struggles around intimacy. Instead, I had quietly elevated myself to the position of his psychological guardian angel. Further exploration of this issue revealed understandings shameful to realize, but ultimately relieving in their implications. I began to recognize how important feeling special had been to me. And how, uncertain of the solidity of my skills as a new clinician, I was looking for validation from my patient for my clinical worth. My patient's idealization of me gave me that identity of being special that I was longing for. It gave it to me packaged in just the right persona—the one I had admired as a child—the all-powerful, perfect mother protector, the guardian angel. And it gave it to me free of charge (i.e., without my having to be aware that I was seeking or needing it). Thus, I accepted the idealization, did not view it as the transference phenomenon that it was, and made some treatment mistakes as a result.

Once I understood that I had unconsciously nurtured Mr. Martin's idealization of me, I could reflect on better ways of managing idealized longing. Over time, I changed my treatment approach to Mr. Martin. I saw the value of modifying Mr. Martin's beliefs that I was the source of his emotional aliveness, that only I could understand him, and that if he had more of me, he would get better. I respected our "good fit"; however, I came to realize that I crippled Mr. Martin by not questioning his idealization. Allowing him to put all his emotional "eggs in my basket" left him vulnerable when our alliance was shaken or when I was not there. It kept him chained to the illusion in life that if only he found the right person, all could be well within him. It robbed him of the chance to adaptively master the destructive wishes that lay behind the need for idealization, thus relegating him to a lifetime of needing to discard relationships once anger and disappointment set in. It selfishly bound him to me as the source of his aliveness and survival, rather than helping him discover the aliveness within himself. (As a cousin to splitting, idealization depleted Mr. Martin of internal strength and vitality by projecting all the good into me [Segal, 1964]). In addition, my providing instantaneous empathy robbed Mr. Martin of the chance to learn that *he* could make himself understood, even when he was not experiencing a sensation of special fusing with another.

These realizations changed me. I began to routinely rely on Mr. Martin's treatment team (e.g., his physician, caseworker, social worker, interim psychotherapist, girlfriend) as valuable sources of emotional support to him. Jock Sutherland (1984) once said, "we can't treat these patients alone" (J. Sutherland, personal communication, 1984). I relinquished the special feeling of being the only one who really understood him and, instead, supported him in his efforts to make himself better understood by others. I let myself be imperfect in his eyes, and allowed him to feel better treated at times by others than by me. Finally, I shifted to respecting his idealization to the degree necessary (Kohut, 1971; Peebles, 1986), while interpreting it to the degree possible.

This professional transformation around issues of idealization changed my personal life as well. I began to understand more how being a "great healer" fit in my psychic life. The wish to be the one who finally figured out what was wrong in an impossible situation, and in short order, fixed it, had its roots in feelings of powerlessness and confusion as a child to know how to understand and somehow transform family tensions into "Father Knows Best," humor-filled bliss. As the emotional trails into the past of this rescuer concept emerged more clearly, the fire driving my zeal to heal became dampened. I had to search for alternative motivations for continuing the work. The enjoyment in helping things grow remained. The belief in the value of leaving the world a better place endured. However, being an omnipotent healer was no longer unconsciously necessary. I could now work on getting a life. I established gratifying sources of satisfaction and self-worth outside my work, long overdue following years of graduate school and advanced training (Guy, 1987; Kupers, 1988). Doing so helped me shift to viewing my job as a skillful trade that helps people, rather than as a life-consuming mission with moralistic overtones.

TREATMENT PHASE II: THE SEDUCTIVENESS OF THE PATIENT'S LONGINGS FOR GRATIFICATION ("LOVE CAN CURE ALL"), AND THE PATIENT'S ABUSIVENESS ("TURN THE OTHER CHEEK")

This second phase of the work lasted from the time I returned from that initial month-long vacation to 3 years into treatment. More convinced of the importance of a predictable, titrated therapy schedule, I adhered to the twice weekly frequency pace. However, demands for more from me continued to emerge in varied ways. Mr. Martin continued to write long letters between sessions, bringing these in for me to read. To read one of these several-paged letters within the session consumed one third to one half of the session. Therefore, after trying that approach a few times, I yielded to his request to read these communications between hours, being ready to comment on them the next time we met. I was begrudging of the extra time but felt ashamed of my seeming stinginess. My reluctance to give more seemed selfish and did not match my ego ideal of being all giving to those to whom I committed myself.

Mr. Martin then began to bring other things in to me. An article from the *Atlantic Monthly*, excerpts from literary works, pictures of his family, letters from family members to him, a book of poetry with underlined passages, and so forth. The line between treatment material and gifts became hard to discern. He began asking me to keep some of these things overnight in my office, ostensibly for us to discuss the next time. Only the next time never came, and I found myself clearing out a desk drawer to accommodate the accumulation of his things. Again, I felt a niggling resentment but guilt about this resentment silenced my taking it seriously or expressing it.

Mr. Martin inadvertently discovered when my birthday was, and the next session brought in a card, handmade with much time and thought. I felt uneasy about accepting the card; yet, to not accept it felt ungracious and rejecting. Surely part of the real relationship (Greenson, 1967) involved allowing Mr. Martin to acknowledge thanks for the work we were doing together? Didn't my uneasiness reflect rigidity on my part (Gabbard & Wilkinson, 1994)—a rigidity that signaled shortcomings in my ability to fully accept and take in Mr. Martin? The card was followed over time by little trinket gifts: a star-filled key chain, a tiny clay figure meant for my office bookshelf, a little book of jokes. These things eventually reached my threshold of felt intrusiveness, and I raised the gift giving for therapeutic inspection. Mr. Martin was hurt; he retreated into silence. It took me several sessions to coax him out of his shell, and when he emerged he remonstrated me for my insensitivity. He accused me of not wanting him "in" me, of "sending him away" as his mother had. He pointed to secretly amassed data on my tones of voice and facial expressions as proof that underneath my so-called kind demeanor was the reality of my irritation with him. He accused me of resenting him and being relieved that I only had to see him two 50-minute sessions a week.

The incisiveness of his sudden insight into me and the intensity of his voice after sessions of his silence stilled me. I felt guilty under the harsh light of his analysis of me. It was true: I did not want more of him than the two 50-minute hours. Thus, I must be a bad person, meager in my generosity, hypocritical in my invitation to open up. How could I respond to him under those conditions?

My lack of clear-headed, focused response became the catalyst for his verbal abusiveness toward me that escalated destructively over a year's time. Mr. Martin became obsessed with berating me. He seemed filled with psychological blood lust whenever one of his attacks hit its mark in me. Subsequently, he hammered away at the same point again and again. For example, he accused me of inflicting psychological pain on him by cutting him off at the end of sessions. He threw in my face that whereas I have a husband he had no one to go home to (by this time, he had broken off with the girlfriend altogether and had become increasingly isolated at work as well). He raised the early hospitalization episode, accusing me of having mistreated him, by leading him on, knowing I would be going out of town and someone else could pick up the pieces. He belittled my looks, my way of carrying myself, my tone of voice, often mockingly throwing back in my face a saccharine imitation of my efforts to sound empathic. He claimed I hated him and put on this show of being so kind, so good, so in control, when the truth was I did not know how to deal with him.

During this time period, Mr. Martin was also singing my curses outside the hour. He was berating me and my skills to colleagues at his work. He complained about me to my receptionist, to his internist, and even to his pharmacist. Occasionally he shouted diatribes so loudly (and distinctly) in my office, that colleagues of mine at work heard and questioned me about them. He used vulgar language, calling me b____, telling me to f___ myself, and refusing to call me by title, instead oozing out my first name in an attacking, mocking, belittling tone.

This phase of the work left me reeling. I had never been attacked so directly and relentlessly before. I was often paralyzed in sessions, overwhelmed by the force of his hate. I found myself going numb, emotionally and ideationally, literally not knowing what to say next. The one model I knew—empathic resonance—was not only completely ineffectual, it was being ripped to shreds by his mocking imitations. He seemed to enjoy hurting me. This concept left me speechless. It was as if my paralysis were saying behaviorally, "this can't be happening."

I began to dread the hours with him, finding my stomach knotting up and my hands becoming clammy just before a session. Often I had a piercing headache following a session. I felt spun around psychologically, as if what he was saying was true (i.e., I *must be* insincere because I *didn't* want to see him and was pretending to him that I did by continuing to act so kind). Had not I indeed led him on 3 years earlier, caught up in my own narcissism and losing sight of what he needed? I could not shake the sessions; the emotional knives of his hate and my unexpressed anger stayed stuck in me for hours, sometimes until the following day. I felt shame in front of my colleagues, and an irrational shame vis-à-vis the unknown numbers of people to whom he had vilified me. In an image that shamed me further with the exhibitionistic, narcissistic motivations it revealed to me, I felt as if I had been acting on a stage and had suddenly been smeared with eggs and refuse, bound with ropes, and was being paraded through the streets as an example of worthless garbage, mocked for having thought myself to be so good.

During this time period, a supervisor gently raised with me a question about my possible masochism. I remember bridling defensively, but, gradually, I came to face that the patient was, indeed, abusing me sadistically, and I was, indeed, allowing it to happen, masochistically. Understanding his motivation came sooner than understanding mine.

For Mr. Martin, I was the abandoning mother. The flavor of the erupting transference suggested that he had experienced mother as having loved him only narcissistically, as someone to make her feel whole and worthwhile. His introject was of a hypocrite who acted lovingly, and even looked that way to other people but who really (he felt) resented him as a burden. His stance as a child was one of having been knocked from a pedestal of felt specialness, to the garbage heap of rejection. He felt he must be worthless because nothing about him was worthwhile enough to engage his mother to stay (or even to maintain contact after she left). He felt the fool because he had thought he was loved. He felt shame, as if his core were worthlessness and exposed for all the world to see (particularly during the years when he felt he needed to explain to friends his mother's absence). Finally, he felt reduced by this woman to impotent ineffectuality.

The abuse of me was a transference enactment. I became the mother for him. Only this time, he was not ineffectual. He was the powerful one, reducing me to garbage. He was the effectual one, withering me with his rage. He rejected; I lay paralytic from his trashing of me.

In seeing this about Mr. Martin, I could see how the feelings induced in me were truly a window to his internal world via a concordant countertransference (Racker, 1957). It took longer to ferret out my own complementary introjects that had allowed me to be immobilized by the induced projective identification, instead of merely informed by it. In this self-examination, I realized that I had been taught that aggression was wrong and that the only allowable tool vis-à-vis aggression was to "turn the other cheek." This meant I was to fight abuse with kindness. It also meant that I could not allow hate within me toward the patient. The hate that did well up, therefore, was robbed of its chance for verbalization and modulation, and thus was unruly in form—at times, as I discovered, rawly sadistic. The unruliness of this complementary sadism was part of what left me immobilized. As Winnicott (1949) has said, "If, for fear of what she [the mother] may do, she cannot hate appropriately when hurt by her child, she must fall back on masochism" (p. 74). Abashed by such dark impulses within, and stripped of awareness of them, my only stopgap for their expression was silence. Beyond that, I tried the reaction formation of increased kindness and seeming empathy. But Mr. Martin rightly poked holes in that, and considered me to be insincere. He sensed that my empathy was masking darker, unmetabolized feelings. And such a sense within him, resonated full force with his early maternal experience, thus fueling even more his relentless lambasting of me.

The correct thing to have done, which I eventually was able to do, was to set limits on his abusiveness. Doing so was necessary for my psychological self-protection. It was also necessary for the preservation of me as a good object and the preservation of the therapeutic space as one of safety in which people are not destroyed literally or psychologically. One holds the hands of a 5-year-old in a playroom who suddenly lapses into a thera-pist-beating frenzy, as a way of communicating, "I wont let you lose control here and destroy things or people in a way that you will regret later." In the same way, Mr. Martin temporarily needed his hands held metaphorically.

In addition, limit setting was necessary for the therapeutic work to pro-ceed. Mr. Martin was caught up in a temporary *psychotic transference* in which the *as-if* quality of the transference toward me had been lost, and the observ-ing ego could not be enlisted to examine his actions and feelings toward me. He was doing with me what he did (albeit in more muted form) in significant relationships, notably with his girlfriend and with colleagues at work. He needed interpretation of this behavior. However, he could neither hear nor work with such interpretations until he was pulled out from the frenzy of re-lentless transference enactment. Further, my limit-setting of his destructive upsurges could model for him what he needed to do in relationships outside treatment, taking time-outs until he could calm, master what was driving him, and express himself in a more communicative, productive fashion.

Finally, in the concordant countertransference that Mr. Martin was in-ducing in me, he was putting in me the impotence, worthlessness, and pa-ralysis that he had felt as a child. He was doing with me what he used to do to himself internally that inevitably triggered a tailspin of depression within him. Every time I stopped his abuse (in a nonsadistic way), and stayed emotionally connected to him while I was doing so, I modeled for him a way of rising out of the masochistic stance without losing the rela-tionship (Peebles-Kleiger, 1989). He could eventually internalize this new way of relating, which had impact not only on how he interacted with other people but also on how he treated himself.

Unfortunately, it was long before I could set these limits because: (a) ac-knowledging his pure hate, his wish to hurt me in whatever way he could, and his pleasure in doing so *shattered* my assumptions of a world in which people loved each other and treated one another well, particularly if you treated them well; (b) becoming numb and silent, and then "turning the other cheek" were my primary ways of meeting aggression; and (c) poorly modulated sadism within me hamstrung efforts at limit setting: Until I could metabolize my own hate and wishes for retaliation, I could not en-gage in an aggressive act such as limit setting in a constructive way without its being imbued with destructive retaliatory wishes. Through the painful crisis of his abusiveness, Mr. Martin forced me to discover my own sadism and masochism. Only with outside help could I begin to tame and rework this sadism and masochism. This outside help included supervision, my own analysis, voracious reading on the topic, case presentations that made public (and thus discussible) my private anxieties, case consultations with outside consultants, learning from hearing others' cases, learning from other cases of my own, and my own professional teaching and writing (that forced crisper articulation of the issues with which I was struggling). Only with such help could I change my treatment techniques and change the way I handled aggression directed toward me in my personal life.

TREATMENT PHASE III: EVENTUAL "GOOD-ENOUGH" RESOLUTION

As before, outside consultation assisted Mr. Martin and me in our effort to move past the transference-countertransference impasse, to eventual "good-enough" resolution of the treatment process. This final phase of the work was the less dramatic, slow-and-steady, "working through" phase. We had the basic dynamics and conflicts identified; the work consisted of mastering over and over again problems in our relationship and problems in his outside relationships. Each new chance at mastery further solidified the knowledge (and behavioral feel) of why an upset had occurred and how to get out of it. Mr. Martin was eventually able to terminate several years later. At termination, he was not totally satisfied with the therapy, but he was not totally dissatisfied with it either. Above all, he was capable of feeling grateful to me and proud of himself. He wished we both could have done a better job; however, he was grateful for what work we had accomplished.

With the help of both supervision and my personal analysis, I was able to set the necessary limits on Mr. Martin's abusiveness. I was also able to examine my own conflicts around nurturance inherent in my fuzzy boundaries around special, extra-treatment contacts and quasigifts. I came to understand that I had succumbed to gratifying Mr. Martin in numerous small ways with the naive belief that I could cure him by providing a good love that was better than his mother's deficient love. I would thus triumph over his mother (and symbolically mine). In addition, gratifying Mr. Martin gratified the child in me who longed for the perfect, protecting love promised by her and her mother's religion. Finally, gratifying Mr. Martin was a way of staving off the unpleasant discovery of both his and my sadism. I became more clinically sophisticated in understanding that a therapist could not replace lost love from a patient's childhood. Rather, the hard road to wellness wound through the grief and rage of giving up attempts to reinstate what one felt one never had (Gabbard & Wilkinson, 1994). Only by so doing, could one then be freed up to feel satisfaction in what was available. In addition, supervision also helped me realize that when a need-filled patient desperately continues to ask for more, the helpful stance is not to try to provide it (or to feel guilty if one cannot) but simply to ask aloud what is preventing the patient from taking in satisfyingly what is available (F. Shectman, personal communication, August 26, 1982).

The confrontations with previously unknown sides of myself were not easy. In retrospect, part of my dread before Mr. Martin's sessions must have been my unconscious dread at meeting my own darker side that Mr. Martin was continuously exposing to light by his provocations and accusations of me. Had I not treated this patient, I doubt that the sadistic and narcissistic impulses within myself would have emerged in such depth and breadth within my own analysis. These impulses ultimately reached "good-enough" resolution in both of us. Thus, Mr. Martin was in part responsible for treating me. As Searles (1979) said, "The more ill a patient is, the more does his successful treatment require that he become, and be implicitly acknowledged as having become, a therapist to his officially designated therapist, the analyst" (p. 381).

EPILOGUE

It is important to highlight three things simultaneously: how much I read about and discussed with my supervisors aspects of this case that were troubling me; how attuned and sophisticated were the comments of my supervisors and the various consultants I sought out; and nevertheless, how difficult it was to put effectively into practice anything that I was reading about and being taught, until certain intrapsychic changes had occurred within me. As one supervisor often said, "I could tell you the words to say, but until you feel them 'from the inside out,' they probably won't have the effect you're looking for" (F. Shectman, personal communication, November 11, 1983; see also Gabbard, 1991).

How did the work with Mr. Martin change me? I came to believe that most people who present themselves as guardian angels have complicated motives and needs that they have not been able to integrate and work through. I came to understand that being good does not mean that good things happen. My view of the world now incorporates an awareness of human impulses to hurt and destroy, sometimes with pleasure and without regret. I believe now that people vary in the amount of primary aggression with which they are born into the world (expressed as infants in temperamental differences in reactivity, emotional expressiveness, and raw aggression). I now understand that love can not cure all. In fact, misleading a patient into thinking that the therapist's concrete expressions of caring are necessary for survival can actually cripple a patient by tethering him or her to dependency on the concrete (rather than dislodging impediments to more liberating symbolic internalizations). I have learned that "turning the other cheek" can be injurious to both self and other. I have also come to understand the normalcy and acceptability of hate feelings and destructive wishes toward patients and all people. Accepting, metabolizing, and channeling such feelings into constructive, creative activity is the "fulcrum around which treatment [or relationships in general] fails or succeeds" (Gabbard, 1989). Finally, I still hold to my image of the Little Blue Engine. However, daily I try to appreciate and accept my small size vis-à-vis the world and to realize that not all mountains have to be scaled; sometimes tunnels can be found, paths around can be made, or some very nice towns and villages on this side can be discovered or constructed.

REFERENCES

Gabbard, G. (1989). Patients who hate. *Psychiatry, 52,* 96–106.

Gabbard, G. (1991). Technical approaches to transference hate in the analysis of borderline patients. *International Journal of Psychiatry, 72,* 625–637.

Gabbard, G., & Wilkinson, S. (1994). *Management of countertransference with borderline patients.* Washington, DC: American Psychiatric Press.

Greenson, R. (1967). *The technique and practice of psychoanalysis.* New York: International Universities.

Guy, J. D. (1987). *The personal life of the psychotherapist: The impact of clinical practice on the therapist's intimate relationships and emotional well-being.* New York: Wiley.

Heisenberg, W. (1930). *The physical principles of the Quantum theory.* Chicago: Univeristy of Chicago.

Janoff-Bulman, R. (1985). The aftermath of victimization: Rebuilding shattered assumptions. In C. Figley (Ed.), *Trauma and its wake (Vol. I): The study and treatment of post-traumatic stress disorder* (pp. 15 35). New York: Brunner/Mazel.

Kohut, H. (1971). *The analysis of the self: A systematic approach to the psychoanalytic treatment of narcissistic personality disorders.* New York: International Universities.

Kupers, T. (1988). *Ending therapy: The meaning of termination.* New York: New York University.

Menninger, K., Mayman, M., & Pruyser, P. (1963). *The vital balance: The life process in mental health and illness.* New York: Viking.

Modell, A. (1978). The conceptualization of the therapeutic action of psychoanalysis: The action of the holding environment. *Bulletin of Menninger Clinic, 42,* 493–504.

Peebles, M. J. (1986). The adaptive aspects of the golden fantasy. *Psychoanalytic Psychology, 3*(3), 217–235.

Peebles-Kleiger, M. J. (1989). Using countertransference in the hypnosis of trauma victims: A model for turning hazard into healing. *American Journal of Psychotherapy, 43,* 518–530.

Pruyser, P., & Menninger, K. (1976). Language pitfalls in diagnostic thought and work. *Bulletin of Menninger Clinic, 40,* 417–434.

Racker, H. (1957). The meanings and uses of countertransference. *Psychoanalytic Quarterly, 26,* 303–357.

Searles, H. F. (1979). The patient as therapist to his analyst. In *Countertransference and related subjects* (pp. 380-459). New York: International Universities.

Segal, H. (1964). *Introduction to the work of Melanie Klein.* New York: Basic Books.

Shectman, F. (1979). Problems in communicating psychological understanding: Why won't they listen to me?!. *American Psychologist, 34,* 781–790.

Winnicott, D. W. (1949). Hate in the counter-transference. *International Journal of Psychoanalysis, 30,* 69–74.

Winnicott, D. W. (1965). *The maturational processes and the facilitating environment.* New York: International Universities.

IV

CHANGES IN TECHNIQUE

12

Myths in Collision

Stanley Krippner

Myths are often seen as irrational, superstitious conjectures about the world. But others find it more useful to take an anthropological perspective and describe myths as internalized constructs expressed in implicit or explicit stories, formal or informal statements, or social infrastructures that address existential human concerns and issues and that impact behavior (Feinstein & Krippner, 1988, 1997). Myths can be cultural, institutional, familial, ethnic, or personal in nature. Hence, a personal myth can be conceptualized as a psychological unit composed of imagery and narrative that interprets sensations, constructs explanations, and directs actions.

This case study demonstrates the clinical efficacy of my interaction with a client who chose to identify those personal myths that directed his dysfunctional performance and relationships and how he changed these myths to permit a fuller actualization of his potential. This case study also demonstrates the way that my own personal myths were modified as a result of our encounter.

OVERVIEW

Ethan, an unmarried 23-year-old junior high school teacher at the time of our first meeting in 1990, was self-referred for counseling with the specific request that hypnosis be utilized. He cited a lack of joy in life as the key

151

reason he was seeking professional help. At the end of 11 months and more than 20 counseling sessions, the client left for Peace Corps service in Asia. He remained in contact with me during his 27 months overseas and paid me a follow-up visit when he returned. During this visit, he expressed his satisfaction with the counseling sessions, citing specific ways in which "joy had emerged" in his work, in his solitary activities, and in his personal relationships.

ETHAN

Ethan was recommended when he requested counseling from someone who would use hypnosis. He rarely smiled; a dour expression contorted his handsome face when in repose. Ethan stated that he carried "a suitcase in my stomach" and that he suffered from both digestive and sleeping problems. It was my impression that he was experiencing periodic episodes of subclinical depression.

As an attractive young man, he had no problem obtaining dates with women but took little pleasure in shared activities, in discussions about life events, or even in sexual intercourse, which he described as perfunctory and constrained. Ethan felt that he was competent in his work as a teacher, and he received high ratings from the school administrators, but it was difficult for him to go beyond his task as an instructor and a disciplinarian. Ethan suspected that he could do more to inspire his students were he not so inhibited.

When I explained that my approach began by assisting clients to identify and explore the underlying beliefs and attitudes that impacted their life, Ethan expressed considerable interest. Our discussion about belief systems, attitudinal habits, and worldviews struck a resonant chord, and he said that this seemed to be the basis of his continual conflict with his parents, especially his mother. Because Ethan seemed highly motivated to experience hypnosis, we decided to proceed with a formal hypnotic induction. After his response to various arm levitation challenges convinced him that, indeed, he was hypnotized, I suggested that he would re-experience feelings associated with the recall of his early years at home. Within a few seconds, Ethan cited guilt as the overriding emotion. When I asked him to associate to this feeling, he almost immediately replied, "in the church, the whole idea is personal salvation; I believed that if I led a life without pleasure, this would save me." Thus, Ethan had identified an *outdated myth*, a belief system that may or may not have once served him well, but that was now inappropriate.

I explained to Ethan that his statement about salvation and a life without pleasure qualified as a personal myth because it addressed existential human concerns and impacted his behavior. I gave him a copy of the workbook Feinstein and I (1988) had prepared, suggesting that he might consider working through some of its 31 personal rituals as homework assignments. By the time of our fourth session, he had begun this process and showed me a notebook in which the results were assiduously described.

As he examined the roots of his personal myths, Ethan recalled, "my father's devotion to my mother was certainly unwavering, but it seemed to be a duty-bound love." Ethan had few early vivid memories of his father who "simply went to work, provided for his family, and attended Mass each Sunday."

Ethan's memories of his mother, especially those evoked during the hypnosis sessions, were more dramatic. Described by Ethan as a person of mercurial temperament, his mother reportedly tucked him tightly in his crib as a baby and restrained him in his stroller as a toddler with a seat belt so firm that it was often painful. In retrospect, incidents of this nature initiated a confusion between pain (the tight seat belt) and pleasure (the comfort of security). Ethan recalled that when he was about 3 years of age, his mother screamed at him for a thoughtless misdemeanor and beat him repeatedly. Ethan jumped in his bed crying, pulling the blankets over his head providing a blindfold to the outside world. It established a maneuver he often put to use in the future; whenever a painful event (such as his mother's punishment) began to overwhelm him, Ethan would counter it with pleasure (the comfort of his bed).

Ethan got along quite well with his older brother who was in elementary school at this time. Ethan recollected the times his brother would come home from school with licorice and would invariably share this treat. Because his father's temperament was stolid and bland and because his mother was volatile and unpredictable, the gift of licorice and other sweets from his brother was the only sustained pleasure he could recall in his early years. Ethan remarked, "candy gave me a momentary feeling of life. Until my brother returned home from school, I felt that I was living in what the Bible calls the valley of the shadow of death." Ethan remembered that his mother kept their home dark, ostensibly to save electricity, but that his brother turned on the lights when he returned. Here again, Ethan's mother was associated with death and darkness and his brother with life and light.

When he was 4 years old, Ethan was sent to a parochial nursery school. He was pleased to leave his home for prolonged periods of time, but the school was a mixed blessing. He enjoyed interacting with the other children, but the nuns exerted strict control. Once again, he felt as he had when tucked tightly in his crib and restrained by his safety belt. When he expressed his curiosity concerning other rooms and events at school, he was physically punished and threatened with "hell and damnation" in the afterlife. On occasion, he was given treats at the nursery school but only if he had been a good child. Ethan began to wonder if the moments of pleasure he experienced at nursery school were worth the price he had to pay for them; it was difficult for him to stifle his inquisitiveness and to sit quietly when there were so many interesting boys and girls in the classroom.

At this point in therapy, a *countermyth* began to emerge. Ethan did not recall any specific words by which this attitude could be described but did recall recurring imagery in which he broke loose of the seat belt, jumped out of the stroller, and ran far, far away from home. In retrospect, he articulated this countermyth as "I'd like to have some fun, even if I am damned for it." He also recalled a recurrent childhood dream in which he was in a sweet shop eating licorice and other delicacies. A shadow appeared in the door. It was the devil, ready to take Ethan to hell to pay the penalty for his indulgences.

For Ethan, pleasure and pain continued to be intermixed during family interactions. When he was about 5, his father took him on a trip to see an open-top reservoir. Ethan stood in awe of this mammoth construction but could not enjoy it because he imagined "falling off the deck into the water and drowning in a slow, painful death." Easter was a special occasion for the family. When Ethan was about 6, the family went to Mass. Shortly afterward, Ethan's brother played Easter Bunny and passed out baskets of candy to the three other members of the family. But Ethan could not fully enjoy this treat because his mother kept interrupting his enjoyment with such statements as "don't eat so fast," "candy always gives me a stomach ache," and "you'll probably get cavities from sucking on all this licorice."

During our hypnosis sessions, Ethan frequently evoked metaphors and symbols, especially after it was pointed out that both are frequent concomitants of both cultural and personal mythology. During one hypnosis session, Ethan described his mother as "nurturant, loving, angry, and venomous." In his imagery, she took the form of a 3-foot, coiled black snake, her head leaning toward him, intimidating him, "ready to strike." Ethan commented that this image was accurate because:

> my mother constantly threatened to harm me if I didn't do what she wanted me to do. And my mother's punishment was not the end of it; she vowed that God would send me to eternal damnation if I did not follow her orders. I did not have a choice so I just stayed out of her way as much as I could. And I had to look away from the snake; if I was afraid, she would know it and would move in for the kill.

During this hypnosis session, I proposed that Ethan confront the snake-mother in some way. Ethan responded by telling her that he no longer needed her nurturance and that he could now take care of himself. He stared her directly in the eyes—a task he described as extremely difficult because of her power. I encouraged him to claim his own authority, and to maintain the gaze until she backed down. After several tries, this gambit was successful.

Ethan shared his notebook with me. He had considered several names for the subpersonality dominated by his outdated but still prevailing myth—the *Vulnerable Man*, the *Still Life*—but he settled on the *Little Torturer*. This label acknowledged that the renouncing of pleasure was originally imposed by an outside oppressor but now was maintained by an internal scourge. The part of Ethan that represented the countermyth (i.e., "I'd like to have some fun even if I am damned for it," was designated the *Bouncing Ball*). This moniker resulted from a hypnotic session in which Ethan visualized himself turning into a "large, light, red bouncing ball that can travel far and have lots of fun." People enjoyed the Bouncing Ball because they would "hold it, play with it, stick it between their legs, and sit on it." The ball cherished these interactions just as much as the people who played with it; the ball was always available, always resilient, always playful. It could not be hurt unless it was popped. Ethan recognized this outcome as going to hell as a consequence of his pleasure, but when I pointed out that holes can be patched, a smile crossed his face—an unusual event given his usually morose countenance.

Further exploring the sources of his Little Torturer, Ethan produced ample material during our hypnosis sessions. When he was about 6-years-old, he found a turtle in a nearby woods and brought it home, placed it on the dining room table, and implored his mother to let him keep it. While making his plea, the turtle urinated on the table. Ethan recalled that his mother "threw a fit, took the turtle outside, and immediately washed the table, berating me all the while." More than once she asked, "what will other people think?", and "what would the neighbors say if they smelled turtle piss all around the house?" Once again, Ethan had attempted to bring some vibrant pleasure into his home and some joy into his life. Ethan, of course, blamed himself for the fiasco, never questioning whether his mother's behavior and statements might have been inappropriate.

Returning from school one day, Ethan let out an unaccustomed laugh. When his mother asked what had amused him, he recounted an incident at school when a boy's loose pants accidentally fell down, "and we could all see his ass, even the girls." Ethan's mother exploded. She hauled him to the bathroom, washed his mouth out with soap, and told him never to use dirty language again or he would go straight to hell. Once again, an attempt to lighten up the dark ambience at home had led to punishment and retribution.

Ethan's father did not threaten hellfire and damnation, but his faithful attendance at church services gave tacit approval to his mother's admonitions, as did the nuns' threats and the priest's constant prattling about the necessity for salvation. When Ethan's brother spent time with him, the Bouncing Ball came to the surface. His brother skipped Mass as often as he could, spent a great deal of time away from home with his friends, but according to Ethan "knew how to charm my mother and say all the right things so that she never took it out on him like she did on me."

As therapy progressed, Ethan and I moved toward a clarification of the prevailing myth and its competition with the countermyth. Ethan's life-without-pleasure myth was in collision with his desire to have some fun, and the Little Torturer and the Bouncing Ball were appropriate symbols for the two myths. During one hypnosis session, I suggested that Ethan take the voice and the posture of the Little Torturer; he slipped into this role-playing procedure easily. Ethan's face took on a maniacal grin, and he began to speak in an almost deranged cadence:

> Yes, I really enjoy torturing Ethan because it is so easy. He is very vulnerable because he has bought into the crap that his mother has fed him for so many years. He actually believes that if he had some fun in life, he would go straight to hell. So every time he laughs or takes some pleasure in what he does, I lay on a dose of guilt. And, boy, does he suffer!

I next suggested that Ethan become the Bouncing Ball. Almost immediately, the lines of tension disappeared from his face and his body lost much of its characteristic rigidity. He sighed, "I stay away from the Little Torturer as much as I can, but he's always just around the corner. I'm happiest with my brother because he cheers me up. I like being with my lady friends, but I wish I could feel as relaxed with them as I do with my brother. Someday I'm going to bounce away from all my troubles and have a really great time."

When Ethan attempted to bring the two subpersonalities into dialogue, the Little Torturer showed contempt for the Bouncing Ball whereas the latter entity displayed fear and wariness toward the former, as well as anger that he was so vulnerable. During almost every session, Ethan shared his notebook with me, and on this occasion he showed me a list of personal myths that supported the Little Torturer:

> "Curiosity killed the cat," "The less I think about my own needs, the better off I will be," "A good baby sleeps a lot and stays in his crib," "If I stay out of peoples' way, I will avoid trouble," "I am still the baby of the family," "I am cursed, and will carry the curse for the rest of my life," "It is better to bear the pain than to experience pleasure because I know more about suffering than I know about bliss."

During several hypnosis sessions, Ethan evoked feelings in his body and later described them, oftentimes in symbols and metaphors. Anger, for example, was "a pissed-off black cat." Affection was "travelling through space to pay attention to another person." Fear was "hiding from a snake that is out to bite and poison me." Sexual desire was "a combination of affect and fear; I want to give pleasure to my partner and to myself, but I am afraid that my penis is poisoned." In discussing the latter image, Ethan reported a recurring dream:

> I am in bed with a woman and we are having intercourse. It is delightful, but the woman begins to feel sick. I know it is my fault. My penis is poisoned. My semen is poisoned. I have been poisoned by my mother, and now I have passed the sickness on to someone else. I have disobeyed the church's teachings. Not only am I being punished, but my girlfriend is paying the price as well.

Ethan described in great detail how his sex life reflected both the Bouncing Ball and the Little Torturer. Ethan's sexual experiences would begin by being enjoyable activities and an escape from his depression and torment. Before long, guilt and remorse would permeate the experience, often leading to premature ejaculation. A similar pattern characterized his conversations with women. Just as intimacies were being shared, he would hold back and change the subject knowing that if he continued to talk he would behave like the *pissed-off cat* and expose his anger toward his mother, the church, and his teachers. His mother's words echoed in his ears: "What will other people think?" What would his lady friends think if he revealed his animosity and resentment?

The symbol of the *poisoned penis* came up repeatedly, not only in dreams but in Ethan's mental imagery. I mentioned that poisons have antidotes and, during a hypnosis session, asked him to imagine an effective antidote for his infection. Ethan reported an image of his mother injecting him with the poison, an image that also imbued many of his dreams. But this time, he grabbed the hypodermic needle from his mother's hand, smashed it on the floor, and said, "you will never do this to me again." Reflecting on these images, Ethan remarked, "I know that I have the strength to heal myself if only I could stop getting those injections."

Christmas 1991 was only a few weeks away, and Ethan had planned to make his customary visit to his parents' home, several hundred miles away, resolving to take some type of affirmative action that would "stop the injections." During the subsequent hypnosis sessions, we rehearsed several scenarios in which he would display the strength of his convictions and make himself invulnerable to his mother's berating and belittling. We tried to use the Bouncing Ball symbol to represent the buoyancy he would need for this encounter. It became apparent that buoyancy was not enough and Ethan, in a hypnosis session, evoked the image of a red hammer—something that was the same color as the ball but impervious to being punctured by his mother's hypodermic needle or her caustic remarks.

When our sessions resumed in January, Ethan entered my office smiling. He cited no fewer than seven instances when he had stood up to his mother, contradicting her statements. He defended his sex life, although his mother felt that premarital intercourse was sinful. He admitted to such human frailties as feeling angry from time to time, and occasionally using rough language—but saw no need to change his behavior.

The most extraordinary event occurred near the end of his visit when his mother began to cry, exclaiming, "the way you talk, you make me feel like I was a failure as a mother. But I did the best I could. I only raised you the way that I had been raised." Ethan knew that his grandparents were extremely strict disciplinarians and very devout in their religious convictions. He could imagine a vulnerable little girl kowtowing before them, introjecting their myths and making them her own. He saw remnants of this little girl in his mother's face, walked toward her, and hugged her for the first time in years. All this while, Ethan's father maintained his usually passive role, but his brother tactfully encouraged him, eventually placing his long arms around both of the protagonists.

I knew that my task in this stage was to skillfully mediate and facilitate the process as Ethan's opposing myths groped their way toward a natural synthesis. During one session, Ethan again orchestrated a dialogue between the Little Torturer and the Bouncing Ball. I had him physically assume the posture of both as they carried out a heated debate and, later, a discussion of their differences.

Ball:	Look at how stiff and rigid you have become. I could give you new life. I'm soft and buoyant; you're hard and dry. But you don't trust me at all, do you?
Torturer:	Why should I trust you? You are so damn vulnerable that any little puncture could deflate you. If I didn't torture you, somebody else would. So why shouldn't I get the fun out of doing it?
Ball:	I am tired of being such a damn masochist. The only way I can have any fun is to bounce away from you. But the guilt catches up with me whether I am at work, with a woman, or simply out in nature.
Torturer:	At least my actions are deeply rooted in my religious faith. What sort of spiritual life does a bouncing ball have?
Ball:	You bet your grounding is religious. What you do to me is straight out of the Spanish Inquisition! Whatever happened to the gentle Jesus and the loving God I read about but never experienced at home, in church, or in the parochial schools?
Torturer:	But in pain there is power. The church is powerful. And I am powerful.

> *Ball:*   You are not powerful at all. You are just a "little" tor-
>   turer. I am a big red bouncing ball. And I am about to
>   turn into a big red hammer.

To me, this latter statement indicated that the countermyth had outlived
its usefulness and saw the advantage of taking on some of the attributes of
the prevailing myth. The softness of the ball and the dryness of the torturer
were rejected whereas the ball's buoyancy and the torturer's hardness were
maintained. The Bouncing Ball realized that his vulnerability needed to be
tempered by the resiliency of the Little Torturer. He also admired the torturer's groundedness, although the religious convictions they represented
were abhorrent. Ethan began to explore meditation as a form of spiritual
development, and I gave him some references both to books and to meditation classes in the area. Ethan's image of the Red Hammer occurred in
dreams, in meditation, and in our hypnosis sessions. He spoke about it,
drew it, and began to establish it as a viable mythic symbol.

Ethan felt that the Red Hammer represented a synthesis of what was
most functional in both his prevailing myth and his countermyth. The Red
Hammer, Ethan's *new myth*, could be put to immediate use; when appropriate, he could be angry and coarse. But a hammer is used to build, and Ethan
felt he was constructing a new life for himself, a life based on a new myth he
verbalized as "I take pleasure in my power, but it is a power that nurtures
and builds." Ethan found that he was becoming more effective in his work.
For the first time, he was able to express humor in the classroom; for the first
time, students would come to him for one-on-one discussions, and Ethan
felt that he was actually making a constructive difference in their lives.

When Ethan returned to his parents' home for Easter, he did not resent
attending the Easter Mass with the family. He told his parents that he had
begun to explore Eastern religious systems and did not receive the condem-
nation he had expected. One reason was that his brother had chosen this occasion to tell his parents that he was homosexual, and was about to move
into the home of his lover. This revelation surpassed in drama and confrontation anything that Ethan could have provoked. However, Ethan was supportive of his brother just as his brother had given him what sustenance he
could over the years.

The essence of Ethan's changes can be conveyed in an old Hassidic saying that counsels: "We should each carefully observe what way our heart
draws us and then choose that way with all our strength." In the earlier
stages of his therapy, Ethan carefully observed the way his heart beckoned.
Choosing to follow that path meant focusing on the day-by-day details of
his existence as he attempted to integrate the new mythology in his life.

One of the most effective ongoing tools for Ethan was his daily ritual of
morning meditation. I urged him not to combine meditation (which, in es-

sence, has no specific goal) with autosuggestion (which is goal oriented). Both are forms of self-regulation, and as such, both are tools for empowerment. Another example of Ethan's integration involved joining a theatrical group in his neighborhood where he found that his prior experience in enacting his mythic subpersonalities could be put to good use in this new venture.

From time to time, Ethan had discussed with me the possibility of joining the Peace Corps. Our early discussions had focused on whether or not this would be escapist behavior, just the type of maneuver the Bouncing Ball would use to distance himself from his mother, his church, and his daily problems. But the idea persisted, and Ethan filed his application. He had no problem being accepted and notified his school that he would not be returning for the fall semester.

Ethan was assigned to teach English in a Southeast Asian country. This was a serendipitous choice because it gave him a chance to deepen his meditation practice and learn more about Taoism, the Eastern perspective of most interest to him. He lived in an area with a high incidence of AIDS so maintained a relationship with only one woman during the 27 months he was overseas. Because she was a single mother, the practical difficulties of bringing her to the United States were insurmountable. For Ethan, it was just as well because he felt no urgency to get married.

There was one incident that Ethan took great pleasure in relating. In his work as an English teacher, he had several opportunities to interact with the local Roman Catholic priest, an American. When the priest suggested that he should either marry his lady friend or abstain from intimate relations, Ethan flashed back to his upbringing. In as calm a manner as he could muster, he told the priest that he had been raised a Catholic, and had made considerable efforts to work his way through the guilt and torment that resulted from this early indoctrination. He also voiced the opinion that his relationship with the Asian woman was based on mutual respect and enjoyment, as well as the knowledge that they might never see each other once he returned to the United States. They both accepted the Eastern adage that "nothing is permanent," including their relationship. Ethan felt positively about himself as a result of this confrontation, especially as the priest was left speechless at the end of their discussion and never raised the issue again.

On his return to the United States, Ethan arranged to see me for a 2-hour consultation. He expressed gratitude for our work together and had continued to use autosuggestion, monitor his mythology, and to lead a more joyful life. He had brought renewed vigor and inspiration to his work as a junior high school teacher, and was dating one of the other teachers at this school. I last spoke with Ethan in early 1996 at which time he was continuing to do well personally and vocationally; Ethan made specific mention of his intense involvement in the homework assignments he had completed when we worked together on his personal myths.

PROCESS UNDERGONE BY THE THERAPIST

Ethan's story affected me very deeply on an emotional level, and I believe that my ability to express these feelings was a helpful model for him. I have known countless people who have been attracted to both mainstream religions and cults, only to suffer abuse, betrayal, and disillusionment. I could not sit by calmly and remain nonjudgmental while listening to the threats heaped on a young boy by his church and its representatives. Perhaps my emotional reaction would have been more subdued if I did not value spiritual experience so highly. But, for me, *spiritual* is not a synonym for *religious*. I conceptualize a religion as an institutionalized body of believers who accept a common set of beliefs, practices, and rituals regarding spiritual concerns and issues. One who is religious may or may not be spiritual; nor is it necessary to be religious to be spiritual.

I did not condemn Ethan's mother, suspecting from the first that, as she later put it, "I did the best I could. I only raised you the way that I had been raised." Her concern with what other people might think probably ingratiated her with members of her church and of her community. These good people would have denied to outsiders that this dedicated, godly woman was capable of inflicting suffering on her son. Curiously, I had less sympathy for Ethan's apathetic father who had abdicated child-rearing responsibilities to his wife and, knowing her temper, was not about to come to the defense of his son. My feeling about Ethan's brother was one of begrudging admiration; he had found a way to cajole his mother, perhaps pretending to share her activities and interests. I hoped that his final denouement brought about some humility on her part rather than self-condemnation.

Ethan's story evoked the recognition of two personal myths on my part. The first was an interest in applying those postmodern approaches to psychotherapy and counseling that had previously been only of theoretical interest to me. The second was a renewed acknowledgement of my competence as a therapist.

The postmodern psychotherapies admit that their premises (whether psychoanalytic, behavioral, cognitive, or humanistic) hardly qualify as a universally acceptable body of psychological knowledge, and that those principles they find most useful might need to be adapted or abandoned when dealing with varying ethnicities or socioeconomic levels. Postmodern therapists realize that, like Ethan, their clients need to learn a variety of coping strategies to live in a world of increasingly multiple realities (Anderson, 1990). The personal mythology approach is one of many narrative psychotherapies that discern a coconstruction of the therapist and client that takes place in their interaction (DeBerry, 1993).

Some of my own myths were in collision: the old myth of modernism (universal laws leading to understanding) versus the countermyth of postmodernism (adapting and changing universals to fit specific situations), the old myth of little confidence in my abilities as a counselor versus the countermyth of sudden empowerment. The two new myths that resulted were (1) a version of the postmodern approach that appreciates its insights but avoids a relativism that would give equal credibility to the values of the "old" Ethan and his mother; and (2) a modest acknowledgement of my competence with clients with an appreciation of my ability to work with individuals with problematic sexual and spiritual issues.

Over the years, I have heard psychotherapists admit their reluctance to discuss spiritual or sexual issues with their clients. From my perspective, however, these topics permeate most of the problematic concerns that clients bring to their sessions. In my opinion, human beings are sexual creatures. They are also spiritual beings. By virtue of genetic predispositions and environmental events, and eventually through volition and decision making, sexual and spiritual matters are dealt with in ways that enhance or inhibit one's quality of life. Sexuality and spirituality permeate much of a person's mythology; avoidance of these topics can be a disservice. To be most effective, practitioners needs to be well-grounded in their own sexual and spiritual orientations. My own mythology envisions sexuality and spirituality, at their best, as embodying love, joy, passion, and commitment. I could not help but reinforce these qualities in my discourses with Ethan, but in so doing, noted that they were self-reinforcing as well.

For example, I was haunted by Ethan's quotation of his mother's words: "The way you talk, you make me feel like I was a failure as a mother. But I did the best I could. I only raised you the way that I had been raised." It is likely that Ethan's mother was steadfast in her conviction that premarital sex was evil, as was homosexual activity. I could imagine her confrontation with the possibility that both her sons were at risk for eternal damnation for their sexual behavior. It was not simply a matter of "what would the neighbors say?" but how God Almighty would deal with the sinner. I reinforced Ethan's direction in our work together, but was fully cognizant that in the eyes of a considerable percentage of the U.S. population, both of us would suffer dire consequences as a result.

I recognized the possibility of countertransference in this case, in which I could have projected unresolved issues of my own onto Ethan's process. It was easy for me to identify with Ethan and his struggles as they paralleled both personal and professional conflicts that I have encountered. My recognition of this similarity, and my determination to allow it to facilitate rather than to aggravate Ethan's growth (as would have been the case in countertransference) was an unanticipated outcome of this counseling process.

For example, Ethan's interest in the Peace Corps occupied a considerable amount of our time in the latter stages of our work together. Shortly after my graduation from Northwestern University, I was invited to apply for a position with the newly formed Peace Corps as a counseling psychologist, working with Peace Corps members who encountered culture shock and other sequelae of finding themselves in radically different environments. I bypassed the invitation because it would have meant leaving my graduate students at Kent State University before the semester had ended but have often regretted my decision. To hear of Ethan's curiosity about the Peace Corps and what it would entail might have given me a chance to gratify my own needs through his activities.

Was Ethan's journey to Southeast Asia a case of the Bouncing Ball escaping the family and church issues that had so dramatically surfaced during our time together? Or would this endeavor be an opportunity for the Red Hammer to nurture and to build anew? I was convinced that Ethan's decision was a life-affirming one and subsequent events confirmed this conviction. As a result, my own self-assurance as a therapist was bolstered.

Another change that transpired during the course of this treatment was my surprising ability to broaden and deepen treatment. I sensed that Ethan had sought my counsel because of a malaise of which he was only dimly aware. However, the evoked symbols and metaphors (e.g., the snake mother, the Bouncing Ball, the Little Torturer, the Red Hammer) were pertinent to Ethan's existential life issues. Could they have been as easily elicited had he simply relaxed, breathed deeply, and closed his eyes? Perhaps. But it is my feeling that working in the context of what Ethan considered to be hypnosis brought a conviction and an authority to the material that would have been otherwise absent. Furthermore, Ethan was a client who had been taught to distrust bodily feelings. Hypnosis gave Ethan tacit permission to get in touch with anger, fear, and pleasure, and to accept and own these feelings. It also initiated a course of self-regulation that led to a disciplined meditative practice, the use of autosuggestion, and the control of his premature ejaculation. These concepts originally were foreign to Ethan—but hypnosis was not. By starting with the known, we proceeded to learn about and to master the unknown.

However, my own mythic conflict reached syntheses. I realized that a therapist could continue using whatever skills and orientation he or she had previously assimilated, as long as they were utilized with humility, propriety, and respect for the client's individual nature. Having a full-time, and fulfilling, position at Saybrook Graduate School, I gracefully left clinical work to teach, hoping to give something to the next generation. It has been gratifying to teach hypnosis to my students, who, in increasing numbers, are using hypnosis.

In the meantime, it has become increasingly apparent to me that hypnosis in its various forms is a valuable modality in psychotherapy. But much of its effectiveness is due to client expectation and the mystique that, for better or for worse, has surrounded the practice. The social construction of hypnosis in the Western world has played an important part in the alleviation of human suffering. Demand characteristics and role-playing are important components of this success. But without the expectation that hypnosis would help him, without the ability to play the role of a successful hypnotic subject, and without the motivation that adhered to the tasks given him, it is unlikely that Ethan would have revised his personal mythology to the point that he could "take pleasure in my power ... a power that nurtures and builds." The same could be said for hypnosis itself.

REFERENCES

Anderson, W. P. (1990). *Reality isn't what it used to be.* San Francisco: Harper.
DeBerry, S. T. (1993). *Quantum psychology: Steps to a postmodern ecology of being.* Westport, CT: Praeger.
Feinstein, D., & Krippner, S. (1988). *Personal mythology.* Los Angeles: Jeremy P. Tarcher.
Feinstein, D., & Krippner, S. (1997). *The mythic path.* New York: Penguin/Jeremy Tarcher.

13

Changing the Use of Hypnosis in My Practice

Albert Ellis

I started using hypnosis in 1949 when I was supervised at the N.J. State Diagnostic Center in Menlo Park by a psychiatrist, Dr. Ralph Brancale. I found it useful in some instances, especially to reveal my clients' thoughts and feelings that they did not easily disclose. I got my Boards in Clinical Hypnosis in the 1950s and kept using hypnosis from time to time when I originated and started using Rational Emotive Behavior Therapy (REBT) in 1955 (Ellis, 1962, 1994, 1995). At first, I mainly used authoritarian-oriented hypnosis.

Various other therapists have also combined REBT with hypnosis, and have presented studies showing that it can be useful. Donald Tosi and his students (Tosi & Murphy, 1995) have published a number of these studies. Stanton (1989) also published two studies showing the successful use of REBT with hypnosis. Several clinical cases back up these studies (Araoz, 1982; Ellis, 1986; Golden, Dowd, & Friedberg, 1987; Hoellen, 1988).

Despite these reported successes of using REBT in conjunction with hypnosis, I first used this combination only occasionally because it seems to have distinct disadvantages as well as advantages (Ellis, 1986, 1993). Some of its advantages are: (a) As indicated in the case presented later, I usually conduct REBT hypnotherapy by recording the hypnosis session and having the clients listen to this recording 20 or 30 times. As they do so, they hear the REBT messages on the tape continuously and feel increasingly urged to do REBT

165

homework. They therefore are likely to respond to the rational self-statements that are on the tape and to keep doing their REBT homework; (b) each hypnotic taped session usually includes working with one or two of the client's main problems and helps the client concentrate on solving this neurotic problem before going on to other issues; (c) the general philosophy of REBT that people largely upset themselves and can therefore choose to unupset themselves is repetitively shown to clients, so that they can adopt it and keep experimenting with applying it; and (d) REBT hypnotherapy is rarely used by itself but is combined with regular REBT nonhypnotic individual or group therapy so that clients are fully encouraged to think for themselves as well as to follow the suggestions of the hypnotist.

On the other hand there are some disadvantages of using hypnosis along with REBT, including these: (a) REBT holds that people preferably should think for themselves and not unthinkingly adopt the suggestions of a hypnotist (or of anyone else). Suggestion is a low-level form of thinking and not high-level falsification practiced by good scientists. Old-fashioned authoritarian-oriented hypnosis, which I used in the 1950s, includes too much suggestion and therefore conflicts somewhat with the REBT emphasis on self-directed thinking; (b) REBT holds that people had better be fully conscious of their dysfunctional beliefs and not merely cover them up with more productive rational beliefs that they tend to parrot as in Emile Coué's (1923) and Norman Vincent Peale's (1952) positive thinking but not really firmly hold and follow; (c) clients often want to be hypnotized because, having low-frustration tolerance, they view hypnotism as an easy and magical way of changing themselves. However, REBT emphasizes that people almost always have to work hard and consistently practice new ways of thinking, feeling, and behaving, until after some time they semiautomatically begin to become self-conditioned to them; and (d) REBT aims to show clients how to be on their own and independently construct self-helping methods for the rest of their lives. When I first used hypnosis I sometimes did it too much in an authoritative manner and found this to be inconsistent with REBT. Today, hypnosis is used much more permissively and counteracts clients' tendencies to use it by rote and to let the hypnotist do all the work.

For several years I rarely used hypnosis with REBT because some of my clients relied too much on me rather than on their own constructive abilities and because it often took me several sessions to put my clients in a fairly deep trance state. In that period of time I could teach them regular REBT and frequently show them how to use it successfully with themselves. So why bother to add hypnosis to its methods, which include a number of cognitive, emotive, and behavioral techniques?

I got a different slant on using REBT along with hypnosis when, in the late 1970s, I worked with Susan, a 40-year-old teacher who had been severely depressed since childhood, who had obsessive-compulsive attachments to several "wrong" men, and who had made little progress during 12 years of psychoanalytic and interpersonal therapy. When I saw her, she was still obsessed with a 27-year-old male, Steven, a "loser" and an alcoholic, who had lived with her for 2 years and then cruelly broke off their relationship 10 months before I saw her.

Susan was impressed with REBT because she had read my book with Robert A. Harper, *A New Guide to Rational Living* (Ellis & Harper, 1975), and for the first time in her life started to unconditionally accept herself despite her foolish obsessive-compulsive behavior. During our first five sessions, Susan worked hard at finding and disputing her main irrational beliefs, especially: (a) "I *absolutely must* be loved by a bright and attractive man, or else I am worthless!"; (b) "If I treat my lover well and he treats me badly, as he *absolutely must* not do, he is a rotten person! But I am also no good for staying with a rotten person like him!"; and (c) "Conditions in New York are so bad that a really good partner is almost impossible to find. Such atrocious conditions *absolutely must not* exist and I *can't stand it* when they do!"

By actively disputing these irrational, self-defeating beliefs, Susan made some progress and felt less self-damning, less enraged, and less self-pitying. But even by using a number of REBT's cognitive, emotive, and behavioral methods, she only mildly accepted herself, her delinquent lovers, and the world. She still more strongly felt that all three of these people and things definitely had to be better than they were.

Using some of REBT's forceful emotive methods helped Susan most of all. For example, she used Rational Emotive Imagery to vividly imagine being rejected and alone, to let herself get solidly in touch with her unhealthy feelings of severe depression, and to work at changing them to the healthy negative feelings of keen disappointment and sorrow. She very strongly kept repeating rational coping statements to herself, such as, "I can stop thinking about Steven! There is no reason why I must obsess about him and avoid getting involved with someone else!" She role-played with me, so that I took some of her irrational ideas, deliberately held on to them very strongly and rigidly, and gave her practice in forcefully arguing me out of them.

All this worked lightly. For a week or two, Susan felt much better, less depressed and less obsessed with thoughts about Steven. Then her obsession would return. She would blame herself for not being more patient with him and for not leaving him sooner. She would tell herself, "I knew he was an alcoholic and never should have lived with him." But then again: "I should have insisted he go to AA meetings and even should have gone with him for at least 90 days." She would blame, blame, blame herself, and then return to her obsessing. Temporarily, her strong and persistent REBT methods would work. But then she would convince herself that she absolutely should have got Steven to use them too, that she hadn't done that, and that she was therefore a weak, stupid person—no go—her use of REBT then fell off.

During my ninth session with Susan, I suddenly realized that I was not following REBT too closely myself but was down-playing one of its main aspects. REBT holds that people like Susan keep insisting not merely strongly wishing that they, others, and world conditions must improve, that it is awful when they do not, and that they and their intimates are therefore no damned good. A great many studies have now shown that disturbed people actually do have several irrational, imperative beliefs and that when they are helped by REBT and by other forms of Cognitive Behavior Therapy (CBT) they often significantly improve (Hajzler & Bernard, 1991; Hollon & Beck, 1994; Lyons & Woods, 1991; McGovern & Silverman, 1984; Silverman, McCarthy, & McGovern, 1992).

But REBT holds that many disturbed people, such as Susan, also have irrational demands about their agitation . They insist, "I must not be disturbed! It's awful to be neurotic! I'm no good for upsetting myself!" Then they make themselves depressed about their depression, obsessed about their obsessions. They thus create a secondary disturbance that is even worse then their primary disturbance and, moreover, that often preoccupies them so much that it effectively stops them from dealing with and eliminating their primary symptoms.

In Susan's case, she clearly blamed herself for her primary behavior her getting attached to wrong men, her being impatient with them, her not insisting that they take care of their serious problems, and so forth. So I rightly figured out with her that her main symptom was self-denigration and that, presumably, if she stopped seriously putting herself down she would distinctly improve. She agreed with this, and we kept working with REBT to help her overcome her abysmal self-downing.

During her ninth session, Susan indicated that she was most upset because she was not using REBT well enough to stave off and continue to overcome her self-flagellation. She still hated herself for her "stupid" behavior with Steven, but she seemed more concerned with her "idiotic" failure to use REBT, "which is such a fine form of therapy," to overcome her original "stupidity."

I then saw that Susan really had two main secondary symptoms: She severely put herself down for being depressed and obsessed about her attachment to Steven as well as for acting weakly with him; and she clearly berated herself for not using REBT effectively. Led by Susan herself, and by her insistence that she now was more upset about her symptoms and about not overcoming them than she was about her original weaknesses with Steven, I planned with her an attack on her secondary symptoms, and then we agreed we would also get back to her original problems of acting too weakly with Steven.

At this same session, Susan indicated that she had taken a teaching job in Europe and would only be available for a few more sessions in New York.

Could we therefore do something to help her work better on her problems before she left? I at first thought of continuing our sessions on the phone, which I do in quite a number of cases and which I find usually works very well. But the phone rates to Europe, especially in those days, would have been very expensive. So I thought about recording some sessions with Susan, which I also encourage many of my clients to do, and giving her the recordings to take with her when she went abroad.

Susan then suggested that perhaps we could speed up things by using hypnosis. So I immediately agreed that, yes, we might try that, and might combine REBT with hypnosis and also with recording.

We quickly arranged to do this. I had Susan bring in a cassette tape, and we recorded three hypnotic sessions. During each of these sessions I put her in a light state of trance, using Edmund Jacobson's (1938) progressive relaxation technique for 15 minutes. While she was in trance, I told her that posthypnotically she would use REBT in three main ways: First, she would clearly see that she was telling herself, "I absolutely must work harder with REBT to overcome my depression and my obsession for Steven! If I don't succeed, as I absolutely must, I am an ineffective, inadequate person!" Second, Susan was to get in touch with her depression about being depressed and obsessed, and would see that she was telling herself, "I must not be obsessed! I must not be depressed! It's awful to be afflicted in these ways! I'm a stupid person for indulging in my depression and obsession!" Third, she was to get back to her original symptoms, and see that she was strongly convincing herself, "I must succeed in getting Steven to really love me! I can't bear losing him! I need him and must not do anything to turn him off!"

As she saw her irrational musts, demands, and insistences about ineffectually using REBT, about making herself depressed and obsessed, and about needing Steven and not succeeding in getting him to truly love her, Susan was to do what I firmly told her to do during the hypnotic sessions: strongly dispute and challenge her irrational beliefs; act against them by forcing herself to cut off all contact with Steven; and use several other regular REBT cognitive, emotive, and behavioral methods to give up her depression and obsession and stop deprecating herself for being disturbed and for not using REBT methods effectively enough.

My three hypnotic sessions worked very well with Susan because she listened to the tape recordings of the sessions at least once a day for the next few weeks that she was in New York. She found that she kept going deeper and deeper into a trance state as she listened to the tapes, and she reported that the posthypnotic instructions to dispute her irrational beliefs and use other REBT methods became easier to carry out. Some of her original resistance to doing this vanished, and she was able to use disputational methods more forcefully and effectively. She continued to use the three tapes that we made when she was teaching in Europe and wrote me to say that they kept working. At first she used them every day, but after a few months she did so only occasionally. She also discovered that the first of the hypnotic recorded sessions was sufficient in itself and that the subsequent ones were repetitious and unnecessary.

During the time I was working with Susan, I also used REBT to thoroughly overcome my own guilt about not more quickly seeing that her main problem was not only building a good relationship with Steven and castigating herself severely when she did not achieve it. In addition to this, and often more importantly, her secondary symptoms of severely blaming herself for making herself disturbed and for not using REBT effectively to overcome her disturbances created more emotional havoc for her. I honestly admitted to myself as well as to Susan that I had not used REBT with her as carefully and thoroughly as I could have used it. But I worked on only criticizing my careless behavior, and not my self or personhood for doing this behavior. So I remained healthily sorry and disappointed with my performance but not damning of my self or being.

As a result of working with Susan, of inventing my new technique of using hypnosis with some of my more difficult clients, and of giving them the tapes of only one or two recorded sessions, I have continued to use this method over the years. I usually first have several sessions of regular REBT with my clients and work on both their primary and secondary problems during these sessions to show them how to use several cognitive, emotive, and behavioral REBT methods. Usually, this suffices and they get going on their way to significant improvement. When unusual resistance occurs, and especially when they are quite willing to undergo hypnosis, I use the method just described, and often find that it works well to overcome their resistances, to help them use REBT disputing irrational beliefs and other methods more forcefully, and to persist at therapy largely on their own by listening repetitively to the tape or tapes that I have made for them.

What were my important feelings as this case progressed? They covered quite a range. First, I liked working with Susan from the beginning because she favored REBT, knew something about it from reading my book, and made some real progress during the first few weeks of therapy. I concluded that she was not a difficult customer and was optimistic about her improving in spite of her long history of depression and obsessive-compulsive behaving.

Soon, however, I felt somewhat discouraged because she only cavalierly followed the main REBT procedures, only lightly and temporarily gave up her abysmal self-denigration, and sank back to doing little therapeutic homework. I became almost impatient with her insistence that she really was doing badly with her obsessiveness and therefore could not realistically stop blaming herself for this. I forgave her for having some degree of obsessive-compulsive disorder because even in the 1970s I was beginning to see that it included some biological tendencies. But I insisted that even if she were responsible for some of her stupid behaviors, she never had to damn herself for any failings and could still give herself unconditional self-acceptance. I felt irritated when I worked so hard to get this philosophy over to her and when she stubbornly refused to buy it. Her insistence that REBT was not working was "catching" and was almost hypnotically convincing me that it might never work for her.

During our ninth session, when I began to clearly see that Susan was excoriating herself more for her depression and other symptoms and for not surrendering them than she was for her weak and foolish behavior with Steven and other men, I came close to feeling quite upset. I felt disappointed and guilty about my partial misdiagnosis of Susan's main problems and had to strongly use REBT disputing on myself. As noted earlier, I finally convinced myself that I was okay, although some of my therapy was not. REBT really worked for me.

When Susan and I, spurred by her approaching venture to Europe, decided to try some hypnotic sessions, I was happy that I was sufficiently trained and practiced in hypnotic methods to experiment with them. I also was very curious to see if my use of recording our hypnotic sessions would really work out. So I welcomed this experiment. I also was happy when I learned from Susan that the recorded hypnotic sessions were quite effective and that only three of them seemed to suffice to produce good results.

Over all, I had my own ups and downs in the course of this case, but I was grateful that I learned a lot from it and obtained some evidence that hypnosis can be combined effectively with REBT, especially in some cases where clients at first fail to successfully use regular REBT methods. The additional forceful and highly emotive quality that recorded hypnosis adds to therapy has some real advantages. In Susan's case, her being able to take me with her on tape, and feel that I was still on her side, may have possibly helped her do the work that I was trying to encourage her to do. Hypnosis has a relationship and an emotional quality that can serve as one of the emotive-evocative techniques that are commonly used in REBT and that makes it a multimodal form of therapy.

REFERENCES

Araoz, D. L. (1982). *Hypnosis and sex therapy.* New York: Brunner/Mazel.

Coué, E. (1923). *My method.* New York: Doubleday, Page.

Ellis, A. (1962). *Reason and emotion in psychotherapy.* Secaucus, NJ: Citadel.

Ellis, A. (1986). Anxiety about anxiety: The use of hypnosis with rational-emotive therapy. In E. T. Dowd & J. M. Healy (Eds.), *Case studies in hypnotherapy* (pp. 3–11). New York: Guilford. (Reprinted in *The practice of rational-emotive therapy* (pp. 231–237), by A. Ellis & W. Dryden, 1997, New York: Springer.

Ellis, A. (1994). *Reason and emotion in psychotherapy* (Rev. ed.). New York: Birch Lane Press.

Ellis, A. (1995). *Better, deeper and more enduring brief therapy.* New York: Brunner/Mazel.

Ellis, A., & Harper, R. A. (1975). *A new guide to rational living.* North Hollywood, CA: Wilshire Books.

Golden, W. L., Dowd, E. T., & Friedberg, F. (1987). *Hypnotherapy: A modern approach.* New York: Pergamon.

Hajzler, D., & Bernard, M. E. (1991). A review of rational-emotive outcome studies. *School Psychology Quarterly, 6*(1), 27–49.

Hoellen, B. (1988). Hypnosisverfahren im Rahmen der RET. In J. Laux & H. J. Schubert (Eds.), *Klinische Hypnose* (pp. 73–80). Pfaffenweiller, Germany: Centaurus-Verlag.

Hollon, S. D., & Beck, A. T. (1994). Cognitive and cognitive-behavioral therapies. In A. E. Bergin & S. L. Garfield (Eds.), *Handbook of psychotherapy and behavior change* (pp. 428–466). New York: Wiley.

Jacobson, E. (1938). *You must relax.* New York: McGraw-Hill.

Lyons, L. C., & Woods, P. J. (1991). The efficacy of rational-emotive therapy: A quantitative review of the outcome research. *Clinical Psychology Review, 11*, 357–369.

McGovern, T. E., & Silverman, M. S. (1984). A review of outcome studies of rational-emotive therapy from 1977 to 1982. *Journal of Rational-Emotive Therapy, 2*(1), 7–18.

Peale, N. V. (1952). *The power of positive thinking.* New York: Fawcett.

Silverman, M. S., McCarthy, M., & McGovern, T. (1992). A review of outcome studies of rational-emotive therapy from 1982 to 1989. *Journal of Rational-Emotive and Cognitive-Behavior Therapy, 10*(3), 111–186.

Stanton, H. E. (1989). Hypnosis and rational-emotive therapy—A de-stressing combination. *International Journal of Clinical and Experimental Hypnosis, 37*, 95–99.

Tosi, D. J., & Murphy, M. A. (1995). *The effect of cognitive experiential therapy on selected psychobiological and behavioral disorders.* Columbus, OH: Authors.

V

CHANGES IN TOLERANCE FOR UNCERTAINTY

14

Countertransference and the Torture Survivor

John R. Van Eenwyk

Countertransference is a concept difficult to define, yet we generally recognize it when we see it. Experience gives us the best definition. Imagine, for example, how it might feel to dial a patient's telephone number to ask for the loan of his private jet to fly to another country to make a clandestine rescue of the daughter of another of your patients. Would you stop to question yourself? Would you examine your motives?

As countertransference varies from patient to patient, let me share with you my own voyage of discovery during my work with a young couple who were referred to me several years ago. We all lived in Chicago then, although they were illegal immigrants who had fled their native land. My experience with them became so intense that only 6 months later I was on the verge of making the aforementioned telephone call. What could possibly have transpired in the meantime that had led to such an unacceptable boundary violation? Humanitarian motives? Sheer foolishness? Countertransference? I was rapidly discovering how easily the first two can become part of the last.

OVERVIEW

Those of us who volunteered our services at the Marjorie Kovler Center for the Treatment of Survivors of Torture (Chicago) rarely knew what to expect when a call came in asking if we could take a referral. In this case, a fortuitous impediment—that neither the couple nor I spoke each other's languages—led me to a translator who proved to be much more than that. Dr. Marianna Capriles-Viney was a Venezuelan-born and trained psychiatrist who was fluent in Spanish. Her intelligence, openness, and humanity led me to trust her immediately. We quickly became cotherapists who could depend on one another as we negotiated the utterly demonic labyrinth of psychological sequelae left behind by the torturers.

When we met, Marianna and I shared information about our backgrounds, motivations for working with torture survivors, and hopes for the process. It seemed a good fit. On our arrival at the Kovler Center, Roberto and Maria were waiting for us. He was bright and accommodating, she was sullen and distant. Roberto jumped right into the work—did all the talking, in fact—while Maria sat with her head against the wall, eyes closed, looking miserable.

Roberto had left his home country about a year ago after government agents put a price on his head. As the owner of a small business with four employees, he had joined with many others to protest the deterioration of the political and economic climate after the takeover of the government several years earlier by a military dictatorship. Soon, however, at the urging of his mother, Roberto cut back on his attendance at demonstrations for fear that he would be eliminated by one of the many death squads roaming the land. It was not an idle concern: 10 years earlier, a death squad had killed his father.

Unfortunately, he had already been noticed. At first, he was regularly beaten and robbed. Then, when his home and family were placed under constant surveillance, he moved his family to another part of town and slept in his small shop. One night his shop was sprayed with machine-gun fire. After repeated attacks, he was in such bad health that he had to sell his business. Soon after, he was jailed without charges, tortured, fined, and released. Friends began to disappear or to be shot in the streets. The government was closing in.

He felt that his only option was to leave the country. With his family in hiding, perhaps he could throw the government off their trail by disappearing. However, after he left, they found where his wife and children were hiding. They came to the house at night and did something—something terrible—but Roberto never found out exactly what it was. Maria had never told him, and from her fragile emotional state he knew not to ask. Since then an awkward silence hovered between them.

As Roberto told his tale he became increasingly depressed. Maria sat and cried softly. Marianna and I felt the weight of their oppression, for undoing the damage of torture is an immensely daunting task. First, security has been totally destroyed by the torturer, the memory of whom lives on in the psyche of the survivor. Second, because there are so many survivors that the quotas established by Congress can accommodate only a small fraction, most are illegal immigrants. As a result, the few services available depend on the limited means of small private charities. Finally, training in how to treat torture survivors was virtually nonexistent. Marianna and I, as well as our colleagues at the Kovler Center, were literally writing the books. We pondered our next step.

Roberto had told his story. What was Maria's version? She confirmed all that Roberto had said, adding only that she had followed him 2 weeks after he left, when government agents had attacked them in their home late at night. After arriving in the United States, a Canadian relief agency managed to find Roberto in an American detention center, and reunited them. Eventually, the relief agency moved them and the children to Chicago, where they were now living in hiding.

As usual, Marianna and I asked nothing about where they were living or details of their lives at the moment, for security is a central concern in treating torture survivors. Most Americans would be astonished to know how many agents from oppressive regimes regularly search the United States for refugees from their home countries. For instance, foreign visitors to the Kovler Center routinely ask suspiciously specific questions about the people we are treating. We learn quickly to cover everything we do with a cloak of secrecy. Sometimes, we become infected by the atmosphere of terror, which produces some very interesting parallel process issues in supervision. Then the supervisor must treat the practitioner as the practitioner is trying to treat the survivor, for example, calming fears of surveillance by foreign or domestic agents (wiretaps, stakeouts, interdiction of mail, etc.).

As Maria completed her story, she began to weep in earnest, for she had been unable to bring her oldest daughter with her. She knew that if her country's government should manage to locate her, they would never see her again. She would become yet another desaparecido. Every time she even thought of her daughter, she was plagued by splitting headaches and abdominal pain. With a weary look she then asked Marianna and me if there was anything we could do to reunite her daughter with the family? Our hearts sank.

TREATMENT COMPLICATIONS

So, there it was. No therapy with Roberto and Maria could possibly succeed without the return of their daughter. Even worse, they seemed to believe that we could do it, as if we were magicians who could accomplish the impossible. Such are the transference relationships between torture survivors and their therapists. Often they see us as their only hope of undoing the damage that has ravaged their lives. Certainly, living in the United States and being doctors must give us tremendous clout. Wouldn't the government have to do what we said? It is as if they thought we could write a prescription that would bring their daughter home. Wasn't it reasonable to assume that doctors can solve most problems simply by calling the immigration authorities?

Inclinations to identify with such projections are short-lived, for treatment is a long and frustrating process. Marianna and I looked at each other warily. Clearly Roberto and Maria were placing their most fragile hopes in our hands. They wanted their daughter with them. So did we. But we had been down this road before and knew it was unlikely to happen. Nevertheless, in order to retain their trust, we had to do something for them right away. Before this first session was over, we had to give them something to hope for, something to work on, something other than anxiety and despair to engage their energies. But what?

We noticed that they seemed to avoid each other. Either Roberto would speak, or Maria would speak, but they rarely spoke to each other. If Maria had never shared with Roberto all that had happened that night, would she ever share it with us? We decided to take a chance. If we could put things in a context that might bridge the gulf between them, maybe they could work together and with us. We said:

> It is like the oppressors came into your lives and dropped a small, foul-smelling box in your midst. They hope you'll never open it. They would prefer that you organize your lives around avoiding its smell. Now that you are here, let's try to open the box. Whatever it is that has come between you, no matter how unpleasant, we must open it up and look at it. Only then can we clean it up and remove its stench from your relationship.

As Marianna translated the words, light began to dawn in their eyes. It seemed to make sense. Yet our goal of creating a therapeutic alliance among the four of us was a double-edged sword, for we were allying ourselves together against the oppressors. How far would this go? Would we begin to identify with their projections of power? We were soon to find out.

In the second session we decided to address their physical symptoms. At first we encouraged them to massage each other gently. But it soon became obvious that neither was in any shape to do so. Both were hypervigilant: In their heightened state of agitation, they could hardly relax and trust each other. Clearly, we had to demonstrate it for them.

I asked if they had ever experienced hypnosis. They said no. I explained that hypnosis is a self-induced state of relaxation that allows us to focus on things undistracted by extraneous influences. They said they would try it. I assured them that I was simply supplying procedures and ideas to facilitate their own relaxation strategies. If they preferred, they could keep their eyes open as we proceeded. Neither Marianna nor I wanted them to experience the fear of not knowing what is going on that characterizes survivors' encounters with torturers.

Although Marianna and I had not been pursued by the death squads, we began to feel what it must be like to be so pursued. As we encountered the remnants of the influence of the oppressors in our patients, and as we joined with them in neutralizing that influence, we were in a very real—if only psychological—way experiencing the oppressors ourselves. The seeds had been planted for us to become surprisingly active in fighting the only external activity of the oppressor that continued in the present: the pursuit of Roberto's and Maria's daughter.

But for the time being, we concentrated only on relief from symptoms. At the beginning of our third session, Maria was absolutely transformed. She had painted her nails, was wearing her hair loose and flowing, and was all smiles. She said that the hypnosis had helped a great deal, that she was virtually free from pain. Even better, she said, she and Roberto were beginning to touch each other again, and neither was feeling troubled by it.

We had seen this before. It is not at all unusual for the typical patient—let alone a torture survivor—to have a great investment in the power of the therapist. Whether or not the salutary effects continue is for time to tell, but in the meantime they provided a means to deepen our work. Marianna suggested that as Maria was feeling so much better, perhaps she could begin to describe in more detail what she remembered of the night of the attack. With great anxiety, but bolstered by determination, she completed the story.

The night after Roberto left, three men had broken down the door, tied up the children, and put them in the kitchen. After heating oil on the stove, they poured it on her as they grilled her for information as to Roberto's whereabouts. She refused to cooperate and eventually passed out from the pain. When she came to, her abdomen was badly burned, and she could hardly walk because the pain in her groin was so bad. The next day one of the men accosted her on the street and threatened to come back for the children. Knowing their lives were in danger, she fled the country with three of her four children. Because the oldest had been with Maria's mother that night, she had not been seen by the attackers. Because she was a teenager, she was in danger of being kidnapped and sold into prostitution during the long and hazardous journey to the United States; Maria's mother persuaded her to leave the child behind with her.

At this point Roberto became very agitated and said it was his duty as a father to risk all to return to retrieve his daughter. Knowing that this was not a wise course of action, we counseled him against doing what his instincts urged him to do. But what could we offer in return? The Center has lawyers who volunteer their time, one of whom was working on legalizing the family's presence in the United States. Another group was quietly looking into hiring someone in the underground to clandestinely spirit their daughter out of the country. Unfortunately, all of these courses of action take time. Meanwhile, a life was in danger.

As I began to feel a strong and compelling wish to rescue her—and them—from any more torture, I realized that my countertransference was growing more powerful. What's more, I had just returned from visiting my daughter, who had left home 6 months earlier to attend boarding school. I missed her very much and took it very hard when I could not be with her to help her with life's difficulties. Like Roberto, I wanted to be at his daughter's side.

All three of these elements—missing my daughter, feeling that for the safety of the family we had to come up with something, and sharing a strong bond with Roberto and Maria through sharing in the therapeutic alliance—led me away from my strict psychoanalytic maintenance of the frame. Nevertheless, even as strict an adherent of frame maintenance as Langs (1976) wrote that "it remains an important clinical principle that before we can deal with the patient's internal dangers, and the anxieties derived from her intrapsychic conflicts and her pathological instinctual drives, we must deal with and resolve the external dangers and real fears with which she is confronted" (p. 369). Essentially, our dilemma came down to this: Is it possible to deal with the internal remnants of the torturers' activity without addressing the external continuation of that torture?

I began to feel like I was losing my grip on the principles by which I conduct therapy. On the other hand, a life was at stake. Could I possibly place principles above a life? As the weeks went by, during which we spent a great deal of time on symptom relief and interpersonal relationships with their family and with the others in their place of hiding, Marianna and I agonized over the slow pace of efforts to retrieve Roberto and Maria's daughter. Then, after about 4 months, they learned that a stranger had accosted their daughter and her cousin on the street. Their daughter escaped, but her cousin had been detained. He had not been seen since.

Soon after, despairing of her father ever coming to rescue her, their daughter left for a neighboring country with two of her friends. The police intercepted her and took her back to her own country, handing her over to the authorities there. She had since been returned to her home.

Marianna and I considered this to be good news, for if the authorities had taken no action, perhaps they were no longer interested in pursuing her. Roberto and Maria were beside themselves with despair, however, for they had seen this pattern before. Initially the authorities would behave according to the law. Several weeks later, however, unknown assailants would come in the night and take the child away. Children taken this way are rarely seen again. Roberto was adamant. He was leaving whether we approved or not. I begged him for more time. I began to share my fantasies of how we might retrieve her on our own. If he had waited this long, a week longer could not hurt.

It was the next day that I suddenly became aware that I was dialing the number of one of my analytic patients. He was about my age and had been in analysis for 3 years. Very adventuresome, he was an aficionado of the *Indiana Jones* movies. This was exactly the kind of action he would love. And he owned a jet. Why not ask him for help?

It suddenly occurred to me that even if we could sneak her out of the country, how would we ever get her past Customs and Immigration in the United States? I stopped before dialing the last number. This was a big step. Like Caesar at the Rubicon, if I crossed this boundary I could never return. Maybe I should think about this a bit. Could countertransference be getting the best of me? Well, perhaps. But so what? What could possibly be more important than a life?

In therapy Marianna and I had consistently reminded Roberto and Maria not to act when swamped by their emotions, for emotions can lead to impulsive acts. They were under strict orders not to do anything about their daughter without discussing it in therapy first. Clearly, I was in need of my own advice. It was time to consult my colleagues.

Usually such consultations help us to recognize our feelings and give us some gentle advice to think about, but do not do much to solve the problem. That task is generally acknowledged to be ours alone. However, this time was different. When I confided in my colleague about my dilemma, he reminded me that I had performed many tasks pro bono for a very important person (VIP) in Chicago. Why didn't I contact him? Perhaps he could help.

The VIP was more than helpful. He knew someone who might be able to facilitate the whole process. A dinner party was arranged, the man was invited, the favor was asked. He agreed to do what he could, but was not terribly reassuring.

In the meantime, my wife and I had made plans to move to Washington State, where she had been offered a new job and career promotion. I had to reveal this to Roberto and Maria, as well as to all the patients in my private practice. Thus began several weeks of heartbreaking experiences. Roberto and Maria were particularly upset, but the continuing presence of Dr. Capriles-Viney promised to make the transition more palatable. Besides, there was now more hope than before for the recovery of their daughter.

In fact, after the move, things began to progress remarkably well. Legal channels opened, paperwork was expedited, and very shortly a visa arrived for their daughter, Joanne, to come to the United States. All that remained was for arrangements to be made to find her and bring her here. A few weeks later, a Kovler volunteer, who was fluent in Spanish and known for her chutzpah, left to pick up Joanne. Joanne made her way to the American embassy, from which the volunteer took her to the airport. The authorities tried to interfere—as expected—but the volunteer prevailed. She simply stood her ground and refused to be cowed. Just as the last call for boarding was announced, they were reluctantly allowed to leave. Moments later, they were in the air. A long and awful ordeal was drawing to a close.

Several months later a call came through on my answering service. A party was planned for Joanne's 16th birthday. Could I possibly attend? My wife encouraged me to spend the money and go. I could hardly wait. Once again, my countertransference came alive.

Or did it? True enough, my contacting people in Chicago to intervene on Joanne's behalf stretched the bounds of analysis further than ever before. But does working with torture survivors qualify as analysis? Or would it be more accurate to consider it a form of psychotherapy? Even so, I maintain the same boundaries for psychotherapy as for analysis. Maybe psychotherapy with torture survivors is unique, requiring its own perspective on boundary issues. Important as these questions are, they brought me back to the question of countertransference.

Again I sought counsel, this time in C. G. Jung's (1946) writings. In Volume XVI, I read: "The doctor, by voluntarily and consciously taking over the psychic sufferings of the patient, exposes himself to the overpowering contents of the unconscious and hence also to their inductive action. The case begins to 'fascinate' him." The effect, Jung said, is that "doctor and patient thus find themselves in a relationship founded on mutual unconsciousness." Furthermore, "The greatest difficulty here is that contents are often activated in the doctor which normally might remain latent" (Jung, p. 176).

That certainly sounded accurate. However, Jung continued:

the psychotherapist in particular should clearly understand that psychic infections, however superfluous they seem to him, are in fact the predestined concomitants of his work, and thus fully in accord with the instinctive disposition of his own life. This realization also gives him the right attitude to his patient. The patient then means something to him personally, and this provides the most favorable basis for treatment." (p. 176)

These were the words I needed to hear.

Torture survivors comprise a unique client population. Their premorbid functioning is generally good. Whatever psychological symptoms they display are a direct result of the torture experience. Threatening a family member is one form of torture. Consequently, if the families of torture survivors continue to be threatened, the torture itself continues. It is absurd to presume to treat the sequelae of torture when the torture is not yet over. Thus, Roberto and Maria's treatment could not proceed without directly addressing the threat to their daughter.

As I began to ponder Jung's words, however, I realized that he was addressing not only psychotherapy, but psychoanalysis as well. No matter what the therapeutic milieu, psychic infection is inevitable. One can try to eradicate it, which, according to Jung, is impossible, for psychic contents never disappear; they simply take forms that are invisible to us. One can learn to work with it. Thus began a crucial change in the way I do analysis.

Today I find myself much more involved emotionally with my patients. I still maintain a tight frame: eschewing contact outside the hour, searching for commentaries in patients' responses to interventions, and avoiding physical contact. But I feel more present in the therapeutic alliance. I feel more alert, more involved, more human.

Life is an ongoing process of learning and transcending the lesson. In his introduction to *Family Therapeutic Techniques,* Sal Minuchin (Minuchin & Fishman, 1981) may have said it best: "Training in family therapy should therefore be a way of teaching techniques whose essence is to be mastered, then forgotten. After this book is read, it should be given away, or put in a forgotten corner.... The goal, in other words, is to transcend technique" (p. 1). And yet, much as each of us knows how important it is to step into the world on our own, to take our own unique place in a tradition of inquiry, messing around in people's lives can be awesome, intimidating, even frightening. Who could fault us for clinging to the admonitions of those who have gone before us?

As I have reflected on my experiences at the Kovler Center, the Jung Institute, private practice, and writing this chapter, one lesson stands out, to wit: The misgivings I have had about venturing forth into uncharted territory are basically archetypal. That is, they are common to all. Everyone who comes to me for analysis faces the same misgivings. As a result of working with Roberto and Maria, I have come to realize that these misgivings, rather than leading us to be wary of one another, can bring us together.

And so, I have become much less sure of myself in the work I do with others. But I have also become much less uncomfortable with that lack of assurance. What brought Roberto, Maria, Marianna, and me together in a close therapeutic alliance was our vulnerability in the face of inexplicably horrific behavior, that is, torture. The mutuality of that vulnerability gave us a common ground from which to explore that terrain together.

To resonate fully with the turbulence of life is to utilize countertransference to its best advantage. I am not a complete person. I have many unresolved conflicts, both current and left over from the past, with which I continue to struggle. My patients understand this. Their respect for my vulnerability and mine for theirs unites us in a common endeavor that emphasizes cooperation, forbearance, and trust. I look out for them, and they look out for me. Together we venture forth into the unpleasant, the unknown, and the inconceivable.

POSTSCRIPT

I arrived unannounced at the birthday party. I wanted it to be a surprise, so I told only the Kovler volunteer who gave me directions. In a brightly lighted school gym, several young people danced to blaring rock music, while about 30 adults stood to the side.

Suddenly, Maria saw me. Turning toward me, she burst into tears and held out her arms. We embraced. Then Roberto noticed what was going on. He rushed over, grabbed my hand, and as he pumped it vigorously, told me excitedly in English that Joanne was here. "Where?" I asked. "There," they pointed.

Among the group of teenagers was a beautiful young girl swaying softly to the music. Apparently unaware of the gravity of the moment, she was simply dancing with her friends. On her were the eyes of all those who had worked so hard for this moment: her parents, the lawyer who volunteers his services to the Kovler Center, the woman who had gone to retrieve her, a couple who loaned houses to refugees rent-free in return for repairing them, the people who maintained the living facility for refugees in Chicago … and me. Our eyes were brimming with tears of joy, gratitude, and relief. But anyone who observed us closely would have seen a haunting sorrow as well: for those who have yet to be freed, for those who continue to mourn those left behind, for those who never made it, and for those who never will.

REFERENCES

Jung, C. G. (1946). The psychology of the transference. In *Collected Works. Vol. 16*. Princeton, NJ: Princeton University.
Langs, R. (1976). *The bipersonal field*. New York: Aronson.
Minuchin, S., & Fishman, H. C. (1981). *Family therapy techniques*. Cambridge, MA: Harvard University.

15

Living With Uncertainty

Karen Olness

INTRODUCTION

The consultant to families who have children with chronic medical problems has a number of difficulties to face. Anxious, depressed families may have low expectations with respect to any new consultant. Much study and thinking must be done in order to help these children and to help their families. Unfortunately, sometimes this means helping them understand the limitations of some of their children and the limitations of what child health professionals can do. Cultivating a tolerance for uncertainty and helping my younger colleagues to accept this is a must. The tendency of many medical specialists to dismiss symptoms as *psychogenic* when diagnostics are not clear, does more harm than good. Often, the consultant must become an advocate for families who perceive themselves as being misunderstood. Although I followed many children over many years, none involved more of my time, or exemplified the issues listed better than did the complex problems of Denise.

SUMMARY OF CASE HISTORY

Denise was 10 years old when first referred to me to learn self-hypnosis and biofeedback in management of her cyclic vomiting. The cyclic-vomiting episodes began when she was 5 years old. Many times these were precipitated by upper respiratory infections. She had been evaluated at three major medical centers before I saw her. The previous evaluations had included a 6-month stay in a child psychiatric unit when she was 9 years old during which there were no significant changes in symptoms. She was hospitalized for diagnostic tests and rehydration 14 times in a 3-year period at our hospital, and I was involved in her care during 10 of those hospitalizations. I ultimately served as her primary physician as well as her therapist.

Denise was evaluated by specialists from many disciplines over the years. These included gastroenterologists, psychiatrists, metabolic specialists, neurologists, endocrinologists, epidemiologists, and allergists. She saw consultants in Boston and in Chicago and laboratory specimens were sent as far as Norway for special assays. A specialist in geomagnetic fields even did an assessment of possible geomagnetic factors involved in the vomiting episodes. Many of her symptoms suggested neurotransmitter abnormalities probably triggered by mast cell dysfunction. One specialist wrote, "Denise has some kind of dysautonomia." This was typical of the imprecision in proposed diagnoses for Denise. Many consultants suggested various medications to relieve symptoms, but no one was ever able to explain the cause of her debilitating symptoms or to suggest steps to prevent recurrences.

In the meantime, Denise continued to go through recurrent episodes of severe vomiting that would last 2 to 5 days after which she would feel well, happy to be free of the symptoms, and would resume her active life with school and friends. She did well in school, had many friends, and enjoyed extracurricular activities such as soccer. Her family included two older brothers, devoted parents, and grandparents. After hearing about so many possible diagnoses over so many years, the parents were skeptical about specialists, very knowledgeable about whatever was to be known about cyclic vomiting, angry about the frequent suggestions that her symptoms were psychogenic, and, in total, psychologically exhausted.

Although the initial referral to me was for a trial of hypnotherapy and biofeedback, I found myself both stimulated and frustrated by the lack of a specific diagnosis. I, like each of my predecessors, made more diagnostic efforts. Because many children with similar symptoms had been referred to me previously and because we had identified 17 such children as having a rare metabolic disorder that made it difficult for them to handle normal amounts of protein, I believed this was likely to be the cause of Denise's difficulties. When the diagnostic tests for this condition came back as normal, I was surprised but determined to persist in the quest for a biologic explanation. After all, we had been able to find biologic explanations for many children referred to us with peculiar behavioral symptoms. I also referred Denise to a child psychologist who followed her for many months. However, she said that the emotional problems of Denise were less than those of most children who have recurrent, uncomfortable chronic diseases. She pointed out that Denise had many friends, related well within her family, and did well in school despite many absences.

Denise was very willing to learn self-hypnosis. She demonstrated skill in temperature biofeedback, and she enjoyed our practice sessions. However, whenever she was in the throes of a vomiting episode she was unable to use self-hypnosis. She achieved some comfort during the episodes when I would coach her through relaxation but the duration of the episodes did not decrease. As years went by, she demonstrated less and less interest in reviewing her self-hypnosis and biofeedback skills. I found myself perceiving increased personal distress whenever Denise was admitted. She was so sick, so miserable, and her parents were so anxious. Ultimately, because of the frequency of the episodes and the fact that her venous sites had all been used, we placed a heparin lock in one of her veins for easy intravenous access during her admissions.

I also found, as was true with every child I observed with cyclic vomiting, that hospital staff did not like her. When children with this condition are ill, they are often unpleasant, irritable, and complaining. They assume a fetal position and do not want to be disturbed. This was true of Denise as well. Many casual observers of Denise and her parents were convinced that the episodes were psychogenic and all sorts of behavior modification plans were hatched and just as quickly abandoned by members of the nursing staff. I had found similar interventions made by nursing staff members for other children with cyclic vomiting who were later documented to have the rare metabolic disorder involving the inability to assimilate protein easily. Although I was convinced of an as yet unknown biologic explanation in the case of Denise, I could not persuade members of the nursing staff that this was so. We had many care conferences and parents were also invited to these. Now chronically depressed by the frequency of the episodes and the uncertainty about disruption of family life, they usually sat mute in the care conferences. I perceived myself as a buffer between this family and nursing staff, residents, and my colleagues, who disliked having to care for Denise when I was out of town. This was because the parents hovered over her during admissions, asked many questions, and second guessed physicians.

Long ago, I had developed a technique in working with families of chronically ill children that seemed to reduce their anxiety and telephone calls to me. It was to initiate calls to the family regularly. I did my best to call Denise's parents frequently, and they appreciated it. They also became dependent on me. I was aware that I had become enmeshed but kept hoping that a breakthrough would bring psychic relief to everyone involved.

Some years before Denise became my patient, I had initiated a medical education program to train simulator parents who were interviewed by second-year medical students. These interviews were videotaped. Students knew that they might be interviewing a simulator parent or a real parent with a true story. About 2 years after I began seeing Denise, I received a call that one simulator parent had failed to come in. The new group of medical students did not know who I was and the current program director asked me to fill in, suggesting that I simulate Denise's mother for a medical-student interview. After reviewing the video-taped interview with a student, the tutor routinely asked the student his or her opinion about whether the parent figure was a simulator. The student who interviewed me as well as each of the other students who observed the tape were unanimous in concluding that I was a "real" parent. This event really made me aware of how intertwined I had become with Denise. I was concerned about my ability to be objective with respect to Denise's illness.

As time went on a new management problem developed. "Managed Care" hit the area where I practiced, and I soon found myself on the phone several times a week with the medical insurance company paying for Denise's care. They questioned the recurrent hospitalizations for the same problem, questioned the diagnostics, and wanted her cared for at home. I prepared a detailed summary of Denise's case, listing the justifications for each test and treatment. I asked the medical director of the insurance company to review this in detail and told him I would welcome any suggestions that might resolve the recurrent cyclic-vomiting episodes. After several weeks he called and said he had concluded he could add nothing and would approve the accumulated charges.

The frequency of vomiting episodes decreased when Denise was 13 years old. Now there were months instead of weeks between episodes. When I was recruited to another University, I was greatly concerned about how this would impact Denise and her family. Although I informed them about my plans 6 months before my move and recommended they choose another primary physician, they did not do so until the month before I left. I had a farewell party for my patients and their families at the hospital. Denise's parents came but Denise did not; she was in the middle of a vomiting episode. However, I did see her before I left and gave her a tape recording of our last session. The transition to the new primary physician went smoothly. Denise wrote to me and I to her a few times yearly for 2 years and then our communication was limited to holiday greetings.

MY PROFESSIONAL RELATIONSHIPS

The child health professional who works in a hospital setting is rarely the only professional involved in the care of a particular child. A well-known pediatrician, Abe Bergman (1975), from the University of Washington once wrote, "Decisions made in a hospital are made in a collusion of anonymity" (pp. 111). The opinions of colleagues impact decision making for patients even when overt opinions are not sought. In my case, relationships included not only other physicians and nurses but also students who were either assigned to specific rotations with me or were house officers assigned to Denise during her frequent admissions. I noted the reactions of some of my colleagues to Denise and to her family. In fact, after experiencing the looks on their faces or negative comments, I not only felt guilty if I took days off but I feared that Denise would suffer from inadequate attention in my absence. Consultants, on the other hand, were usually enthusiastic and certain they could solve her problems when I made referrals. I would feel a few days or weeks of relative respite as they did more tests. However, as they inevitably withdrew without having provided a diagnosis or treatment, I would sense that they avoided me, feeling guilty because of failure. This phenomenon is one that I believe has not been studied but that affects most health professionals at some time. One specialist, after reading my extensive documentary on Denise, said, "This evokes the response, 'My God.' This requires someone who can devote a lot of time, not me."

The other response that I noted repeatedly from nurses and students was that they projected blame on the parents. I have noted that this phenomenon is less evident in older child health professionals, possibly because they have followed more children over longer time periods or have experienced personally the complexities of parenting. When blame is projected on parents, a vicious circle ensues. Parents sense the hostility from staff, fear that their child will suffer, and become either demanding or reticent. Either response is interpreted as evidence for parental responsibility. This is not to say that there are not psychological problems in such families. When children have chronic illnesses that disrupt normal family life, there are problems, and most families would probably benefit from individual or group therapy.

In Denise's case there were particular problems with respect to house officers, young pediatric or family medicine residents. As previous director of Medical Education, I had been adamant that house officers should see each patient and that primary physicians should not have the option of choosing to have or not have a house officer assigned. Now I had parents who were asking that Denise not be examined by yet another physician. When she was admitted she was always unpleasant, hostile, and house officers often reciprocated with anger. I had many conferences with students and house officers about their attitude toward Denise, the generic issues of chronic illness in children, and relationships with parents. Eventually, when I moved to another city, the physician who assumed Denise's care was one of the former house officers at whom Denise had yelled.

HYPNOTHERAPY WITH DENISE

I do not believe that the training in self-hypnosis was very helpful to Denise with respect to reducing the symptoms of nausea and vomiting. However, she benefited in two ways. Via the adjunct of biofeedback, she observed that changes in her thinking resulted in physiologic changes, and she was proud of her ability to control peripheral temperature measures and electrodermal activity. We talked about the use of similar strategies by Olympic competitors. She said that she applied self-hypnosis in sports activities. During hypnotherapeutic sessions I also encouraged her to focus on a pleasant situation in the future when she would no longer have the episodes of vomiting and would be engaged in doing something she enjoyed. I never asked what future event she was imagining. She said she enjoyed this practice and also did it at home. Eventually, Denise graduated from high school, went to college, and studied in a health-related field. My view is that a focus on a desirable (and reasonable) outcome in the hypnotic state may facilitate that outcome at some considerable time after the initial therapy, especially if the child reinforces practice at home. For many years, in teaching about pain management with children, I have asked nurses and physicians about their recollections of childhood pain. I am invariably astounded at the large number that recall traumatic experiences in hospitals or dental chairs when they were children. I wonder if that is an important psychodynamic factor that leads them later to choose to work with children in pain. This may have been true for Denise in her choice of a profession.

In a recent letter she said:

> you will be happy to know that I have not gotten sick since my junior year in high school.... I have learned to deal with it. It doesn't happen very often. I can throw up once and be done, I know it will not continue. Dr. _____ monitors me. Besides you, he was the only one who believes that I did not cause the sickness. My experiences in the hospital have seemed to be paying off. Whenever anyone mentions a drug, 9 out of 10 times I know what it is since I have been on everything! I also seem to know how to run those IV pumps better than most. I guess there are some good things that end up out of bad things. I don't look down on my childhood. I accept it and realize it has made me who I am today.

PRAYER AND OTHER FACTORS

I believe it is important for therapists to assess all support systems available to families who have children with chronic diseases. In the case of Denise, I learned that the family was Catholic and devoted to their church. Their priest was a support person. Family members believed in prayer, as I do. A recent study from Walter Reed Hospital documented that hospitalized patients who are prayed for do better than those who do not receive support. Prayer may be a surrogate marker for a number of psychological supports, so important for those who are ill (Dossey, 1997). For Denise as for other children with serious illnesses, I asked my mother to include her in her prayers. My mother prayed for Denise on a daily basis for several years and periodically asked me how she was doing.

YOUR FAVORITE PATIENT

Denise would occasionally give me cartoons (that she had clipped from papers or magazines) that she said represented me. They were usually horrible looking characters. She was expressing some angry feelings via these approach. It was understandable that she was angry about not having a diagnosis, angry about not getting better fast enough, and about losing control during the recurrent vomiting episodes. Although she had a lot of positive feelings toward me, there was also some ambivalence. I thought it was healthy for her to express this, however indirectly. She began writing to me when I moved to another city. By this time she was well into puberty and her vomiting episodes were much less frequent. The hormonal changes seemed to provide mitigation of the symptoms but, as usual, no physician seemed to know why. Or was it Denise's programming? Or was it prayer? I so much enjoyed the letters, telling me about school and family and signed, "Your favorite patient, Denise." The fact is, after all these years, I feel enormous warmth and affection for Denise.

PSYCHOTHERAPY

I believe that psychotherapy is a facilitation of insight and positive change for an individual provided in a kind and hopeful manner. And, ideally, regardless of the strategies used, when therapy is complete, the client believes that what he or she has accomplished, he or she has accomplished it himself or herself. The client acknowledges the therapist as a wise teacher, counselor, or coach. Denise's most recent letter suggests that she has learned to cope with her disease and she has done this herself.

   I wonder how anyone, including myself, can know that he or she has become a therapist. Perhaps the genes that impact on personality have a lot to do with the potential to be a therapist. Then there is the gift of intuition. Marvin Ack, whom I considered an extraordinarily gifted child therapist, spoke often about this quality of intuition. This is the ability to sense what a client needs and to direct therapy toward that end. I believe that my own intuition has improved with experience. Perhaps I have observed subtle cues over many years that relate to certain diagnoses or messages. If I had video taped each of the more than 100,000 patient encounters I have had, I might be able to explain what I term *intuition.*

It is important that the therapist be skilled in ascertaining the learning style and preference of a client. This was never explained to me as a young physician and I was fortunate to have stumbled into some basic education courses that made me aware of how learning styles and strengths vary from person to person. I observed that some people have auditory processing difficulties and do not learn best by hearing information. I learned to be creative with drawings, art work, readings, and chalk boards. LeShan (1996) recently published a book in which he emphasized that therapy must be tailored to the individual in both time and technique. I spend a lot of time thinking about children, what I know about them, and how I can facilitate a therapeutic process that recognizes their individual differences and needs.

UNCERTAINTY AND LONG-TERM OUTCOMES

A few years ago I initiated a special conference in general pediatrics. This conference was for faculty only and I consciously intended that it should be a sort of therapy for therapists. Participants took turns presenting medical histories of children with problems but only those for whom they had a minimum follow-up of 2 years. After presentation of the initial history, examination, and laboratory findings, the faculty member stopped in order to allow comments from colleagues. What did they think about the diagnosis? What outcome would they predict? Following this discussion, the faculty member then told the rest of the story. Senior faculty members were able to present the stories of children whom they had followed for more than 30 years. One faculty member had early video tapes and now, 15 years later, drives 2 hours to videotape an update of a child with multiple handicaps. What we all learned was how difficult it is to predict long-term outcomes. Younger faculty tended to speak more confidently about what were the likely diagnoses and outcomes. Many times we were all surprised about the successful, productive lives of the adults who had such serious, complex problems as children. There were also numerous examples in which the initial diagnosis seemed straightforward but ultimately proved entirely wrong. The teaching mode in most hospitals is to present current or recent cases, and the learners rarely have the opportunity to know about the long-term outcome. It is only when we have the opportunity to follow our patients over time that we really understand the complexities of mental and physical development, variations in responses to treatment, and the limitations of our predictive ability. We cultivate humility in ourselves and increase our tolerance for uncertainty. I believe that the tolerance for uncertainty level can be increased in therapists who participate in cross disciplinary forums and practices, who continue to study not only their own but related fields, and who spend time outside of their own cultural milieu.

CONCLUSIONS

As I do this summary and analysis some years later, I think that, indeed, Denise may have been my favorite patient. From her I learned much about the limitations of medical diagnosis and a tolerance for uncertainty. Despite many efforts to turn every stone of diagnostic possibility, we still lack a precise explanation for Denise's symptoms. And we are left to tolerate uncertainty. Someday we may have a diagnosis for Denise. As has been true for many conditions affecting mankind, we may learn about a precise treatment that will result in rapid resolution of symptoms. I may say, "why didn't I think of that?" Happily, a parent group, Cyclic Vomiting Association, has become active during the past 6 years. This group is networking among families and professionals and not only provides comfort to families but also sheds light on causes and treatment of cyclic vomiting.

Although I was often frustrated by the reactions of colleagues and students, this experience provided me many good teaching opportunities. Did I become too enmeshed with Denise and her family? Probably, but my style has been to get intensely involved with families. The experience of working with Denise has not changed that. Denise has had the opportunity to read this chapter. Hopefully, she may learn not only from her experiences but also from my reactions in a way that will benefit her patients as she enters the health-care field.

POSTSCRIPT

In April 2000 I attended the wedding of Denise, a wonderful joyous event. Denise was a beautiful and gracious bride. Her parents were radiant. The priest who conducted the wedding ceremony was eloquent. I had not met the groom previously. Yet, at the reception he said to me "You made this possible. You helped Denise through those difficult years." I was acutely embarrassed. I knew that Denise had been the one who made this possible—Denise now the caring, competent nurse who specializes in oncology. And words cannot express the incredible joy I felt at this special event—the ultimate reward for a therapist.

REFERENCES

Bergman, A. B. (1975). Pediatric education—for what? *Pediatrics, 55*(1), 109–113.
LeShan, L. (1996). *Beyond technique.* Northvale, NJ: Jason Aronson.

16

In Harm's Way: Thoughts and Reflections on an Unwelcome Struggle

Richard P. Kluft

Dr. Sandra Black was a familiar face from my lectures, seminars, and study groups. Attractive and intense, yet shy and private, she seemed liked and respected by everyone, yet close to no one. When she requested consultation on her work with dissociative disorder patients, we went over a number of tapes of therapy sessions she had conducted. I found her to be an astute clinician with excellent skills, judgment, and insight. When I told her this and wondered (in jest) why she would waste her time and money to receive consultation when she was qualified to be a consultant, she blushed with embarrassment at the praise but became clearly uncomfortable. The next time we met she told me that she had been sexually abused as a child; she admitted she had really come for consultation to size me up as a potential therapist. Over the years, many colleagues have approached me for treatment after "auditioning" me in this manner. It is a mixed blessing: the traumatized colleague feels he or she knows me well enough to be safe with me, but usually learns so much about me in the process that the transference becomes somewhat contaminated and muddied.

Once she admitted her true agenda, Dr. Black's carefully crafted composure and reserve crumbled. "All I have is my appearance and my professional role. People like what they see of me. The rest is chaos." I learned that she was 37-years-old and had always retained conscious memories of sexual abuse by her father and brothers, and of brutal physical abuse by her mother. Her family had opposed her going to college. She had applied secretly and ran away to attend the school of her choice, living on the street her first semester and subsisting on menial jobs. Despite this, her grades were superb. She never returned to her family. A supportive professor took interest in her and earned her confidence. He became her advocate, and was instrumental in arranging for her to get a scholarship. She lived with him and his wife during school vacations. She managed to complete college with high honors, married, and continued on to graduate school. She became a successful psychologist. As much as she had run away from her family, she had run away from herself. She forced herself from one demanding project to the next, never allowing herself to look inwardly for fear the pain of her past would catch up to her and destroy her. At 37 she had three failed marriages and nasty divorces behind her. *Disastrous* would understate the nature of her relationships with men, but she was a devoted and caring parent to her two children. To oversimplify, in order never to be at the mercy of a strong man who might misuse her, she had become attached to men who were safe by virtue of their inadequacy as persons and as providers. When she realized this and tried relating to stronger men, she found herself in sadomasochistic submission to partners she realized too late were barely disguised facsimiles of her father. Many of the same concerns had kept her from therapy. Not only did she fear that examining her past would destroy her, she feared that any therapist, male or female, who was strong enough to help her might also come to dominate and exploit her. In fact, one supportive supervisor in whom she had confided had converted their meetings to therapy sessions and seduced her after she lowered her guard.

This raised a red flag at once. I asked if this was a concern between us. Dr. Black was blunt. She said that she was unsure whether I was safe. I seemed trustworthy, but she wondered whether my high praise of her intellectual and professional abilities and my failure to comment on her striking physical appearance was my clever indirect technique for seducing professional colleagues. She went on to say that she was confident that she could protect herself from me if I began to show any improprieties.

I heard this with a mixture of relief and concern. I was glad that Dr. Black had not defensively idealized me and that negative expectations and transferences would probably not be blocked by her prior interactions with me. On the other hand, I was worried that Dr. Black's confidence in her ability to defend herself was a combination of denial and whistling in the dark. Revictimization is all too common in incest victims, and I had spent years studying incest victims who had been exploited by prior therapists (Kluft, 1989a, 1990a, 1990b). Many demonstrate what I have called the *sitting duck syndrome*, a pattern of profound vulnerability for repeated misuse. I suspected that Dr. Black was much more at risk than she could allow herself to see and was saddened in anticipation of what more I might learn about how she might be suffering without immediately realizing her plight.

As we began to explore her depression and despair, it became clear to us that her past was continuing to intrude on her present. As much as she wanted to do a treatment centered on her problems in the here-and-now, we had to deal with her past. She feared this meant she would never get well. "I am one of those patients who will plague you. If I don't kill myself, we'll grow old together." I soon learned that one of the other motivations for her seeking treatment from me and trying to keep the focus on the here-and-now was based on her belief that I was so busy and involved in my work that I was insulated from the impact of any personal pain or strife. Under my tutelage she hoped (by modeling) to become an emotion-free workaholic.

It was difficult for me to get a grasp of Dr. Black's day-to-day life. Her narratives had an elusive quality. I did not find her deceptive. Instead, I had the impression that something was being held back both from herself and from me, so that her most candid accounts still left me puzzled. I resorted to a technique I often find helpful: I asked her to take me through her week day by day, hour by hour. Dr. Black became nonplused and then agitated. By the time we reached Wednesday it was clear that there were hours she could not account for in every day. After composing herself, she asked, "is it alright to tell you something? You won't be angry?" I told her I could not vouch for my response in advance but that anger was unlikely. I wondered why she would expect me to be angry.

Dr. Black said that when I had asked her certain questions during my assessment of her she had given me her own understanding of the questions, but she had not given me additional answers that popped in her mind as vivid thoughts but that often had a vocal quality, like voices inside her head. She tried to persuade herself that these phenomena meant nothing and were not really her; if she ignored them they would not really be there. "What if the answers I didn't give you meant I was crazy?" she asked.

I told her that because it was her style to put her best foot forward, despite her inner pain, I would not be surprised if she had carried that defensive style right into our work together, and had held back things she thought would make me think less of her. She was silent for several minutes, and then said, "what would you think if I told you there are voices in my head, and they tell me things I can't, I don't want to believe?" I responded, "I would tell you that I am beginning to see how important a sense of self-control is for you, and how threatened and ashamed you are when you realize that a lot goes on that you don't know about or control. Sharing this with me is an experience of terrible mortification for you."

Dr. Black wept silently for several minutes. Then, clearly forcing herself to say every word against the opposing pressure of her own reluctance, she described terrifying traumatic nightmares that seemed to be repetitions of her childhood abuses by her father, but in these dreams she was an adult and her father was older. She revealed losing hours every day, and occasionally being unable to recall periods of as long as a week. She described hearing many voices in her head. "It's as if there were a world in there, with people arguing, fighting, telling me that what I am doing is stupid. When I block it all out I get terrible headaches."

The history of child abuse, the lost time, the inner voices, the sense of inner dialogues, the headaches, and the traumatic nightmares were very strong indicators of a major dissociative disorder, quite possibly dissociative identity disorder (formerly called multiple personality disorder; Kluft, 1991; Putnam, 1989; Ross, 1989). As Dr. Black continued in her recital, I was not surprised when her voice became stronger, her posture more erect, and her language lost its beseeching and apologetic quality and became more assertive. "I think you have figured it out, Doctor. We brought her to you. Do you think you can help us?" I replied that I thought we could work together, and that the quality of our ability to work together would determine our success—I had no magic independent of our collaboration.

Dr. Black as I usually knew her had no recollection of that interchange. When I appreciated she was "back" she complained of a headache and was transiently confused and dazed. When she composed herself, she inferred she had lost time and I had spoken to another part of her mind. "I guess I knew, but I didn't want it to be true." We spent a few sessions discussing how treatment would proceed. Dr. Black wanted me to eliminate the other parts of her mind, and any unpleasant memories they contained. The other parts wanted me to help Dr. Black accept them and their recollections so they could be unburdened of the pain they had carried for years. It seemed like a fairly routine beginning to a fairly routine psychotherapy for dissociative identity disorder.

Once I had persuaded Dr. Black to work with the others and convinced the others I met to be patient with Dr. Black, keep her coconscious with their activities, and to hold their painful feelings away from Dr. Black except in therapy sessions, the periods of time loss dropped dramatically and Dr. Black's distress was reduced. I was in familiar territory with what appeared to be a bright and motivated patient. I anticipated no major difficulties and began to teach my patient some techniques to contain her misery, her traumatic memory, and her unsettled alters.

I first ascertained that Dr. Black had no current or anticipated legal involvements that might be a contraindication to our using hypnosis. In many jurisdictions persons who have experienced hypnosis may be held to have contaminated memories and to have concretized their recollections so that they cannot be cross-examined. When this was clarified to our mutual satisfaction, I helped her experience a wide range of hypnotic phenomena and demonstrated their potential application in treatment. For example, I taught her to experience glove anesthesia, and to transfer the absence of sensation to other parts of her body. Then I taught her how to use this anesthesia for emotional pain. Having seen the hypnosis could block a genuine painful stimulus to her hand, she had confidence we could use hypnosis to block genuine emotional pain from unpleasant material.

We did not pursue traumatic material; instead we worked on stabilization and containment techniques facilitated by hypnosis. Trauma therapies ideally go from a phase of stabilizing and strengthening the patient to a phase of metabolizing the patient's traumatic experiences and conclude with a phase of integrating the patient's self, social roles, and interpersonal relationships. In Herman's (1992) useful terminology, a stage of safety is succeeded by a stage of remembrance and mourning, which in turn is followed by a stage of reconnection. I tried to make Dr. Black safer and stronger by a number of techniques useful in the initial phases of therapy (Kluft, 1993).

Soon we moved on to her mastering how to put uncomfortable alters in a safe and healing place between sessions, to putting unsettled alters to sleep between sessions so their pain would not intrude on her daily life, and to remove the affect and physical pain from alters working with painful material and place them in a vault between sessions, or until we were ready to work them. She mastered these temporizing techniques (Kluft, 1988, 1989b) with great skill and facility, but even when she used them she had the vague and unsettled feeling that something was very wrong.

I shared this concern. It is unusual for me to "take my work home," but I found myself worrying about Dr. Black between sessions. It seemed to me that my apprehension expressed my sense that something was going on that I was missing. My natural suspicion was that either some alters remained unknown, and I was intuiting or inferring the indirect manifestation of their presence, or that some of the alters I was beginning to meet were holding back information of great importance.

Matters came to a head rapidly because by achieving coconsciousness, Dr. Black was more aware of apparently trivial everyday events than she had been in the past. She came to one session trembling and terrified. In the mail that morning she had found a birthday card addressed to her daughter and bearing her parents' return address. "How could this be?" she wailed. "I haven't seen them in 20 years. They couldn't possibly know where I live, or all about my kids." She was confused because her daughter did not seem surprised or curious about the card.

We considered alternative explanations. One brother knew her address and was occasionally in touch. He might have given the parents this information. Initially Dr. Black wondered if her parents were trying to establish a relationship with their grandchildren. We explored her feelings about this. We used hypnosis for anxiety relief and I made her a tape for use at home.

The card remained a mystery, but to me much more puzzling was her daughter's reaction. Perhaps what was strange to Dr. Black was familiar to her youngsters. If that was so, what might that mean? My worry about Dr. Black continued unabated.

One week later another letter to the daughter arrived, and its contents implied that Dr. Black's parents not only knew their grandchildren, but also that they continued to have an ongoing relationship with Dr. Black. This drove Dr. Black to despair and suicidality, on the one hand, and almost manic hysterical defensive humor, on the other. "This is all just too absurd to be happening. I could not possibly be having ongoing relationships with people who abused me, whom I hate, and whom I have not seen in 2 decades!" But if this were possible, had she betrayed the children she had tried to keep safe and protect from what had occurred to her? Was she truly crazy? If so, she feared, the only solution was suicide.

I was on the phone with Dr. Black several times a day for a period of 2 weeks, trying to keep her safe. Finally, she restabilized. We were able to discuss possible courses of action. It was clear that her parents had knowledge about her that was current and had to come from her or from someone who knew her well. The prime candidates seemed to be Dr. Black herself, one of her former husbands (who was still in contact with her due to their children), her brother, or someone in contact with any one of these suspects. Dr. Black knew from experience that she could not trust the candor of her former spouses or her brother. She was uncertain of the honesty of her alters, and her alter system had not yet been explored. That had been postponed, awaiting her mastery of techniques useful in keeping her safe and stable when approaching difficult material.

We discussed many approaches, all of which were impractical for one reason or another, and concluded that the most reasonable source of information would be Dr. Black herself. Unfortunately, direct inquiries to her alters failed to yield useful material. Some hinted something was amiss but that they did not have the knowledge themselves. That left us the possibility of using techniques to access additional alters and memories, and raised a number of questions and issues that concerned both of us.

Retrieving currently unavailable material is a time-honored application of hypnosis that has come under virulent attack in recent years. I was very familiar with the problems associated with all forms of memory retrieval (of which hypnosis is only one), and had made a point of expressing these concerns to those who attended my seminars and workshops. Dr. Black not only had heard my concerns, but had also taken courses from colleagues who were very sympathetic to the False Memory Syndrome Foundation. They had taught her that material retrievable with hypnosis was inherently unreliable. She was very reluctant to accept any explorations that might yield information of uncertain reliability.

We reviewed her situation in terms of the risk–benefit ratio of exploring with hypnosis or a drug-facilitated interview. I took her through a review of what is currently known about hypnosis and memory, and outlined for her the highly politicized and polarized viewpoints being expressed in both the media and professional publications. I used the "informed consent as a process" approach advocated by Applebaum and Gutheil (1992), making sure that each time major issues arose, they were reconsidered in the context of the therapy so that Dr. Black could make a decision based on truly informed consent.

The stance I took is that all forms of interpersonal influence may exert postevent influences on what is recovered as memory, and that hypnosis is only one of these forms of influence. I pointed out that created expectancies and hypnotizability rather than the induction of hypnosis was responsible for the distortions of memory earlier attributed more globally and imprecisely to hypnosis (McConkey, 1992). I told her candidly that because she was hypnotizable and that she knew in advance hypnosis might be used to make inquiries about her parents' activities, her expectations, past experiences, hatred of her parents, fears, and fantasies might influence what emerged as apparent memory. I also helped her appreciate that the consequences to herself and her children of leaving this unexplored were not inconsiderable. I helped her reflect that although explorations of the past were unlikely to be confirmed by external evidence, anything that emerged under hypnosis about planned future actions would be subject to external corroboration. I emphasized that whatever emerged would be food for thought, not proof of historical events unless corroborated. I warned her that what might be useful for therapy and prudent with respect to her contemporary life would not necessarily be scientifically accurate or hold up in a court of law. I reiterated the warning that exploration with hypnosis might disqualify her from giving testimony with regard to her current circumstances, and possibly about other matters as well.

Dr. Black's decision to proceed with hypnotic exploration was made with reluctance, but with an appreciation that her daughter had just achieved the age at which her own abuse had proceeded to full sexual intercourse. We carefully took a prehypnotic history from all accessible alters about contemporary contact with her family, and proceeded.

Dr. Black readily entered a deep trance. All known alters were explored for relevant information. The hypnosis was used for disinhibition and circumvention of defenses because my prior research (Kluft, 1986) had demonstrated that age regression and allied techniques with dissociative identity disorder patients can be reasonably complex to achieve and difficult to interpret. Then I asked if there were any other alters who could contribute to our understanding of the situation.

Dr. Black's body strained and fidgeted. After several minutes I heard a childish whining voice complain, "But Daddy says I'm his special little girl. Sandra is mean to her Daddy. She doesn't talk to him any more. But I do. He loves me and I love him and I don't want anyone to take me away from him." I learned that I was talking to "Missy," who was totally dedicated to her father. She treasured a shoe-box of cards and letters he had sent her, and kept them concealed in a rarely used room of Dr. Black's home. She boasted that she called her father on the phone frequently, and that father continued to visit "just me" and continued their special relationship, which included sexual intercourse.

Dr. Black was aghast at these revelations. She tried to beat her head against my office walls to "make it go away." When I tried to protect her from herself she pushed me away, briefly attacked me, and blamed me for creating "Missy and her dirty lies." The session ended in a very painful atmosphere of perceived betrayal. Dr. Black felt abused and tricked by me.

Although I consoled myself that I had taken reasonable precautions and introduced useful safeguards, I was very upset. I was sure of the clinical truth that something very complicated was going on, and that my patient was potentially in harm's way because of her dissociative disorder. However, I had no reason to be sure that what we had retrieved was accurate, and, in today's litigious era, I had no way of knowing whether my efforts to help my patient might land me in a lawsuit. To add to my anxiety, the Ramona case had just been adjudicated. In Ramona, mental health professionals who had used drug-facilitated interviews to uncover memories of incest had been found guilty of harming their patient's accused father. My patient might react in a way that could place her at risk, turn her against me, and destroy the therapy. I did not sleep well.

It is one thing to talk in the abstract about the consequences of child abuse, or to deal with the treatment of a patient whose alleged perpetrators are deceased. It is quite another to probe a situation in which all of the participants are very much alive, and in which real consequences to third parties to therapy may follow from what therapy discovers. I searched myself to find some trace of wanting one result or another to come from the inquiries I had made, and was not surprised to find myself wanting to believe the hypnotic results were inaccurate. In workshop after workshop, when I am asked what I find most difficult in treating trauma victims, I reply that it is the anguish of bearing witness to their revictimization in the course of treatment. I did not want to contend with the implications of Dr. Sandra Black's remaining in an incestuous relationship with her father. I liked Dr. Black. I wanted to find no evidence of ongoing abuse. I wanted to be able to reassure her she was safe, that her hurts were in the past, and that her future was bright with promise. Speaking selfishly, I was not eager to remain empathetically attuned to someone who might be submitting herself to ongoing exploitation. Caring trauma therapy exacts a high toll from the therapist. It is hard enough to remain connected when someone you have come to care about must relive the pain and betrayal of the past. I did not want to have to "hang in there" with a patient who might be reexperiencing this anguish every few weeks in the here and now.

The next morning there was a message from Dr. Black on my answering machine. She had found Missy's box of letters and cards. Missy's own diary was there as well, detailing clearly erotic encounters with her father in a handwriting very unlike Dr. Black's own. The most recent letter from her father indicated he would arrive at a nearby motel 2 weekends hence. He expected to see her and wanted to spend an afternoon alone with her daughter. Dr. Black had lacerated her vagina in a dissociated state. I saw her on an emergency basis that evening.

Dr. Black was too agitated to speak coherently. For the first time in her career she had canceled her practice hours—she could not recover her composure, and had been bleeding through her clothing until she went to a gynecologist I recommended. I spent the entire session using hypnotic and other methods to calm her. At the end she both apologized for accusing me of misleading her. Demoralized and hopeless, she contemplated submitting to her father's wishes in exchange for his leaving her daughter alone. Although I generally am permissive and respect my patients' choices, I do not hesitate to become directive when my patient's well-being is at risk. I insisted that this option was not acceptable. At the time I intervened I believed I was calm and compassionate, and appropriately protective of my patient. I was surprised by the look of shock on Dr. Black's face. Only when I reviewed the session that evening could I realize that as I had begun to empathize with her sense of helplessness and masochistic surrender to rape and sexual sadism, my own defenses could not tolerate my vicariously experiencing myself choosing such passive submission for even a microsecond—I had to be active and protective. My own countertransference plus my concern probably had generated a much stronger response than I could have acknowledged in the immediacy of the moment.

Dr. Black's denial, encouraged by Missy and an alter based on her father, rapidly reestablished itself. She experienced a distressing derealized and depersonalized state of mind in which the actuality and importance of the current situation was disavowed. It became clear that her main motivation was to protect her daughter from abuse and herself from the painful knowledge that had emerged. She considered giving in to Missy if Missy would insist on her daughter's safety. She finally reached a state in which she, unaware of the mutual incompatibility of aspects of what she was experiencing, simultaneously assured herself that the material from the hypnosis and the letters could not be real, continued to recover memories of Missy's making the arrangements for Father's upcoming visit, and, in searching her old telephone bills, was finding that she had made dozens of calls to her father over the last calendar year.

It was hard not to be swept into the melange of conflicting "realities" that Dr. Black was entertaining. As I empathized with one alter's accounts, I was transiently immersed in its realities, only to plunge into another with the next switch. When my mind rebelled at remaining closely involved with this "multiple reality disorder" (Kluft, 1991, 1994), I lost empathic contact with Dr. Black, and had to scramble to reconnect with her. I worried that if I got either too close or too far from her emotional world I might make a false step that would encourage her to place herself and her daughter at risk. As I struggled with this, at times my turmoil became obvious. On one occasion Dr. Black asked me what I was thinking. While I experienced myself reflecting thoughtfully, I heard myself blurt: "You would lay down your body or your life for your daughter without a moment's hesitation, but you treat yourself as badly as your father treated you. When it comes to helping you, most of the time I feel I'm out there alone and you're rooting for the other side." I had become depersonalized in the countertransference (Loewenstein, 1993).

With exquisite kindness, Dr. Black told me that she now was confident that one of her alters had indeed retained a long-distance relationship with her father, but that she could not endorse the idea that visits occurred or that the relationship remained sexual. She was sure this was the result of Missy's superheated imagination and smiled charmingly when I groaned audibly.

Throughout this period of time I had used hypnosis to bring the problems to the attention of the remainder of the alter system, trying to bring the resources of the entire mind to bear on what might prove to be a false alarm, but that might pose a genuine crisis. As the weekend of father's possible visit neared, the alters that had emerged early in the therapy and protested Dr. Black's denial of their existence and their memories became much more active. They made incessant comments on Dr. Black's "pigheadedness" and Missy's "stupidity." I used hypnosis to access them and bring their arguments to Dr. Black's attention. With their help, in the last session before the fateful weekend I was able to persuade Missy and the alter based on her father to go to sleep until the session after the weekend. Dr. Black said as she left that she anticipated a boring weekend and was beginning to worry that I was succumbing to the hysteria of the parts she doubted were real and felt she would be better off without.

The next morning I received a panicked call from Dr. Black. Her father had come to the door. Immediately he had put his arms around her and tried to kiss her passionately. She had fought him off, and locked her doors. Over the next several days her father laid siege to her and her family, sitting at the end of her driveway in a rental car until she went to her office, and sitting in the waiting room at her office. He filled her voicemail with entreaties, angry harangues, and, at night, drunken protestations of his love for her and reminiscences of their sexual relationship. He sounded like a jilted lover. He accosted her children, introducing himself as "Grandpa" and asking them why their mother was so mean to him. The children, who were starved for male affection, brought his accusations to their mother and asked her to have their "nice grampa" over for dinner.

Despite my advice, Dr. Black refused to take any action to protect herself until one day her father tried to force his way into her office and then went to the children's school and tried to take them away. I had anticipated this, and insisted that Dr. Black inform the school that no one but herself could pick up her children. At the time she protested vigorously that it would cause her shame in her community and injure her professional reputation if she took any actions, but acceded to this one demand. When she saw that her children might have been kidnapped and abused because of her denial, she filed charges against her father despite her mixed feelings. A court order prohibited him from being closer than a certain distance from her home. The police picked up her father outside her home and removed him. Within an hour he was back, placing himself exactly 1 foot beyond the proscribed distance. After several days of such behavior and intense telephone harassment, he apparently left the area.

Dr. Black tried to convince herself that the danger was gone and that she was safe. However, her father continued to try to coerce her compliance with a series of telephone assaults. In one he left a message that he could not live without the love of his daughter and would kill himself. Then there was a sharp sound like the discharge of a gun and the line went silent. She called me and reported she was ready to cut her wrists with a razor blade out of guilt for killing her father.

I hypnotized Dr. Black over the telephone because not only was I afraid she might kill herself or self-mutilate, but also because I thought these coercive emotional blackmail tactics were sure to activate Missy and an alter based on her father. I learned that Missy had already reserved airline tickets to fly to her parents' home. We held an emergency session. Only by calling the appropriate authorities could I satisfy the patient that the whole affair was an elaborate ruse to bring her to her father because he could no longer come after her with impunity. Using a speakerphone I called her parents' home during a session. Her father answered the telephone. This episode finally broke Missy's dedication to her father, and the patient became far more resistant to his efforts to reengage her.

As the dust from this series of episodes gradually settled, I made hypnotically facilitated inquiries across all the alters to ask not about the details of traumata, but to ascertain the family's usual strategies to bring Dr. Black under control. I needed this information urgently, and did not hesitate to ask very leading questions, eliciting either ideomotor signals or inner verbalization of the answers. I considered it very important to anticipate what might happen next and to protect Dr. Black. There was already sufficient evidence that the family was as pathological as Dr. Black had described, and was invested in reestablishing its pathological equilibrium.

The answers suggested that the family's next strategy might be to use the brother with whom Dr. Black had retained some relationship to forward its goals. Dr. Black had called him in connection with her father's stalking her and asked for him to validate her recollections. He had done so, but assured her that he still was afraid of their parents and wanted to inherit their wealth. Therefore, he would not back her story to any authorities, and would say whatever the parents wanted him too. He also protested his love for her, and begged her to renew their childhood sexual relationship.

Dr. Black was very protective of her brother, about whom I took a decidedly negative stance. His own declarations branded him as selfish and still invested in perpetuating her misuse. I was concerned that he would exploit her love and protectiveness to forward his own interests, both sexual and financial. I also feared that Dr. Black might have an alter who loved her brother, much as Missy had been dedicated to father. Dr. Black preferred to see her brother as a fellow victim without predatory traits. She declined to let me probe to identify any such alter and interdict its likely course of action.

Approximately 1 month later her brother appeared at her door. He approached her sexually and she kicked him. She had no recollection of the next several hours. In session the following day her arms were bruised, her wrists were abraded, and she had a slightly swollen and blackened eye, which she had tried unsuccessfully to disguise with make-up. No alter could or would give me additional details. When I asked her to describe her sensations from head to foot she admitted with great shame that she had terrible rectal pain and was bleeding from her anus. Using hypnosis, I explored to see if there was a previously unknown alter that could be of help. I found "Helen," who was particularly dedicated to her brother. I learned that when the brother had been kicked, he groaned in pain and Helen emerged. Helen became nurturing and protective toward him. She had brought him into the house and let him lie on a couch. When her brother recovered sufficiently, he beat her into submission, tied her wrists to a piece of furniture, and raped her anally. The personalities who told me this kept their eyes fixed on the floor and wept softly. Had Dr. Black looked in my direction, she would have seen tears staining my cheeks even as I struggled to keep from showing rage of murderous dimensions, for fear she would think I was angry at her rather than at her assailant.

Although I knew this reaction was irrational, I was overcome by a profound sense of failure and despair. I had anticipated the difficulty and proposed preventive interventions, but my patient had not been ready to do what had to be done. I poured over my notes and tried to recreate the sessions from memory, trying to see what else I might have done to bring her to protect herself. I stopped only when I realized, to my amusement, that my self-interrogation was creating pseudomemories in myself that contradicted my contemporaneous notes and alternately blamed and exonerated both me and my patient. Dr. Black's love for her family was stronger than her anger or her self-protective impulses. She still yearned for their affection. She could change gradually, but not abruptly. I had to accept this and help her endure its consequences when they could not be prevented. Although I felt optimistic about the long run, my sense of impotence in the here and now of day-to-day events troubled me. I hated the experience of empathizing with her struggle to extricate herself from her circumstances, and mentally flinched when I foresaw situations in which she might suffer yet again. It was difficult to restrain myself from making interventions and giving advice that would have protected and helped most people, but that imposed on Dr. Black the burden of guilt for disobeying her family and the onus of terror over her inevitable separation from persons who clearly wished to exploit her, but to whom she was bound, in many alters, with ties of profound, albeit conflicted, attachment and affection. My street-smart reaction—"how can she be so stupid?"—battled with my psychodynamic appreciation of the complexity of human object relations.

I used hypnosis to provide Dr. Black analgesia while she healed. Once it had been revealed, the rape experience became intrusive. Dr. Black was so upset she could not return to her home, the scene of the rape. She relocated temporarily to a motel. For several days she suffered flashbacks most of the day and had traumatic dreams at night. She refused to allow therapy to attempt to contain and process the material; instead, she tried to dissociate it anew. These efforts failed. Finally, demoralized and exhausted, unable to recover her composure and incapable of working, she agreed to address it in treatment. We had not done deliberate trauma work until that point in time, but she had mastered all of the techniques that are useful in making such efforts relatively safe and unlikely to disrupt function (Kluft, 1988, 1989b). I explained the technique of fractionated abreaction (Fine, 1991; Kluft, 1988, 1989b, 1990c, in press), in which traumas are processed piecemeal and the patient is restored to a position of mastery and containment after each partial review and abreaction of the traumatic scenario.

We began with her reliving, under hypnosis, the first 15 seconds of her encounter with her brother in Helen alone, with all physical sensations ablated and retaining only 10% of the affect. When she mastered that we proceeded to increase the temporal dimensions and the affective force in small increments. Gradually, the physical sensations were added at low intensity. In seven sessions over 2 weeks we covered and abreacted the entire scenario without her decompensating or having crises. She became able to return home without discomfort, and was so pleased with her mastery of this experience that she became willing to allow the mapping of her alter system (which allowed the discovery and containment of other alters that were dedicated to or identified with her abusers) and the beginning of work on past traumata.

Gradually Dr. Black got her life under control, and settled into working through the impact of the past on the present. When her mother and other brother attempted to approach her, preventive work on the alters dedicated to them and identified with them deprived them of power. They had no impact on Dr. Black, and finally her family stopped pursuing her. She continues in treatment for her dissociative disorder and her interpersonal difficulties, but is much improved in all dimensions. She has developed a wonderful sense of humor, and is no longer as shy and reserved. We have much work yet to do, but we do not appear in danger of growing old together.

In treating Dr. Black I was moved and at times unnerved by her suffering, furious at those who abused her, and, as much as I was moved by her, at times I was exasperated, enraged, and even disgusted by her propensity for revictimization and her difficulties in dealing with the facts of her life. It was wrenching to watch the power of her attachment to her abusers at work, and heart-breaking to empathize with its emotional aftermath. Work with Dr. Black was painful, but I never was tempted to withdraw because as awful as the negative aspects of the treatment were, the opportunity to help and witness the growth and recovery of this decent and courageous person were always more powerful motivators. This aspect of the psychotherapy was virtually without conflict. I find in myself no trace of regret for fighting the good fight.

On the other hand, my struggle with the intellectual and political issues that surrounded this therapy were profound and anxiety provoking. Treating Dr. Black at the height of the media coverage of the "recovered memory debate" forced me to revisit problematic and provocative clinical and research questions virtually dozens of times a session. I was both distracted and edified by the fact that at times every intervention I did would have provoked scathing rebukes or fervid cheers from partisans of one point of view or the other. Dr. Sandra Black and many other patients like her forced me to appreciate that the entire false memory debate and the issues that spring from it are, like so much that has become politicized and polarized, oversimplified, and prematurely disambiguated, essentially mindless and heartless. Real life is a complex tapestry not easily reduced to simple blacks and whites, yeas and nays. One must not succumb to such reductionism. To do so is to introduce denial, depersonalization and derealization into one's cognitive processes and to endorse a deeply dissociated and distorted rendition of reality.

Day after day I would arrive at my office under the temporary influence of the most recent article I had read on the subject, only to find its arguments broken on the shoals of the anguish of the suffering woman before me. I learned how dangerous it would be to approach a real human being armed with the a priori assumptions of many of the self-proclaimed experts in the field. To have endorsed these abstractions and generalizations might have blinded me to Dr. Sandra Black.

Had I not used hypnosis I would have been squeaky-clean in the eyes of many, but my patient, and perhaps her daughter, would have been victimized. Her anguish would have overwhelmed her and destroyed her practice and her financial stability. Had I avoided leading questions when my experience and clinical intuition told me to do so, I would not have had the opportunity, albeit an unsuccessful opportunity, to prevent still further mishap. Had I been permissive in the face of her masochism and press to re-enact past scenarios, many would have approved, but I would have ignored my own hard-won knowledge and Terr's (1981) cogent advice that traumatic reenactments take on a life of their own and must be interrupted in order to break the vicious cycles that they can perpetuate.

I came away convinced that the clinician must allow himself to be informed by the debates of the moment in the field but must rise against them and above them to fight for the recovery of his or her patients. It seems to me that patients must be allowed to reveal themselves to their therapists, and their therapists must allow themselves to help their patients make these revelations. Neither can be allowed to slip into generating materials or selecting for emphasis materials in the service of confirmatory bias. Therapy that adheres rigorously to the most cautious and scientific advice is neither safe, nor good. It places a priori assumptions above the patient and the therapeutic process. Ultimately it becomes the antithesis of what is circumspect and scientific. (For a more scholarly discussion of these concerns, the reader is referred to the more objective reviews of Brown, 1995; Hammond et al., 1995 Brown, Scheflin, and Hammond, 1998.)

I would never want to treat a patient without state of the art knowledge, but I would never want to mistake state of the art knowledge for compassionate and caring psychotherapy. State of the art knowledge is the fruit of scholarly debate and academic dispute. It represents the state of an art other than psychotherapy. Its relationship to the process by which patients are healed remains to be established. The therapist who enters the therapeutic dyad with the utter certainty about what is right and proper as defined by academicians and scholars who are not responsible for the recovery of that particular patient is not a scientific therapist. He or she is the contemporary descendent of the medieval mountebank. I find this realization reassuring as I continue to study, to do research, and to do psychotherapy, and appreciate the differences among these processes.

As I reflect on my work with Dr. Black, and ask myself how I can understand how I have changed in the process, I find that I am certain that I have changed, but I struggle when I try to specify what form that change has taken. I have always wrestled with the impact of scientific findings on the practice of psychotherapy. I have always been aware, from my education in both psychoanalysis and hypnosis, of the vicissitudes of memory and of the pressures that the uncertainty of human recollection impose on clinical practice. I have always been passionately involved in the work I do while maintaining my emotional privacy in the interests of my patients' recoveries. These are not new awarenesses. They accompany me to my office every day. They whisper in my ear at conferences. They sit beside me like a loyal cat or dog when I write at my word processor, trying to give order and expression to my experience. They are not always intruding, but they frequently demand my attention whether I want to give it to them or not.

The images of change that come to my mind are not particularly elegant. They are those of a snake shedding its old skin, and of a maturing hermit crab moving from one shell home to another. In each case simultaneous change and continuity coexist. The lessons I learned in my work with Dr. Sandra Black were not so much learned as relearned. Time and again the issues involved in dealing with trauma must be encountered anew. We learn them only to turn away from them in order to protect ourselves, and then we must face them and master them once again. Those of us who work with the traumatized are no more immune to the natural human tendency to distance ourselves from the reality of trauma and its raw anguish than the most hardened skeptic who rushes to dismiss the high incidence of child abuse and deny the dissociation of traumatic material. What distinguishes us and renews us may well be those moments, those clinical encounters, like my own with Dr. Sandra Black, in which we see with eyes opened anew and encounter with perceptions and emotions resensitized and revitalized what so many forces in our own psyches and society at large encourage us to discount and disavow. I would like to retain the changes my work with Dr. Black has brought to me, and would like to reassure both the reader and myself that what I have learned will always be fresh and poignant in my work. But I would not be surprised to find I am more human than otherwise, and will have to undergo this process again and again.

REFERENCES

Applebaum, P. S., & Gutheil, T. G. (1991). *Clinical handbook of psychiatry and the law* (2nd ed.). Baltimore: Williams & Wilkins.

Brown, D. (1995). Pseudomemories, the standard of science and the standard of care in trauma treatment. *American Journal of Clinical Hypnosis, 37,* 1-24.

Brown, D., Scheflin, A.W., and Hammond, D.C. (1998). Memory, trama treatment, and the law. New York: Norton.

Fine, C. G. (1991). Treatment stabilization and crisis prevention: Pacing the therapy of the multiple personality disorder patient. *Psychiatric Clinics of North America, 14*, 661-675.

Hammond, C. D., Garver, R. B., Mutter, C. B., Crasilneck, H. B., Frischholz, E. J., Gravitz, M. A., Olson, J., Scheflin, A., Spiegel, H., & Wester, W. C. (1995). *Clinical hypnosis and memory: Guidelines for clinicians and for forensic hypnosis.* Seattle, WA: American Society of Clinical Hypnosis Press.

Herman, J. L. (1992). *Trauma and recovery.* New York: Basic Books.

Kluft, R. P. (1986). Preliminary observations on age regression in multiple personality disorder patients before and after integration. *American Journal of Clinical Hypnosis, 28*, 147-156.

Kluft, R. P. (1988). On treating the older patient with multiple personality disorder: "Race against time" or "make haste slowly." *American Journal of Clinical Hypnosis, 30*, 257-266.

Kluft, R. P. (1989a). Treating the patient who has been sexually exploited by a previous therapist. *Psychiatric Clinics of North America, 12*, 483-500.

Kluft, R. P. (1989b). Playing for time: Temporizing techniques in the treatment of multiple personality disorder. *American Journal of Clinical Hypnosis, 32*, 90-98.

Kluft, R. P. (1990a). Dissociation and revictimization: A preliminary study. *Dissociation, 3*, 167-173.

Kluft, R. P. (1990b). Incest and subsequent revictimization: The case of therapist-patient sexual exploitation, with a description of the sitting duck syndrome. In R. P. Kluft (Ed.), *Incest-related syndromes of adult psychopathology* (pp. 263-287). Washington, DC: APA.

Kluft, R. P. (1990c). The fractionated abreaction technique. In C. D. Hammond (Ed.), *Handbook of hypnotic suggestions and metaphors* (pp. 527-528). New York: Norton.

Kluft, R. P. (1991). Multiple personality disorder. In A. Tasman & S. Goldfinger (Eds.), *American Psychiatric Press annual review of psychiatry* (pp. 161-188). Washington, DC: APA.

Kluft, R. P. (1993). The initial stages of psychotherapy in the treatment of multiple personality disorder patients. *Dissociation, 6*, 145-161.

Kluft, R. P. (1994). Countertransference in the treatment of multiple personality disorder. In J. P. Wilson & J. Lindy (Eds.), *Countertransference in the psychotherapy of multiple personality disorder* (pp. 122-153). New York: Guilford.

Kluft, R. P. (in press). The management of abreactions. In J. A. Turkus & B. M. Cohen (Eds.), *Multiple personality disorder: Continuum of care.* New York: Jason Aronson.

Loewenstein, R. J. (1993). Posttraumatic and dissociative aspects of transferences and countertransference in the treatment of multiple personality disorder. In R. P. Kluft & C. G. Fine (Eds.), *Clinical perspectives on multiple personality disorder* (pp. 51-85). Washington, DC: APA.

McConkey, K. M. (1992). The effects of hypnotic procedures on remembering: The experimental findings and their implications for forensic hypnosis. In E. Fromm & M. R. Nash (Eds.), *Contemporary hypnosis research* (pp. 405-426). New York: Guilford.

Putnam, F. W. (1989). *Diagnosis and treatment of multiple personality disorder.* New York: Guilford.

Ross, C. A. (1989). *Multiple personality disorder: Diagnosis, clinical features, and treatment.* New York: Wiley.

Terr, L. (1981). Forbidden games. *Journal of the American Academy of Child and Adolescent Psychiatry, 2*, 741-760.

About the Contributors

Phyllis Alden is a consultant clinical psychologist working in the Department of Clinical Oncology at Derbyshire Royal Infirmary, Derby, England. She has worked in a number of areas including adult mental health, spinal cord injury, and physical medicine. Her main interest, however, is oncology. She has used hypnosis in clinical practice for many years and is known for her work in pain and cancer.

Brenda Bursch, PhD, is the associate director of the Pediatric Psychiatry Consultation Service and the associate director of the Pediatric Chronic Pain Program in the Department of Psychiatry and Biobehavioral Sciences, University of California, Los Angeles (UCLA), School of Medicine. She has focused her interests on functional disability associated with medically complex children and their families.

Marlene R. Eisen, PhD, is a clinical psychologist in private practice. She has taught and directed programs at the University of Chicago and Harper College. She is currently a member of the Adjunct Faculty of the Illinois School for Professional Psychology. She has been a lecturer and consultant in a variety of settings and has published several articles describing her clinical work.

Albert Ellis, PhD, is the founder of Rational Emotive Behavior Therapy (REBT) and president of the Albert Ellis Institute in New York City. He has published many books and articles on REBT, including *A Guide to Rational Living.*

Erika Fromm, PhD, is a professor Emeritus at the University of Chicago Department of Psychology and has an international reputation in the field of hypnosis for her outstanding contributions to both the clinical and experimental literature. Her research has focused on the phenomena, the theory, and the practice of hypnoanalysis (the combination of hypnosis and psychoanalysis) and of self-hypnosis. She has published more than 100 articles in scientific journals and 8 books. She also has taught many workshops on hypnosis in the United States and abroad. Dr. Fromm is Past-President of both the American Psychological Association's Division of Hypnosis and of the Society of Clinical & Experimental Hypnosis. She has received many awards and honors.

Stephen Kahn, PhD, is an assistant clinical professor at the University of Chicago, Department of Psychiatry and is the director of the Institute for Clinical Hypnosis and Research, a group that trains and supervises both clinical and research psychologists. His private practice includes individual as well as couples work with a specialty in hypnosis and behavioral medicine and hypnosis with couples. Dr. Kahn teaches stress management courses to a number of businesses and schools and also teaches hypnosis workshops to clinicians. He also has directed a number of major research projects at the University of Chicago, one on *hardiness* and stress and another on creativity in artists. He has authored several papers and publications and has presented lectures based on his research endeavors. He is coauthor of a book entitled *Self-Hypnosis: The Chicago Paradigm.* He is both on the faculty and a fellow of the Society for Clinical and experimental Hypnosis.

Richard P. Kluft, MD, is a psychiatrist and psychoanalyst in Bala Cynwyd, Pennsylvania, and is Clinical Professor of Psychiatry at Temple University School of Medicine and on the faculty of the Philadelphia Psychoanalytic Institute, both in Philadelphia. He has authored over 230 scientific articles and book chapters, most of which concern the diagnosis and treatment of dissociative disorders.

Stanley Krippner, PhD, is a professor of Psychology, Saybrook Graduate School, San Francisco and the past president of Division 30 (Psychological Hypnosis) of the American Psychological Association. He has specialized in altered states of consciousness from a cross-cultural perspective, and has written on the use of hypnosis for children with learning problems.

Linn LaClave, PhD, is a clinical associate professor at Indiana University School of Medicine in the Department of Psychiatry. Since the early 1980s she has utilized hypnosis to enhance the treatment of medically ill and traumatized youngsters at Riley Hospital for Children.

Joan Murray Jöbsis, PhD, maintains a full-time private practice in Chapel Hill, North Carolina, and has a clinical appointment in the Department of Psychiatry, University of North Carolina at Chapel Hill. She has an international reputation for her teachings and for her clinical publications regarding the use of hypnosis with severely disturbed patients and focusing on hypnotic techniques for renurturing and developmental repair.

Karen Olness, MD, from the Department of Pediatrics, Case Western Reserve University, has an international reputation in the field of child hypnosis and biofeedback. Her research has documented the ability of children to voluntarily control autonomic responses and the clinical effectiveness of hypnosis in juvenile migraine. With G. Gail Gardner she wrote the first U.S. textbook on child hypnotherapy, now in its third edition.

Mary Jo Peebles-Kleiger, PhD, ABPP, ABPH, is a senior psychologist at the Menninger Clinic in Topeka, Kansas, and faculty and supervisor in the Karl Menninger School of Psychiatry and Mental Health Sciences. She received her training as a psychoanalyst at the Topeka Institute for Psychoanalysis and the Washington Psychoanalytic Institute and has lectured and published extensively in the areas of trauma, hypnosis, and inference making. She is currently working on a book for Analytic press entitled *Case Formulation for the Brief Therapies: A Primer*.

Judith W. Rhue, PhD, from the Department of Family Medicine, Ohio University College of Osteopathic Medicine has conducted research and coedited several books on theoretical and clinical aspects of hypnosis. She has also conducted workshops on therapeutic storytelling, hypnosis with children, and hypnosis research both nationally and internationally.

Rita V. Rogan, PhD, is a clinical psychologist in private practice in Illinois, who specializes in the integration of psychodynamic, cognitive, and behavioral modalities in psychotherapy. She is currently Director of the Institute of Clinical Hypnosis and Research–Michigan (ICHAR–M), which trains professionals in using hypnosis. Her early interest in imagery led to her experimental research in hemispheric function, which has informed her specialty work with artists.

David A. Soskis, MD, a clinical associate professor of Psychiatry at Temple University School of Medicine has specialized in the clinical applications of meditation and self-hypnosis. He has served on the medical faculties of Temple University, The University of Pennsylvania, and the Ohio State University and is the author of papers, book chapters, and a book on his areas of research and clinical interest.

David Spiegel, MD, is a professor and associate chair of Psychiatry and Behavioral Sciences at Stanford University School of Medicine. His most recent book (with Dr. Catherine Classen, 2000) is *Group Therapy for Cancer Patients: A Research-Based Handbook of Psychosocial Care,* from Basic/Perseus Books.

Rev. Dr. John R. Van Eenwyck is the associate rector of St. John's Episcopal Church, Training Analyst at the C. G. Jung Institute of the Pacific Northwest, Clinical Instructor at the University of Washington School of Medicine, and a clinical psychologist in private practice in Olympia, Washington. A member of the Executive Council of the International Society for Health and Human Rights, he travels throughout the world training practitioners in the treatment of torture survivors.

Erika Wick, PhD, is a professor of psychology at St. John's University in New York, teaching in the Clinical as well as in the School Psychology doctoral programs. She graduated from Carl Gustav Jung's Alma Mater in Basel, Switzerland where she was a student of the existentialist and phenomenologist Karl Jaspers. A part of her clinical studies were completed at the medical school. Although her approach in private practice, overall, is eclectic, she emphasizes the benefits of hypnosis and imagery-related techniques. One of her recent contributions is the development of comatherapy.

Lonnie Zeltzer, MD, is the director of the UCLA Pediatric Pain Program, Departments of Pediatrics and Anesthesiology, UCLA School of Medicine, has an international reputation in clinical and experimental research on hypnotherapy with children. She has published extensively on the effects of hypnotherapy in pediatric populations, including medical procedure pain, chemotherapy-related nausea and vomiting, chronic pain, and laboratory pain paradigms. Her research has focused on the developmental psychobiology of pain in children and the role of hypnotherapy in pain relief.

AUTHOR INDEX

SUBJECT INDEX